THE
JEWELLED
FLOWER

The Jewelled Flower
is the
"treasure hard to attain"

"In the darkness of the unconscious a treasure lies hidden, the . . . 'treasure hard to attain'. . . ."
> *Symbols of Transformation*, from Collected Works of C. G. Jung, Vol. 5, Bollengen Series, Princeton University Press, page 330.

". . . only in the region of danger can one find the 'treasure hard to attain'. . . ."
> *Psychology and Alchemy*, from Collected Works of C. G. Jung, Vol. 12, Bollengen Series, Princeton University Press, page 335.

"The treasure which the hero fetches from the dark cave . . . is himself, new-born from the dark maternal cave of the unconscious. . . ."
> *Symbols of Transformation*, from Collected Works of C. G. Jung, Vol. 5, Bollengen Series, Princeton University Press, page 374.

Permission granted by Princeton University Press

THE
JEWELLED
FLOWER

BY LEE JENS

The True Account of a
Courageous Young Man's Life and Death
by His Own Hand

Jewelled Flower illustration originated
by Author

THE NATIONAL WRITERS PRESS

Published in the United States of America by
The National Writers Press
1450 South Havana
Aurora, CO 80012

Second Printing, June, 1987

International Standard Book Number: 0-88100-049-3
Library of Congress Catalog Card No.: 85-61903

iv

TO BE NOTED

All names have been changed except those of our immediate family, Chris's friend Karen (who asked that her name not be changed), and Lee's friend—Richard W. Barton, Ph.D.

Members of the immediate family:

Father—Arthur M., born June 26, 1912.

Mother—(Elizabeth) Lee, born January 25, 1915.

Son—Timothy V., born September 3, 1941.

Son—Christopher E., born February 24, 1944.

Son—Jeffrey A., born August 13, 1950.

The hometown is Glen Ellyn, Illinois.

The family letters from and to Chris which are used in this book do not, of course, consist of the complete correspondence. Some letters were lost; others were felt to be of insufficient importance in the development of Chris's story.

Letters written by Lee to people other than Chris (mainly in Part 2) were selected to show some of the main ideas to which Chris was exposed as he was growing up.

ACKNOWLEDGEMENTS

I wish to express my great appreciation to all the people who allowed me to use their letters in this book; to the authors and publishers who graciously gave me permission to quote from their books; to Robert A. Fitz, Senior Editor, Macmillan Publishing Co., Inc., for his generous and excellent editorial advice; to Richard W. Barton, Ph.D., and Ronald F. Cunat, Ph.D., who read the manuscript, gave me so much encouragement, and wrote testimonials for it; to Harald H. Prommel, Production Manager, National Writers Press, for his many suggestions and editorial advice, including the naming of this book; to my friend, Myra Bakke, who did the original typing, often from hard-to-read handwritten letters, tiny notes on the backs of envelopes, etc.; to my husband's secretary, Mona K. Martin, who did so much further typing as the manuscript went through revisions, and who did the final typing and photocopying; to my friend, Ruthann A. Fowler, who read the manuscript and expressed her valuable ideas about it; to my friends, Robert E. Carlson, Alice V. and Robert H. Dyson, and Margaret L. Snyder, who gave me excellent advice when I asked for it; and to my family: my husband, Arthur M. Jens, Jr., who bore with me so patiently through all my years of involvement with this book and never once discouraged me, and who proofread the galleys; my two remaining sons, Timothy V. and Jeffrey A. Jens, for their interest and reassurance; and last of all, to Chris himself, without whose writings this book would lose its major asset.

Lee Jens

Christopher Edward Jens
February 24, 1944—May 10, 1970

DEDICATION

To all the people who knew and loved Chris, and to all the people who will come to know and love him through this book.

On the First Anniversary of a Suicide

I'm thankful for your thoughts of me today—
It's been a year since I have dealt in death.
I told you, yes, I'm sad. I did not say
The year has devastated me; my breath
Did not grow short, though in my mind I saw
Him jump the wall again, and screamed to stop
His move that killed. You see, he'd felt the flaw
Within him crowd his heart; his nurtured crop
Of soul success did not mature. His hope
Of living all his life for God decayed.
He chose the only way he could to cope:
He sacrificed his body. Thus he made
No trade, no compromise. Some think that none
Failed more completely. But, for him, he won.

Lee Jens

ABOUT THE AUTHOR

Lee Jens, an Illinois homemaker and civic worker, has been interested in the workings of the mind since she changed her major from journalism to abnormal psychology at Northwestern University, where she received her B.S. degree in 1936.

As a volunteer, she has been deeply involved in activities with and for the mentally ill. She has served on the board of the DuPage Mental Health Association—except for a five-year interval—since 1963. In 1966 under the Association's auspices, she organized The Thursday Evening Club, a social organization for persons with mental and emotional problems. It has been thriving ever since.

She has served on the Mental Health Advisory Committee of the Du Page County Board of Health since 1977. Her column "Mental Health and You," written for over 16 years, currently appears in Press Publications, Life Newspapers and Pioneer Newspapers in her area.

She has volunteered untold hours at the state mental hospital in Elgin, Illinois, as a friend to the residents.

As an active member of Homemakers' Coalition for Equal Rights, Lee gives many hours to promoting legislation of benefit to women, especially homemakers.

She has been deeply involved in the development and growth of the Du Page Art League, and is well-known locally as an artist who works in many media.

Concerned about conservation of natural resources, she was one of the first fighters against the use of persistent pesticides, namely the chlorinated hydrocarbons such as DDT and was Pesticides Chairwoman of the Illinois Audubon Society for many years. She also served on the Board and Advisory Committee of the Rachel Carson Council.

Her efforts have been recognized with many awards and honors, and she has been listed in Who's Who in the Midwest and Who's Who Among American Women as a civic worker.

A comment written by Ronald F. Cunat, Ph.D.

This book explores the human condition of one young man without emphasizing the professional jargon of a clinical case history and without the dramatization of a novel. Nevertheless, it is one of those rare books that speaks to both the layman and the mental health specialist by piquing one's interest to know more with each chapter. I believe that between the lines it urges us to open our eyes and to take a second look at our notions of normalcy and illness.

It is engrossing reading for those fascinated by mind and behavior; my guess is that the author wrote this book for all of us, professional and layman alike.

TABLE OF CONTENTS

PREFATORY NOTE

This is a book about an intelligent, talented, well-educated, well-loved, handsome young man who killed himself at the age of twenty-six. Though he had been diagnosed as "mentally ill," as *schizophrenic*, and by one hospital as *schizo-affective*, and had had a very difficult two and one-half years since his "breakdown," going in and out of "sanity," I believe that during the month or so before he died, he was never more sane, and I believe that his decision to commit suicide was made with a clear and reasonable mind. I was with him a great deal during that time, and he was very communicative; that is why I believe this.

The main reason I want this book to be published is to try to help other people who are caught in the same kind of problem—the individual who has the same dilemma, those who are dear to him and to whom he is dear.

This is a very intimate story. Chris and I, and others whose writing appears in these pages, are people who are not afraid to put what they are thinking and feeling in writing. There is very little pretense in this book, if any. I hate pretense perhaps more than anything else (though I recognize that it is unavoidable at humanity's present stage of development).

I believe that a true, intimate story is a great gift to readers and that it helps them in their business of living and growing. Especially in a case like this, when there is a very grave problem which affects many people deeply; and when the reader is involved in the same kind of problem, perhaps within himself, perhaps within his family, or perhaps within his practice as one of the many kinds of professional mental health workers.

Chris was a young man at a certain stage of spiritual evolution. I believe that we are all making progress in our knowledge of ourselves as spiritual beings (as readers will learn in the letters I wrote to friends which appear

xv

in Part 2 of this book); that Chris was at perhaps the most critical stage of that progress; that this fact precipitated a crisis; and that as a result, Chris had an overdose of energy from his unconscious, causing him to exhibit the symptoms of so-called mental illness.

It is my feeling that a person going through this particular crisis could best be guided through his upheaval by an analyst who is educated in the methods and theory of Carl Gustave Jung, and I urge that anyone who is floundering in this situation seek out, as soon as possible, a Jungian analyst. If I had known as much about Jungianism as I know now, I would have wasted no time in getting such help for Chris. I don't know if this would have made it unnecessary for him to make the decision to take his own life, but I feel it might have. In any event, I think it could have greatly helped his understanding of what was happening to him, which would have probably eased his ordeal.

I hope that readers among professional mental health workers who believe that genetic and brain research, chemicals, and behavior therapy will give us all the answers concerning *every type* of person who exhibits bizarre behavior will absorb the material in this book with an open mind. Hopefully they may come to believe that what we should want for disturbed persons is for them to reach their full potential, rather than just to be what is called "well-adjusted."

It is also my hope that many other readers will find this a fascinating study which increases their understanding of themselves and their fellow human beings.

Lee Jens
Glen Ellyn, Illinois
1986

PART I
1984-1986

"The impulse to death need not be conceived as an anti-life movement; it may be a demand for an encounter with absolute reality, a demand for a fuller life through the death experience."

> *Suicide and the Soul*, by James Hillman, Harper and Row, 1964, page 63.

Permission granted by James Hillman, Ph.D.

A Very Special Letter

Letter from Richard W. Barton, Ph.D., to Lee.

September 1984

Dear Lee:

Having read *The Jewelled Flower*, I now want to say something about my reactions. It is a very powerful manuscript and story and has affected me deeply. Whether I can adequately express this or not is another question.

Though I share with you the Jungian perspective, I must emphasize that my thoughts on such matters are not intended to represent the "official" Jungian view, if indeed there is such a thing. While I have had two years of Jungian analysis and have read maybe 3-4 volumes of Jung's writings, I am not a Jungian analyst nor am I an authority on Jung.

I will begin with my most spontaneous, personal reaction; "There, but for the grace of God, go I." The parallels between Christopher's life and my own are many. Our ages are within a year of one another, so we shared the same generational experiences, above all the idealistic quest for perfection (at least among many college students of that generation) followed by the inevitable disillusionment. Chris and I both had fathers born in the same year and both had conflicting relationships with our fathers. My mother was born only a year later than Chris's mother and both under the sign of Aquarius. I'm not sure whether or in what way these parallels matter, but it is the clustering of so many, the synchronicity if you will, that struck me as noteworthy. The parallels in our inner lives are even more striking. We both began seriously encountering the problem and opportunity of inner spiritual evolution at approximately the same time. In both of us this took the form, for a while, of a conflict between spiritual and material forces, altruism and personal ambition, higher and base motives . . . in short, what Jung has termed, "the fight with the Shadow."

In our quest for the treasure it seems to me that Chris and I both became identified with an archetype that Jung called the *puer aeternus*—the eternal

3

child. Perhaps the extraordinarily happy childhoods that we (and others like us) experienced provided such a powerful experience of joy and perfection that we wanted to cling to it, rather than exchange it for the broken, imperfect, often joyless world of adult responsibility and human conflict. In my own life, a nostalgia for this lost paradise began to seep into my young adult years and to produce a vague unhappiness that I attempted to resolve on the level of ideas. Even the way I attempted to solve the problem evidenced an avoidance of the concrete and a flight into fantasy. This nostalgia for the lost paradise eventually saturated my entire existence, and, as it did, the vague unhappiness grew into a full-blown depression. With the *puer aeternus* pulling me back into the past (the only path to eternity that I knew or had faith in), I eventually became completely blocked in my development and sought help from a Jungian analyst. I read in Chris's letters a childlike innocence and an implicit vision of a perfect, if ethereal, world. For this and other reasons I feel that we were in the grips of the same archetype.

Dating from the beginning of my analysis, my experience begins to differ from Chris's, yet there are still important parallels. My quest also contained a jewelled flower as a symbol of the goal, the spiritual treasure. This appeared in an experience of active imagination and I subsequently painted it in watercolor. The difference between my experience of the jewelled flower and Christopher's is, I think, significant. In my experience there was a snake coiled around the jewelled center, which I had to confront and pass through on my way to the treasure. The flower of life contains within it the possibility of evil, symbolized by the snake, which like all symbols has a positive dimension as well . . . in this case *knowledge*. Evil—the Shadow—is an inner problem, something each individual must confront within himself or herself. Though Chris began this process as an inner confrontation (I recall several of the letters in which Chris ruthlessly examined his own darker motives, his Shadow), he often projected the Shadow onto others (yourself, for example) and eventually came to deal with the dark side of the self as the *idea* of Evil in the works of Guénon.

My psyche employed similar defenses, and it was only with the help of my analyst that I was able to cope with the symbols and unconscious material that came flooding through. I too considered suicide. My reasons for not ending my life had as much to do with fear as with concern about the impact of such an act on those whom I loved. I say this in order to indicate my understanding of the courage involved in Chris's final act.

Without the tools for continuing his quest on the symbolic level (as he indicated to you), yet unwilling to succumb to the *puer aeternus* and live a life of backward movement, his suicide signifies a commitment to, as

4

James Hillman put it, "an encounter with Absolute Reality," . . . an attempt to move forward in the only way he could.

In saying earlier, "There, but for the grace of God, go I," I do not want to imply that Chris's solution to a similar problem (similar in the archetypal sense) was somehow inferior to mine. Indeed, it evidences much more courage than I presently have. Grace comes in many forms. In my case, it came in the form of a particular Jungian analyst who made it possible for me to continue my quest in this life. In Chris's case, we must have faith, as he *must* have had, that grace awaited him in his final encounter. This kind of test of faith is much more demanding than was mine and brings to mind the mythic tests of Abraham and Christ. Only special people are called for such sacrifices, and Chris must have been a very special person. The manuscript bears this out by recording the profound effect that he had on other people

I feel fortunate to have come in contact with Chris's life, even if so indirectly, because of the additional light that it sheds on my own. This is too complex to describe any further, and I do want to get this to you soon.

Thank you for the opportunity to read and comment upon this extraordinary manuscript. I am really glad that it is going to be published. I am also glad that our paths happened to cross.

Dick Barton

An Analysis - 1986

It is now 1986. Chris has been dead for sixteen years. His unrest and subsequent death have led me into many pathways of learning. I have become a far richer person since he died.

I have tried to present Chris's story—which is also my story—just as it was, without much of any analysis over and above my knowledge at the time of the book's happenings.

But now as the time for publishing draws near, I find I cannot resist making some analytical observations about the relationship between Chris and me. And more importantly, about his suicide. The extensive writings of Carl Gustav Jung have made it possible for me to attempt this analysis.

The relationship between mother and son seems especially prone to complications. The mother has carried her son in her womb; no physical relationship can be closer, or as close. She is of the opposite sex, and she is his first love.

If she also happens to be a potent individual, capable of loving her son unselfishly, wishing for him to be independent, free to develop his own

5

potential, the relationship can have great spiritual depth. And this can cause even more complications, because of its strength.

Such was the case in Chris's and my relationship as mother and son.

As if this were not enough, not only did I represent his natural mother and his spiritual guide but he projected to me, in the times of his great stress, parts of his own inner conflict and experienced them as being in me. He also projected to me feminine archetypes from his collective unconscious. (The *collective unconscious*, so-called by Jung, belongs to all of us and is "inhabited" by primordial, universal images good and bad, which are called archetypes; it contains the myths and symbols of the human race.) I believe that often in his disturbed years I represented his whole collective unconscious known in myths as the "terrible mother" who would devour her own child, or as the maternal abyss into which one could fall and be lost forever. That maternal abyss is at once so luring (we read of people forever "searching for the mother") and so frightening because it could prevent one from ever growing up and becoming whole. I believe this kind of projection to me was what made him so often turn against me in his late college years and to emphasize the masculine values. Mythologically, the masculine symbolizes consciousness and logic and I believe Chris intuitively felt the coming danger in the path he was slowly choosing. It was then that he would complain about me, be so hostile to me, not because of the need for adolescent rebellion, but because of a need for a much deeper maturity than that which is usually considered in average life as an "adjustment" to adulthood. At those times he would wonder to me, "Why do I do it, why do I treat you this way? I *love* my mother." He knew something was wrong about fighting me, but he didn't realize that what he was fighting was *inherent in his own unconscious*, and that he *was not fighting me at all*. Nor did I.

I wish I had known then what I know now; though I did know considerably more than the average person, not only because of what I had already read, but because of my own feel for the psyche and my own personal dark journey. Though I had had that successful dark journey of my neurosis many years before, had experienced the union of the opposites and come to a realization of my wholeness, come to know my true self, I knew very little consciously about archetypes, symbols and myths as such. It was not until after Chris died that I read avidly about these subjects. (I must stress, however, that I always believed that Chris was involved in a very great experience which in the end included his suicide. I did not, at any time, believe he was simply "mentally ill," merely a victim, say, of a chemical imbalance.)

If I had known more about archetypes and the collective unconscious, I would have been saved quite a bit of confusion and heart-ache, especially

6

during those times when Chris spoke of his great fear of me, or of the inferiority and evil of women, and of the negative archetypes of the feminine. I wish I had known that all those archetypal burdens which were hung upon me had nothing to do with me personally, as Chris's natural mother, but were part of his unconscious.

Certainly all this added to the complexity of an already complex relationship. Yet in spite of all these developments which I did not sufficiently understand (as the reader will see), there was never a time when I doubted the fact that Chris and I had a very great love between us. Nor did I, I repeat, ever doubt Chris was embarked on something much more important than just "mental illness." The truth was that he was in search of *himself*.

Chris's story is, to me, in large part that of the proverbial hero who, as he has appeared in myths from time immemorial in all parts of the world, takes a journey, overcomes a great obstacle and gets the wonderful treasure. The journey is, in an actual person, into himself, into his depths, as far as necessary. The obstacle is the fear of the danger of the unconscious. Jungians believe the treasure is the realization of one's true self and, from my experience with Chris, I ardently agree.

In one of the main versions of the hero myth, the treasure is guarded by a dragon: the hero must kill the dragon to get the treasure, which is symbolized by something of great value—e.g., a pearl—and return home with it, triumphant.

Only courageous, searching persons undertake such a "journey" in real life. To go down into the unconscious is very dangerous. These brave men and women want something better than the "ordinary life."

As Chris finally started on the journey (he had been considering it, in his own way, for years), he felt great joy. He threw over everything that he had been working on, and in his euphoria he felt he had been "reborn·" But he had plunged too quickly from one kind of life to another, and this caused his unconscious to gain power too quickly. Conscious reality lost its grip as Chris experienced the glory and the evil and the power which lie in the unconscious. He was transported to the heights, only to fall into hellish torments. He painted a picture of himself trying to walk and keep his balance on the top sharp ridge of a mountain. Deep down in the valleys on either side of him were treacherous gray rocks; if he leaned too much to either side, he might lose his balance entirely and crash into rocks which would destroy him. Thus he pictured himself in a precarious state in which he tried not to become entirely conscious on the one hand or entirely unconscious on the other. To be entirely conscious was for him to be at the mercy of society; to be entirely unconscious was too full of the horrors and thrills mentioned above, as he encountered the raw evil of negative archetypes that are found in the unconscious along with the unadulterated

7

goodness of positive archetypes. Actually he was not doing a very good job of balancing, and he kept slipping down the unconscious side of the mountain, not quite being crushed by the rocks at the very bottom but having quite a long distance in which he had to work his way back up. No, he really was not balancing very well at all, and as a result he became so involved in his unconscious that we found it necessary to hospitalize him four different times since he was felt to be a danger to himself and others.

After he had committed his death-dealing act and he lay on the floor, waiting for the ambulance I had ordered, I said, "We may not have much time, so I must ask you quickly, why did you do it?" He answered immediately, "Fear of what God would try to make me do."

I did not know what this fear meant at the time, but now it seems clear. He felt God was cheering him on, rooting for him to win, to conquer his fear of the unconscious (slay the dragon) and go on to reap his reward of true selfhood (claim the treasure).

And oh, how Chris wanted to do just that; hadn't he written and illustrated a poem, *The Jewelled Flower*? The flower lying in the water was a symbol of his self, his total self; at last he knew for what he had been searching! But just knowing what it was did not mean he owned it; he must now find the plant it came from (in order to really own it), deep down in the water, which symbolized his unconscious. So down into his unconscious he had to go. But there he found the great horrors and the great beauties, and he was hurled from one archetypal figure to another as he floundered in the collective unconscious. He was getting lost, lost, lost, and he was scared as he had never been scared, and he often lost sight of his goal.

I remembered how he had reacted a few years before, when I had again pointed out, "But Chris, we have to suffer! Otherwise, we'd never grow! We'd never find any happiness!" He had shouted back to me, "I don't *want* to suffer, I want to be happy *now!*"

And yet, this same young man had finally seen that it was not easy. He had searched and searched, and he had found out what he wanted. And he had started on the journey to achieve it; he had plunged into that "water" of his unconscious. And he was scared.

Yet he felt God wanted him to go on and on. But he was so frightened that he would be lost forever in the abyss of the collective unconscious, he couldn't go on. He did not have the strength, the courage. He was the failed hero. He could not "slay the dragon". He could not bring back the treasure. He could not bring back to consciousness wisdom from the collective unconscious and present God with that gift of enlarged and worthier consciousness, grown greater because of being combined with knowledge

8

from the collective unconscious, thus uniting the opposites. He could not come back to consciousness with his own wholeness, a better man for having discovered that *all* opposites need each other, complement each other, must be united for completeness. (Could not find out that even the evil dragon works for good; by challenging the hero, she goads him to fight for the treasure.)

"God did not give me the tools to be the person I want to be," Chris had told me in his late days. His smile was so sad, yet so beautiful, too, as he accepted his lack. At another time, he said to me, "We all have our roles to play." He had faced the fact that his was not the hero role. Not in *this* life-time.

And so Chris, the "failed hero," refused two of the options open to him: to go back to where he'd come from, to the consciousness he felt had been too directed by the competitiveness and pretenses of society; or to lose himself in the dark collective unconscious. He chose the only other option he had, the valiant option of killing his body. He could not "kill the dragon." But he had the courage to kill his own body—to give up his consciousness, to give up the strange powers and the beauties he had found in the unconscious, along with the demons, to give up his life and to give himself back to the God he loved enough to die for.

It is said that each person who kills himself has one way in which he prefers to do it, for his own reason. Chris chose to kill himself by fire. It is my belief that he wanted the purification that fire would give, and that he believed he could try again rising from the ashes in a rebirth.

Thus he reached, I feel, the highest potential of which he was capable.

PART 2
1943-1958

1943 - 1947

In 1943 a young woman, mother of an infant son, enmeshed in a marriage that demanded growth, three times visited the office of an aging psychiatrist in Kansas City, Mo. She told him of her fears of having an impulse to harm herself, or less frequently others (*though she had actually never had such an impulse*); of the advances she had made in her own self analysis with the help, particularly, of Karen Horney's books; and asked him if he felt she should have another child. He saw no reason why she should not, told her that he believed she had enough insight to free herself from her distressing neurosis. He was right.

Christopher Edward Jens was born the following year on February 24, 1944. The doctor held him up for me in the delivery room, covered with pieces of vernix caseosa, red. But in two weeks, he had become as beautiful a baby as was ever seen, and there was not the slightest doubt that he smiled at that very early period at his mother and the nurses.

Except for two bouts of pyloric spasm, which manifested itself before he left the hospital and which temporarily caused him considerable discomfort, and emerged again for a short while when he was six months old causing dehydration and screaming, he spent what appeared to be a totally happy babyhood. He was extremely responsive to others. When I hung a "baby gym" across his bed, he would get almost too excited. I took him for long walks in his carriage with brother Tim hanging onto one side of the carriage and dog, Chica, leashed to the other side. We lived in three homes during that year—the war was on, and we finally had to buy—but Chris, always with his own crib, his own baby gym, and his mother's ever-flowing breasts, seemed not to notice any changes.

He was busy, oh, so busy. As soon as he could navigate by himself, he was into everything and always deeply involved in projects. Of the two boys, he was the "builder" with Tim standing on the sidelines making sly remarks that would make Chris howl with rage. Later he admitted he did a lot of fake howling to get Tim in trouble. They fought, as all brothers do, but never physically. Father was away a great deal of the time, negotiating an airport in New York. As Chris grew older, there were many trips through the woods, much bird-watching and symphony records on the phonograph to make up for the excitement of not having Daddy coming home from work most of the time.

Happy, happy, loving everyone, winning everyone. At the age of two, a rectal polyp required two trips to the doctor and being put in a most embarrassing position, but he never cried. The nurse said, "What beautiful security he has! If you could see the fear that most of the children have who come here." A stay with Grandma in another town for three weeks because we (Tim, Art and I) went to New Jersey—a nursery school—and how he loved it all, never time to be lonely for family, too much to do! And such good food, "My, dat's good egg, Grandma." (He *loved* eggs!)

Excerpt from a letter written by Lee to a friend, M.G. September, 1947.

. . . Then, suddenly, we are adults, and the dreamed-of time is here. And it is not like the dreams. But now there is no escape into dreams of the future, there is nothing to look forward to; there is only the present, the life of the adult is *here*, to be faced.

. . . I think one of the greatest experiences of life is the realization of what living really is—not a dream, not heaven, ever—but a period of *growing*. Here is something real, this knowledge, one feels with its introduction a desire to use the time well, to do a good job. The knowledge of this truth, though it involves the necessity of facing the problem of struggle, is exciting and inspiring to me. Though there be so many times of despair as one seems to slip back instead of progressing, those moments when one knows he *has* made progress, be it ever so little, are so blessedly sweet that they keep one on with the struggles. . . .

Love,
Lee

October, 1947

We moved from Kansas City to Glen Ellyn, Illinois when Chris was going on four years old. We decided to choose our home in the western suburbs of Chicago because we felt the North Shore would involve more social life than we wanted. Glen Ellyn had a hometown atmosphere that we liked, and it was in Art's original home territory. We have never regretted our decision.

1948 - 1958

Excerpts from letter written by Lee to a friend, J.S. Summer, 1948.

. . . I believe that neurotic troubles, based on insecurity and hostility, are deeply involved in the troubles of mankind—on a world-wide scale; war and the necessity for capitalism (failure of communism); lack of cooperation between nations; problem children; divorce and general unhappiness. The neurotic has such great needs and compulsions.

Psychiatry has a long way to go before it is of great value. As it is now, it takes too long and costs too much. And even if people had the time and money there wouldn't be enough doctors. I feel the answer lies in a huge program of child guidance (prevention) and group therapy.

But you and I and the rest of us adults here and now, what of us? There is only one answer, complete analysis. That is, if we are to find our SELVES—and do for the world what we can—and help our children to be free from compulsions. For me, no amount of trouble or ruthlessness with my puny self has been too much to reap the benefits. My psychiatrist in Kansas City told me he felt I had enough insight to do the thing myself and, of course, Karen Horney's book *Self Analysis** really gave me the courage to believe that I could do it. As you know, Horney's other books were invaluable; she got away from the inevitable Freud with whose theories I never got any place. It's all taken an intensity, an avidity, that few seem to feel. It breaks my heart that I cannot pass it on to others, this wish to change. I could only wish for you the glorious freedom, the great spontaneity and love I am able to feel much of the time. And it's getting better every day.

You have said, "Why not just be human and feel things instead of analyzing everything?" I reply that I am now able to be that—I couldn't when I was tied to phobias and obsessive thinking. You said, "You think about yourself too much," and I say, "I must in order to learn not to."

How can we learn what we really are if we are unconscious of our inner conflicts which make themselves felt by symptoms that absorb our energy and creativity and mask our reality? How can we grow if we are cramped by our neurotic needs? We must be ourselves, not what our neuroses dictate—do what we really want to do (not what we are compelled to do)—be selfish, if you will, if we are to grow in our ability to be selfless, i.e., to be channels for God, Who is Love.

Now, I maintain that you are trying to get out of analysis because you are scared to do it. You even said one time that you would be afraid to

*Published by W. W. Norton and Co., Inc., New York.

15

look beneath the surface for fear there would be nothing there at all. You are too bound to your neurotic structure, you are rationalizing yourself out of analysis. And it WON'T WORK. Not if you want to be free. *I know.* I tried it. I hated to give up my ways for fear I would be even worse off, even though I knew in my heart that they were preventing me from living life as it should be lived.

And don't say I can't judge you by myself. *You* know very well how neurotic you are. A cancer will eat at your body just as it will mine. And so will a neurosis eat at your mind just as at mine. Maybe, yes, your manifestations are different—maybe you do things that would shock me, and vice versa. But that's not what is important—those are only manifestations. At the bottom you know darn well we have both been involved in the same ailment.

Now I suppose I am making you uncomfortable. I want to! I think you have the stuff in you to analyze yourself. Making neurotics comfortable (of course, they are insatiable, so one never could, really) in their structures never did any good. The only thing that does any real good is change. There's no other way. Just gotta change those funny ways. Only analysis can show you how completely smothered your real SELF is, how you are being cheated out of life, and how you are affecting other lives in an adverse way.

I wish so much for you and H. You both have such great potential. I pray that you will find the way to make that potential materialize.

I am sure you know some place that I am your same old friend. Use me for one!

Affectionately,

L.

P.S. Here's part of the poem I mentioned when you accused me of unfriendliness and rudeness when I called and complained to you one time (even though you had always insisted we be completely honest with each other, and even though you had exercised that perogative with me whenever you chose) that I felt hurt because when I needed you, you were never available, though you expected me to be available when you needed me. It's also an answer to your saying that "anger is unproductive" (though you indulge in it rather frequently).

From *Chiarscuro**, by Archibald MacLeish
> "But we were lies and never did confess
> The true thing in us. When I should have raged
> And killed you with a bloody sword, I'd press

---

*From *Streets of the Moon*, by Archibald MacLeish.
Permission granted by Houghton Mifflin Company

Your hand and smile; and when your malice waged
Most bitterly with mine you kissed me most.
Alas, I cannot see your face, poor ghost."

1948

Chris sucked the two middle fingers of his right hand until he was going
on five years old. We did not show him anger about this, but we did try
to get him to give it up using various methods. One day he evidently made
a decision to stop, and we never saw him do it again.

His best friend in our first Glen Ellyn neighborhood, where we lived
for three years, was the girl next door. Because she was a few months
older than he, she was able to start kindergarten a year before he could.
He was not as easy to live with that year as he was the year before. He
was very angry that his playmate could be in school and he could not.

1949

The next year, when he was old enough to go to kindergarten, brother
Tim got polio, and Chris was not allowed to enter school for three weeks.
He was furious, and *nothing* would placate him during those three weeks.
I don't think he smiled once. When the day he could start school finally
arrived; he was ecstatic. He entered the school room without a drop of
fear that I could see, as all eyes turned toward the "new boy." He did not
cast one backward glance toward me. He thoroughly loved school from
the start.

Notes jotted down in 1949 by Lee.

My study of neuroses served to change other people in my eyes.

Where before they had appeared as enemies, and in fact were anything
but loving human beings, they now appeared as unhappy creatures wildly
searching for meaning to their lives. I can forgive them for not measuring
up to what I believe is the true purpose of life, loving one's brothers,
which of course has deep implications. They are going against me because
they are *compelled* to do so by their neurotic needs.

Being now able to forgive them much more easily, I am able to be what
I always wanted to be—one who loves a lot, and improving in it all the time.

Excerpts from a letter to Aunt J. from Lee. February 22, 1950

. . . I am sending you this article in the hope that it will make you feel more tolerant toward the suffering neurotic instead of condemning him for his "selfishness" which is brought about by his horrifying feelings of insecurity and fear.

You often say these people should just do things for others and forget themselves. But just trying to force yourself into loving others doesn't work. . . . You must first love yourself. If you have not first learned to know and love yourself, your frantic "do gooding" is simply another neurotic attempt at gaining security. And of course, it doesn't work.

It is because I have learned to respect myself, and therefore truly to feel warm toward others, that I have wished so poignantly to pass on what I have learned. But what I have to offer is "change of oneself," not a magic panacea, and most people, desperate though they may be for any answer, turn away in fear because nothing scares a person more than changing. What gives some people the courage to change in spite of their fears? I wish I knew.

Love,
Lee

Excerpt from letter written by Lee to S.C. May, 1950

. . . There is so very little reality in people. I need very much to touch the reality of them with my reality. I feel so isolated in this artificial world. It is only rarely that I have found any reality at all. In most cases it was too small to stand up under mine. The people who had it, loved me. But they hated me, too, because they were afraid of me. So much of them was not real but neurotic, and the love they felt was beaten down by their fears which were heightened by me because I made them feel ashamed in their neuroses. They cannot rest comfortably in their neurotic structure when reality comes close to them. I spoil things for them, though I am greatly empathetic with their neurotic problems. I believe in change because I know they can never find peace until they do change. They know with their tiny reality that they must change but the neurosis is so much larger than the reality in them that they must hang onto it for a feeling of security, false though it is. In you I feel much more reality than in most. Don't let the neurosis choke it out.

Love,
Lee

18

August, 1950

When Chris was six years old a baby brother, Jeffrey, was born. Chris was delighted with him and never showed the slightest jealousy, even though Jeffrey supplanted Chris as the baby of the family.

Excerpts from letter to S.C. written by Lee. December, 1950

. . . bearing in mind that my thoughts on these subjects are always growing, never basically changing but changing by their growth, let me again present the truth as it appears to me. I know that I have had these basic thoughts since I was a very young child. But they are only now maturing.

Many members of our society are, I think, near the middle of the spiritual ladder, that is, a little more animal than spiritual. They are the ones who suffer the most from the *basic* human conflict between animal and spiritual impulses. This is *not* a neurotic conflict due to repressed material in our personal unconsciousnesses. It is important to solve our neurotic conflicts so we can apply all our energies to this basic conflict, to overcome it bit by bit as we grow in spirituality. The individual at this stage of spiritual development is bent on pursuing his own interests in an animal-like law of the jungle way (refined, of course, by "civilization"), yet he is spiritually evolved enough to be continually bothered by his conscience which tells him to think of the other fellow. The highest good he can perhaps think of is to be the richest man in the world, or otherwise the most powerful, while all the time being a great benefactor with his gifts to charity, etc. And sometimes he actually is truly loving when some situation has touched his spiritual side. The middle group is bent on obtaining animal necessities and pleasures, including power over others, but being beyond the lower level (who are more animal and not so conflicted) in development these people are not satisfied with simple pleasures, but are after luxuries. They are continually in search of new ways to gratify and stimulate their appetites. I think this avidity for ever-new pleasures is born directly from their underlying feeling of dissatisfaction which can be traced to their divinity. Their animal side demands satisfaction; their spiritual side is bored with the everlasting pursuit of this satisfaction and keeps them in a state of unrest. To quell this unrest, they look for more stimulation, more pleasures, more power, something to make them forget their uneasiness. Sometimes they get the idea that this is not the cure and what they need is more religion; their spirituality gets through that much. But they can't be truly religious because the animal keeps interfering, and they just cannot love their brothers or God. Or they turn to creating something and try to become artists to express themselves. But here, too, they cannot go far enough. Their conflicts have made them too rigid and, since real art has spiritual communication, they fail because they have not enough to say. Of course, this is all in a greater or lesser degree, depending on the individual, his degree of spiritual evolvement, and his neurotic structure.

The lower level human, being largely animal and not bothered so much by "conscience," is not as basically divided and conflicted as the middle level because he is over-balanced on the side of animalism.

And the higher level human, being much more spiritual than animal, is not as basically conflicted as the middle because he, too, is overbalanced—but on the side of the spirit. But he does develop a neurosis because of the hostile conditions in which he finds himself; conditions dictated by the conflict of the middle masses. So it is a "happy" world for no one except those at the very *highest* level who have risen above it. The higher level person (who is not yet highest) is faced with getting along somehow in these conditions, and he is afraid and isolated and becomes hostile. He has to develop a neurotic structure in order to feel some security. But because he is quite spiritual and has the underlying ability to be quite loving, he can cure his neurosis. (Often, however, help is necessary.) He will still have conflicts, but not neurotic ones. And he will be able to dissolve his conflicts one by one by making changes within himself; in short, by growing. That's what we're here for—to grow, to become fully spiritual; I am convinced of this.

Love,

Lee

P.S. Don't ever forget that being at a higher level than someone does not make one worth more in the eyes of God. All, all are of equal worth. (If someone is in third grade in school, he is not worth less than someone in ninth grade.) All, all are carrying out their roles. All, all make it to the goal. All will be "saved." No one—not even one—is lost. This I believe.

Excerpts from letter written by Lee to her mother. October 8, 1951

. . . We'll be seeing J. and L. Homecoming weekend. J. calls me his No. 1 soul-searcher. But I do think he can't figure out my basic motives. I tell him no one could have a simpler motive—just plain concern for people.

. . . It's the fake part of people I can't stand. I have a deep love for Truth and Reality, and I can spot pretense as easily as if it were lit up with a neon sign.

. . . Forgive me for going on again about spiritual values. I realize it is a dangerous subject. yet I feel compelled to have you see me, at least to some extent, as I really am. . . .

I suppose you are again exasperated with me. I know what a trouble-maker you consider me by my not going along with conventional ideas . . . I wouldn't talk to you this way if I weren't interested in appealing to the real you, if I didn't care about you.

Love,
Lee

Excerpt from letter written by Lee to her mother. October 21, 1951

. . . always I have been a renegade and that is because I cannot, *will* not, do what I don't believe in. That is, I will not lead the fake life that almost everyone around me leads. You say I have harmed myself by my self-analysis. Can't you get it through your head that I have saved myself by it? I was a miserable fear-ridden neurotic—and now I am at peace and able to be myself, to grow, to *live*. You must forgive me if I have loved people enough to want them to know the freedom from bondage that I now know and in so doing have used the wrong methods. But I've learned and will not bother them much any more (unless they ask for it). But neither must *they* try to bother *me* much, try to get *me* to change to *their* ways. I'll have no part of that kind of limitation.

I believe I get more joy from even the simplest things than anyone I know. I don't have to go out looking for something to amuse me, to titillate me, to inspire my tired appetites.

Love,
Lee

Notes from Chris's Baby Book by Lee, 1952.

Chris is very good at helping Mom. Improving in everyway—less crying and anger—more understanding of the fact that everyone has problems, not only he, and that he is not a privileged character who should have good, no matter what!

Notes by Lee, August 1953

I came to see that were I *not* the one to do this work in the house, I would also not be the one *here* to listen, to guide, to love, to be *mother* to my children. I came to love the "serving" part of my life, keeping my family comfortable and taking care of all the material details. I was both Martha and Mary; and glad to be both and to see the importance of each.

Excerpts from letter to three sons from Lee.* August 16, 1953
To be given to them only if I died.

. . . From that time (1948) to this has been a period of tremendous spiritual growth for me. Many of my ideas have changed. When I started the period I was convinced that if one could be completely non-neurotic, one could be all good (i.e. loving). I now see that one could not be (except in rare cases). To be non-neurotic is wonderful. For one does not have to be limited by symptoms. But to be non-neurotic does not make one perfectly loving. (I mean, of course, loving all one's fellow men, as well as all the universe and its living things—therefore a detached kind of loving, rather than attached, or preferential). We indeed, I now see clearly, come into the world with different amounts of "goodness" based on how far our spiritual evolution has proceeded (in past lifetimes, either here or in some other kind of "learning" place—I'm inclined to think here, for where could there be a better place?).*

My basic belief has always been the same. We must grow in order to love more.

With so much love,
M.

Excerpts from letter to Chris from Lee. August, 1953
(Never given to him, nor was there any intention of so doing, except in case of my death.)

. . . I love you all. For each I have a particular affection, each has his own special attributes. While it is true that your interests in spiritual pursuits have seemed not too great in that you have found such discussions tedious much of the time and have felt that getting to school on time was much more important than helping in a home crisis; it is also true that your boundless enthusiasm for whatever were your pursuits has been heart-warming to me and reminded me very much of myself. This has created a certain empathy between you and me that does not exist between Tim and me. (On the other hand, his penchant for the spiritual creates an empathy between Tim and me that does not exist between you and me; he is able much of the time—and has for all his life since he was three, or thereab-

---

*Often when I talked in this way with the boys, I would say, "Maybe *you* won't feel this way when you grow up." Or, "If you believe this way when you grow up, it will have to be because you've made it *your way, too*. Accept it fully because you've *experienced* it." Or "You may have another way."

22

outs—to comprehend complicated spiritual and psychological subjects. While with you it's just some of the time.)

Somehow I have never wanted to "talk down" to you children. To me, you are souls that happen at the moment to be in children's bodies, souls that may be much more advanced than mine.

As for which of you has been the most difficult for me—or which I have been most difficult for—I couldn't say. Your way of getting down to business, acting, enthusing, your ability to admit when you are wrong, has warmed me; Tim's ability to be a close understanding friend when I needed him desperately has warmed me. Your vacancy in a deep discussion and "boredom with God" much of the time, your preference for self interests, has concerned me; Tim's "nothingness," his lack of aim, his inability to carry through in much of anything or to admit he is ever wrong, has concerned me.

Now, because those are general characteristics does not mean that you have failed spiritually or that Tim is a complete blank in every day life! Actually, you have both improved a great deal—you show great spiritual growth and Tim has become much more dependable by being something rather than nothing in every day life. What I want most of all is to see a better relationship between you two—that is the improvement I long for. I feel more for you in it, because I believe that because you are a "man of action" you are more anxious to do something about it; while he, being an introvertive type, given to no action, no change, lets it slide; getting together is especially difficult for the two of you, for each is the perfect annoyer for the other.

But we have all learned a great deal. We know that real differences or resemblances don't mean a thing and that basically we are all (all of us in the whole world) on the same track, all pursuing God, step by step, whether we know it or not. And while one has an appeal for us in one way and one in another, that is really all very superficial for underneath, deep in our true beings, every human being loves every other.

So, I have not loved you more sometimes because of your liveliness, or loved Tim more sometimes because of his seeming greater (at present) comprehension. I love you both equally.*

I have not commented on Jeffrey for he is just our beloved baby whom we all adore. What "problems" of personality he will present remain to be seen.

I have been thrilled with the progress you have made in these past two

---

*Note: In 1962 I wrote on the side of this letter—Chris at eighteen shows great spirituality.

years; thrilled because to make it, you had to overcome great obstacles (as of course, we all do in all our growths).

I love you,

M

Excerpts from letter from Lee to Art, 1953. (Written during an eight month's separation.)

. . . You are afraid to face your own faults, and I can greatly empathize, for I, too, have been afraid to face mine. Yet I differ from you in that, even though I'm afraid, I'll plunge into them and be utterly ruthless with myself. And because I have done this, I have grown in strength as you well know. And there is only one source of strength. The only way we can tap that source is by being ruthless with our selfishness which shows itself in so many different ways. As we go along the way tapping it—becoming more and more directed by God's strength, shall we say—we have times of the greatest fear as the mass of worldly opinion moves in on us.

The struggle that has gone on in our particular home is the basic struggle between the two ways of man. Not that you are utterly sold on the world, or that I have been perfectly attuned to God—but you are more one and I am more the other. Of course in the end, there is only one way—God's—and I believe completely that we all come to this when we have evolved enough. Just because someone may seem not evolved as far as another does not in any way mean that he is inferior; I fully believe we are all doing the very best we can, and are carrying out God's plan. Remember that poem by James Stephens—on the last day of the world, Satan sits on one side of God, and Christ on the other, and God calls them both sons, and tells them they have done well.* Being animal is just as much part of the process as being spiritual. Yet, I believe, there is the goal of spirituality, which is not attainable until one has done all the rest.

I'd better stop or you'll never read this at all. I hope at least that I have given you the idea that I believe completely that we shall all—all—get back to the Everlasting Arms.

Believe in my sincerity and
love for you,

L.

---

*I had read this poem shortly after I had had a revelation that evil was an important part of the plan, and I was thrilled that Stephens agreed.

24

Letter from Lee to Art.

December 9, 1953

Dear Dad:

The point you seem to be making is that I think I am always right. If I actually did think that, I would not have the constant prayer that I be rid of my selfishness. This has gotten in my way all my life, prevented me from doing the only thing I've ever really wanted to do, and that is to be completely loving. In an effort to get rid of this selfishness I have done many things—some very productive; others have served only to bring on new complications. In my last year of college I switched my major from journalism to psychology—which was no easy job—because I knew that my first problem was to get rid of my peculiarities (which grew into a real neurosis the year after college).

As you know, it was a long struggle for me to get rid of that neurosis. I do believe that it was a success, and that I am rid of the thing in the main. Now I can evaluate myself (which one can never do when one is neurotic). I am very much aware that I have a lot of selfishness left to get rid of, and I sincerely believe I do look my faults in the eye (which is much harder to manage if one is neurotic).

While I used to detest myself for my weaknesses (when neurotic) and had a perpetual feeling of guilt, I no longer do. Now I recognize myself as not the most evil kind of a person in the world but a human being struggling up the spiritual ladder *exactly as everyone else is doing*. At last I have developed some respect for what I am. And even though I make horrible mistakes because of the self that I am still not rid of, I am sure God loves me as well as anyone else!

As to what my evil has been (selfish activity, sins, if you will) there would be great differences of opinion, since all would judge me in their own lights, by their own current moral standards, which would be influenced by the smallness or largeness of their own selves and of their neuroses.

For all the way up the ladder we have different moral standards, and what to me seems good does not to another—even though they are all, of course, based on the one basic drive of all of our lives, which is to progress up the ladder (though we may not know it) and to help everyone else progress. In the latter, we use a lot of peculiar means on each other and don't even know that we *are* helping although they do work. If we were perfectly loving, we would use Christ's ways exclusively. And yet we must face the fact that that way would not work at some levels as well as these peculiar ways men use. We are not ready in our earthly dream to be like Christ or to receive the ways of Christ. The higher we go on the

25

ladder, of course, the more we can comprehend—and long for—the ways of Christ.

In the past year I have been guilty of bitterness in the extreme. I simply was not advanced enough to forgive. Nor have I been forgiven. However, I do sense what it is like to be forgiving, and I feel I can almost "get my hands on it." All I can do is keep trying and, at my own rate, get there. I have absolutely no wish for any other goal than that of love and forgiveness with the far greater part of the sum total of "me."

I have had a great deal to feel bitter about—being what I am, that is, being at the state I am, I have gotten into a terrific amount of trouble with the world; I have frightened people many times when I was really most loving; I have appeared to be utterly non-cooperative when I was really ardently trying to cooperate with what I felt to be the real man. In other words, I, and all like me, appear to be social misfits if we reveal what we really think. We are not good enough to make the top grade, and too good to comply with society.

No, I do not think I am always right as opposed to someone else. But I do think I am just as right as anyone else, whether they be above or below me on the spiritual ladder. I am carrying out the Plan, just like everyone else. And while I do feel that my own type has its own particular reasons for feeling bitter, I also know every other type has *its* particular reasons. No one, therefore, is any worse off than anyone else. And all will get to the top.

Of course, C., in her evangelical fundamentalism, believes some are weeds and some are wheat; all will *not* get there by any means. Believing in reincarnation, or its equivalent, makes it possible to understand why some people appear to be weeds—being in "lower" lifetimes, not having yet decided to put out greater efforts into work for God (most efforts are bungling at all but the topmost levels).

Much love,
L.

P.S. What you and Mother and others have been trying to say to me is that you must be allowed to proceed at your own rates. And what I am trying to say is that I must also be allowed to proceed at mine. If your rate and mine do not blend at this time, there would seem to be nothing to do but stay apart. I do feel that if there is ever to be any empathy between us each must recognize the complication for what it is and stop dwelling on superficiality.

You say you have been forced. I have felt just as forced. You say I have frustrated you. I have felt just as frustrated. At each level, the feelings are the same. The greater the level, the greater the complications; that is, the more subtle, the more intricate.

M.

Note: In 1986 my beliefs are still basically the same and they have served me well. They matured to the point where I began to feel that separation (multiplicity) came about to make Unconscious Perfection conscious. That is, the purpose of the whole creation (with all its good and evil) is to bring what *was* before the world began (which was unconscious) into consciousness.

Lower creatures have very little consciousness and are mostly unconscious; and as we progress through many lower animal and human states (or their equivalent), through the hard business of living, we become progressively more conscious. The so-called truly holy have become almost completely conscious (yet still separate in that they have bodies)—which means the same as almost "completely loving," and feeling one with All, as I formerly expressed it.

Unconscious Perfection (which was all there was), then, wanted (for Its own reasons) to become Conscious Perfection. (In order to do this, I understood it had to know itself in all its possibilities.) This idea of Unconscious Perfection was presented to me one time; it was in a lecture by someone I do not recall given at the Theosophical Society in America headquarters many years ago. I grabbed the idea, hugged it to my heart, and it became part of my beliefs. It satisfies me completely. It's all I need.

We—the many into which the One is "divided"—are carrying out, I believe, by our experiences of living, this divine wish of the One to know itself in all Its possibilities. Gradually, ever so, ever so gradually, all the members of the multiplicity (through countless lifetimes or their equivalents) reach the highest, the most selfless state in which one can be and still be in body, worthy of a return to the One. The returns to the One *shall* be accomplished. *All* shall make the grade. (How else could the One be whole again?!)

Thus, the One became the many, the many shall become the One, as has been said by mystics of all religions. Actually, should not many be spelled with a capital M? For the Many *are* the One. Unconscious Perfection shall have become Conscious Perfection. All the evil possibilities shall have been experienced—and rejected in favor of good—which is Love.

In our limitations, we cannot comprehend this state of Conscious Perfection because we cannot conceive of it. But I feel it is a state utterly sublime. And I believe that, paradoxically, we can move in and out of that state, move from Unity to separateness, when the One wishes for some reason

27

I cannot fathom to reexperience individuality. It is *all* happening *constantly*.

I believe everything that ever has happened, is happening, or ever will happen, is happening right now in the Eternal Now. Probably my conviction of this stems back to the *anaesthic revelation* (as William James called such a happening in *The Varieties of Religious Experience**) I had during what was probably about a 30 second interval when I was given a whiff of gas at the end of a pain when my son Tim was being born. In this revelation, *everything* that ever was, is, or shall be appeared to me (not in a physical way, but in a much more real way); and I saw that everything fit perfectly into the pattern of Being and *everything* was GOOD.

I knew, *while I was having the revelation*, that I would never be able to hang onto all of this when I was in my conscious mind—that is one of the things I *do* remember. But I struggled to hang onto it because, "I must tell Art."

But all I *can* remember is what I have written here. Which is really all I need to know.

I believe it is that revelation which tells me, over and above the basic pattern of GOOD, that *everything* is happening *right now*. I know that ALL was shown to me right then, right in that 30 seconds. And somehow, I find that idea of the Eternal Now comforting—the idea that actually, we are already in timelessness; even though, paradoxically, we are caught in time.

Excerpt from letter written by Lee to her mother. May, 1955

. . . From what I am told, our boys are well-known as three of the nicest kids around. The two older ones have said many times that they are thankful for the bringing-up they have had;** and they have also told me that I am considered one of the nicest mothers in the neighborhood . . . When we have problems, we admit them and try to grow with them. This was something that was not done during my childhood. . . .

Love,
Lee

Notes from Chris's Baby Book by Lee. July, 1956

Chris has improved a great deal in his outbursts and is working to keep on improving. He has lots of friends and is very enthusiastic about sports,

---

*The Modern Library, publisher.
**Jeff was not quite five at the time.

collections (butterflies, rocks, stamps), and in general seems to find life very good. He had a number of female interests this year, but nothing serious (gals are a little too aggressive for him!). He continues to get good marks.

Fall 1956

Oh, so enthusiastic, so full of joy so much of the time. But so sensitive. When I learned Chris would have to stay at Junior High School for lunch, I felt uneasy. It seemed necessary for him to come home in the middle of the day to get reorganized and to talk away the hurts of the morning—of the class-mates pulling off the wings of a fly; of the teasing of Rodney, the brain-damaged boy, by some of the students. And it was in seventh grade that we first noticed a big change in Chris. He became a conformist, and he wanted to be the most popular boy in the class. He seemed to be succeeding quite well at this, but I was worried about him.

Chris was always talkative, and always, always very communicative with me.

Notes from Chris's Baby Book by Lee, November 1957

How he is lengthening and thinning out! He has lost all the chunkiness of the past. He is intent on being a *big shot* 8th grader—and is being just that. Lots of friends, boys and girls. He is again on the basketball team—second string as last year—and has made two especially good boy friends. He earns his own spending money doing lawn work.

PART 3
1958-1962

1958-1960

On into high school. Excellent grades. Popular with boys and girls.
Worked in a drug store. Knew everyone. Quite a wise-cracker.

1961

Letter from Chris to Glenda, high school girl friend. (Not sent.)

Spring 1961

Angel:

Well, here goes in one messy #X@#—you see what you can get out
of it. I suppose I'll never feel okay about much until I get this off my
chest. (The one I'm going to pin all those medals on).

Like I've said, I'm not sure of my ideas. I know what's right and good
and I want to live by them. But I'm so confused all the time about why I
can't. Remember how I quit smoking? I did it because I thought it was a
silly stupid thing to do. I've smoked a fair amount since then, mostly when
I was depressed after a fight or during work while bored stuff. I still think
it's silly and stupid and I quit entirely again since then in disgust, but I
can't figure out why I ever started again. Am I a little phony?

Remember what I said about sex? It repulses me how human beings can
turn into animals when it can be such an affectionate way to show a deeper
than usual feeling toward another person. Yet I've looked at some pictures
and thought the same thoughts that every "red blooded American boy"
has. Sure, it repulses me, and yet I let my mind sink sometimes. Am I
just a silly fool with ideals not cut out for him?

I hate to see anyone with power over anyone else because of money,
and I hate to see people seeking prestige. Yet, I find myself enjoying the
big house, the big car, etc. which has come because of my Dad. I realize
it and try to stop it before it gets out of hand, but nonetheless, the thoughts
are there.

33

There are other things like this which seem to go against my morals; and yet the thoughts are there, the temptations are accepted.

I've told you this because I like you, and because I like you I want you to like me. But it has to be me and not just the "perfect" guy you've been seeing. I can't help feeling guilty and that gives me that low feeling. When I'm with you I can forget usually, but then I get the guilty feelings worse than ever. It's a vicious cycle that cuts me. Had enough?

I'll shut up for awhile.

Love,
Scout, The People's Choice

Summer, 1961

Chris began to get deeply involved in people's troubles. Suddenly very rebellious as junior in high school, very unpleasant. Off on a three week trip in the summer before senior year—hitch-hiking. We hated to see him go.

July, 1961

It was not easy to see him go. This was 1961. Boys from "good" families did not go off on hare-brained trips. We were still a long way from the back-packing, rebellious, drug-filled days of the late sixties.

He had simply announced to me, "I'm getting three weeks vacation from the drug store, and I'm going to hitch-hike to California."

"Hitch-hike! That's awfully dangerous," I remonstrated.

"I've got to go, Ma."

I could tell he meant it. I brought it up after dinner when Art got home from his business trip to Atlanta. "Tell Dad what you told me, Chris. About your idea."

Chris liked to use me for a "go-between"; he would tell me something—maybe bad news, maybe something he wanted—and I was expected to tell Dad, take the guff instead of Chris, get the rough edges all smoothed out before he and Dad would come face to face on the issue.

Chris seemed a bit taken aback to be confronting his father. Not quite so definite, so clear-cut in his explanation to Dad as he was to me. "Uh—I've got three weeks vacation coming, Dad. I—uh—thought I'd like to go to California."

"California! Do you have enough money?" asked Dad. Chris, as we all knew, had had to use most of his drug store earnings paying fines for misdemeanors of one sort or another!

"Well, no. I—uh—thought I'd hitch-hike. I thought I'd just take $20 with me." He was looking at some spot on the ceiling.

"Twenty dollars! How far can you go on that? You have to eat."

"I want to see if I can make it, one way or another. Uh—I've got to prove something to myself. I've got to go, Dad." His voice rose.

"You're not asking me for any money?" Dad stared at Chris.

"No, I want to try to make it. It's important to me."

Chris was like that. He liked to make things hard for himself. He had a certain admiration for hoboes, a wish for their comparative freedom from rules, their disdain for competition. Competition was a bug-a-boo for him. He didn't like that part of himself. Oh sure, everybody competed—but—well, it got in the way of other things he wanted to be—it worried him.

We thought of him swiping corn from the farmers' fields, washing dishes for a night to earn a buck. Other thoughts came into our minds. Men on the prey . . . a kid hungry.

Art and I talked it over alone. "If we don't *let* him go, he'll probably go anyway, the mood he's in," Art said. Chris had been at his adolescent worst; hostile, argumentative. He and his father had almost come to blows, and had pushed each other around from time to time.

We didn't tell him he could, and we didn't tell him he couldn't. With part of us, we both rather admired his guts. We felt he had a right, at seventeen, to make some decisions for himself. If it got too tough, he could always wire for money!

When the day came for him to go, a hot one in July, I was still hoping he'd change his mind. I asked, as he was about ready, "Don't you want me to take you over to Route 66?"

"No," he answered gruffly. "I just want to get out of here."

He left with barely a good-bye. I watched him go up the road. My heart died a little.

It was ten days before we heard from him, a postcard from California. "Well, I made it! I don't miss the family one bit, yuh, yuh!" We were comforted by this message. He was still alive!

I ran into Audrey Meyers whose son was Chris's friend. "I don't see how you can stand it," she said. "I could never bear to have Jack do that. You must have an awful lot of faith in Chris." Was that it, or were we just plain crazy to let him go? Was it that we didn't have any other choice? The only way we could have stopped him from going would have been to threaten him with something drastic like "Chris, we forbid you to go. And if you *do* go against our wishes, we'll never let you use the cars again!" or, "Okay, Chris, if you go, don't look to us to pay for your college education!" But we didn't believe in threats—they might control a young person, but they certainly would not help one's relationship with him. By neither saying he could or he could not, we gave him our tacit consent. And of course, my friend was right. We did have faith in a fundamental decency in Chris which carried us through those three hard weeks he was gone; that, and prayer, at least on my part, that affirmed his divine spark.

Art and I discussed it all while Chris was gone, trying to reassure ourselves. "What if we had forbidden him to go, and he went anyway?" I asked. "Then we would have had to think up some drastic punishment to let him know he couldn't get away with that defiance. But we really wouldn't want to have to carry out some great punishment, would we?"

Art agreed. Then he added, "You know, he has a right to some big experiences. We all have to take some chances. I took some pretty wild ones myself."

"Dad, you know why I think we felt we should let him go mainly? Because it seemed so darned important to him, as if he just *had* to prove something to himself."

Postcard from Chris to family from Whittier, California, August 2, 1961

Hi Family—

Surprise! I made it! I'm at Bob's who used to live in Glen Ellyn and I'll stay for a couple of days then go back to Long Beach. *This is the life.* I've done a million things and had so many experiences, some of which I'll tell you about when I get home. This is just to let you know I wasn't abducted. I stopped overnight in Springfield—what a wild night—then finished in 2 days for a total of 3 days to the coast. Pretty good considering everything that's happened to me.

Love,
Chris

Letter from Chris to friends while on hitchhiking trip. (Not sent.)
California. August 1961

Harry and to whom it may concern:

So you thought I couldn't make it, huh, you jerk! Well, I made it to Long Beach, Laguna Beach and now up here 20 miles out of L.A. where I've looked up Bob and Mary Reeder all in 3 days and nine rides—the shortest of which was 14 miles and the longest 1100; and on top of that I stopped in Litchfield with Ernie and Ben from Springfield where we went to a wild club, had 21 beers apiece, met hundreds of kids from all over, danced to Conway Twitty and his rock and roll band, spent all but $4.00

36

of what I brought with me, and passed out in the bushes; thereby losing almost half a day and any hope of a square meal. (I'd started with $20.)

The last half of the trip came with Don Padder, a 35 year old playboy in a rickety old '53 Ford that blew up as soon as we reached his home in Long Beach. In this town are the most fabulous girls parading the streets in bikinis waiting to pick you up. As Don aptly put it, there's a scarcity of guys and an over-abundance of girls. At any rate, we had a God damn ball! Bob said he could set me up with some nice girls, but if they're too "nice," I'm gonna go back to Long Beach.

I'll tell you now about a coincidence I'm still trying to get over. This will be of interest to Lou. In Long Beach one of the girls we met looked almost exactly like Lou, so much so that I had to look twice to believe it wasn't. We took her home, and believe it or not she had the same address in Long Beach which Lou has back home. Really it was amazing.

At any rate I've squeezed quite a bit into these first few days and all signs show more to come. The only bad thing is the sweat, dust and grime aren't making my complexion snow-white.

With Don I hit about every other bar through N.M., Ariz. and Texas (very few in Texas). Aside from these things it's all been pretty uneventful.
Chris
P.S. If possible let Burther, Hal and my brother Tim read this, also Nat and anyone else who is interested. This is the life!

Luckily the girls are all rich out here. Sleeping is no problem at all. I just don't bother with it. (4 hrs. since I left). Don and I split up the driving about 50-50 the 1100 miles. Don is married—two kids.

(Save this until I get back).

Postcard written by Chris to family from San Francisco, California
August 5, 1961

Hi—

You better mail $130 bail money, yuh, yuh! Too much rushing around to write anything worthwhile but a lot has happened and I've had a lot of experiences, a few of which I'll remember to tell you when I get home.
Love,
Chris
P.S. I don't miss home one bit, yuh, yuh!

August, 1961

Unexpectedly, at about 9:30 A.M., two days before his vacation was up, Chris reappeared. He was wonderfully friendly. He even kissed me hello and shook hands with his brother Jeff, who was as delighted as I to see him. He looked brown and well-fed, even clean.

"Hey, Jeff, wait till I tell you about the bums' camp I stayed in. They called me 'The Kid.' Here, I've got a present for you from them." It was a worn looking steel spoon which had written on it, "U.S. Navy."

"Wow!" Jeff said, his eyes wide.

"You have a new jacket, Chris," I said. "I wondered how you'd get by without yours. I noticed you weren't taking one, but you wanted to do it all your way, so I didn't say anything. How'd you ever buy a jacket?"

"I didn't buy it, Mom. I—uh—found it behind a radiator in a bus station." He didn't look at me.

"Chris! You stole it!"

"Come on, Ma!" he hollered, looking me straight in the eye this time, "I needed it."

The trip had done something for him, made him feel that he was really independent. Which, unfortunately, he really was not. But it did establish that for at least three weeks he could make it without—as he would have put it—a shot in the arm from his family. And I guess he thought that if he could make it for three weeks, he could make it for six, and so on. (Whatever, he was pleasanter to live with the last year of high school.)

Letter written by high school friend Anne* to Chris.

August 17, 1961

Hi Sunshine, Happiness, etc., etc.,

Honestly Chris, I've never met a person with more zest for living than you have! It really was so good to hear your laugh. I only wish I hadn't waited so long to come in and see you, not only because you make me feel so cheery, but mainly cause I'm dying to hear about your trip to and from California! Chris, I'll bet it was absolutely wonderful! Well it just seems like that would be more than an adventure, etc.; it would almost be an education in itself. Just think of all the people (all kinds) one could meet and the places you must have stayed, etc. Well anyway, I can't stand this "just thinking" any longer so hitch yourself up here! No kidding, Chris, there's no one I'd rather hear or see 'cause you've got so much to tell. I don't know how, who or what you are going to get up here on, but

---

*She had moved away.

anyway, anyone, anything is o.k. One ride that you might latch on to is Dave. He was planning on coming up with Kathy, but then I don't know whether they're coming or not. If you can drive up then *you* come.

It really is nice, we've got 52 acres of woods, creek, meadow and cliff! I love it! So many things I could tell you about that I'd go nuts trying to write them all down—you know—when you think faster than you can write sort of brings about a frustrated being.

Oh well, what I really wrote about is to tell you you really are welcome Chris, 'cause I'm going silly wondering about your trip, etc. If you can't make it, do write and let me know all what happened, o.k.? You devil!!

Me,
Anne

Winter, Spring, Summer, 1962

Letter to Chris from Anne.

10 a.m. Friday. January 26, 1962

Dear Chris:

Sometimes a letter brings newsy bits of everyday life, in fact most times, and then it can bring sorrow, joy, a mingling of a mind in today's culture retarded by what the writer perhaps may feel the reader wants to read or rather what the writer wants the reader to read. What he reads is a short note denoted by nothing particularly interesting or really worth the while. But then there are those rare moments when someone somewhere will lead a pen across a page, sign his message, seal and mail. Its arrival and reading represent to the recipient, life, a person—a very real person, a mind. The reader experiences emotion, a twinge of sadness, not grief-type sadness, but rather a sort of gushing joy that comes to the surface in the form of small tears rolling down one's cheeks and swallowed by an upturned or smiling mouth. I guess it's the feeling that one experiences upon the discovery of something one believed could never exist or be found, though one has spent a lifetime pursuing it and hoping it exists.

I read your letter this morning, Chris. How can I write in words what it meant? Above I have tried, but somehow and it seems at always the most important times, feelings know no verbal expression. This letter may seem odd—strange, even disconnected—but because I believe you will understand I am going to write my feelings about the letter; the possible why to the reasons you think and feel life as you do, etc. Not that I am any prophet or know myself through and through but, well—you know how it is to have thoughts that need escape and when they find their opportunity—they explode.

When I first knew and heard about you, your whole life was an existence of glory, self, and lots of "I don't particularly give a damn about anything." Then we somehow got to talking in study hall—my opinions are never engraved as set rules or ideas—Chris, you easily became another person than the original Chris. You had ideas, understood (although right now you perhaps don't think so) people, life and yourself much more than most people. This ability in you I appreciated and respected. If only more could experience a life of understanding and extraordinary feelings, but for only a few men is this possible—and they are the wise, the true successes, the very *real* people.

But then my graduation came and I moved—the knowing of a very real person was to be, perhaps, left behind, placed with other memories and experiences.

However, as a person who saw life's meaning in some other way than the common, you would reappear into my mind many times during my first quarter here. I wondered and I would question myself "I wonder how Chris is—if he still is one of those rare individuals." I would consider writing. I wanted to tell you, "Chris, don't you dare ever change except to develop more expansively than you have." But so oftentimes silly are my urges and thoughts, so—I never wrote—possibly I miscalculated. He might have fooled me, he might not understand a letter. I mean to interpret me is something even my mother has ceased to do. But Christmas and a card—aha—my chance—chance to see if he is what I believe he is or could be. So I wrote and that wasn't enough. I had to see—so, Glen Ellyn and that corner drug store. There I was—and yes, he was HIM! He was what I'd hoped! He had more of his special quality than ever. Someone has to tell him all he has. It is important, not only to himself, but to everyone. He is what this crazy, sometimes "mad" world needs.

That, Chris, in essence, is why I write on. You see, Chris, we live in a society of every man for himself. We become enclosed in a glass tomb. Sure, people escape to some vacation spot, but must always return to earning that cursed dollar lest the other man beat us to it. It is America's existence. People must reach, grab, connive, to get it and keep it. And so it is with the world clinging to a vine entangled with the unreal. With false conceptions of what life is people trample the steps to reach the height of this falsity in living. Some have the courage to remain on solid ground—they are the individuals, the thinkers—the ones who won't race to the top only to discover dissolution. But alas, they are always the ones trampled on as the others rush by, and upward to possibly the greatest letdown this world knows—in easier terms I explain it this way: One man races towards the top. Money, prestige, glory and fame all encouraging him onward. Another man works. But in life he doesn't expect prestige and honor, the dollar sign or popularity quota is not his end. Instead he lives for those moments of deeper expression, of meditation, of honesty and unpretentiousness, of communion with the natural world, of caring about others; seeking to help others see through the same window he sees through. Oh, of course, he enjoys the moments of gaity, parties, dancing, but he also knows and understands the other moments of true living.

You, Chris, perhaps you don't realize it now, but you have this great capacity of being real. However, things don't appear to you to be as simple do they? I think maybe I know why. Frustrated. I always have this inner urge—urge for exactly what, I don't know. I feel most frustrated with others. Life, love, sincerity, they can all be expressed, experienced and seen in so many ways, if only we would seek them, know and understand them when they are in front of our very selves. Most persons see so little. Oh, to me this is so frustrating. I want to grab people when I see something beautiful or touching and say, "Did you notice that? Did you feel that surge of joy rush through you in that moment? Please people—notice these things!" Oh, for everyone to be able to feel that joy!

But alas, I can point these things out to people, yet they can't grasp the feeling or thought and so I return—return to this enclosed self—self that becomes overwhelmed with gloom. There is like a rebellion inside me against the gap between what I so want to see and be and want others to see and be and what seems to me the artificial way that conforming and apathetic people are.

And then, too, there are all those things I speak of doing—yet lack of time or perhaps misuse of time prevents me from doing them. This, too, is frustration. In this running with the clock there are always those brief moments of reality—a smile, a word, a work of art, a work of nature—moments that make all the hours not near so important. If we have the capacity to receive the offerings of those moments as you, Chris, can.

From what you were, Chris, as I saw you at first, there was confusion, but underneath there was direct force in an unknown direction. In the second state—the state of mind you have now—many things seem to have been cleared up. However, now that you know them it appears that you don't exactly understand what to do with that which still confuses you so that you can see the direction towards which you are headed. Somehow there are opposing factors, some unstable ideas, yet some forceful and positive ideas. There appears an inner dynamic longing to do something that you don't quite know how to do. Perhaps, what I briefly describe as what I understood and could see in your two states of mind is miscalculated. Chris, something is bursting within you. Incidents in your life are coming

41

to the surface. There is something, perhaps lots of things, you want to let explode. "Lack of sunshine in my life." Chris, something important was meant by you when you made that statement.

I am going to ask a big favor of you, Chris. Please, at a moment when you feel like guiding a pen across some paper, leaving all of yourself—ideas, dreams, on the paper—do it. There may not be time, do it anyway. And send that paper to me. To you it will be most important—to me it will be too. Sometime after you have done this I will explain why, when you are ready I will tell you. You only *touched* on your true feelings in your letter to me, Chris. Perhaps you were blocked by what I might interpret, that I might think you're a Kook. Don't bury your thoughts, Chris—you have reached a point in your life that few reach 'til they are much older—if they ever reach it. I can see a person developing. I can't sit back or be satisfied until you bring yourself wholly to this person. I believe in your sincerity, Chris, and I think you will write—please do—do it—again, in the future I will explain why—you will see and understand why.

California! This perhaps was one of the most important things you have ever done, Chris. An education in itself. Oh, how wonderful it must have been! Someday we will talk about it. Or you will express your thoughts, feelings, etc. in book form with that trip as the foundation—a book published for the purpose of teaching—helping others to see as you see, to learn what you are learning—perhaps the readers can become familiar with the art of awareness, and of caring, the art of really living. Life is sort of like circles—far-out thoughts—confusion and then "pop"—all of a sudden someday you find yourself.

I should be the one thanking you, Chris. One searches for people like you yet one rarely finds them, and when one does, the feeling is almost impossible to explain. It lifts one from the depressed state of feeling that the world of people is blind—one realizes all is not lost—that there *are* some *real* people—for this lift, thank you, Chris.

I am disturbed by what you said. "I hope I don't lose my enthusiasm."

Perhaps this seems a letter of indirect course—with me pouring out my thoughts in what may seem a cluttered way, but, well, crumb bum—you know me I guess.

School is same—classes, eat, study, sleep. They say it's an education. Jack—one of the guys from the pad—wants very much for you to find your way out here if you can. He feels much the same about you as I do.

Running out of this cruddy scratch paper-type stationery so better end.

Love,
Anne

P.S. Chris, keep your chin up. You've got something wonderful in your make-up. I know there are times when all hell could break loose on this crazy mad world, but Chris, in some form we all hit our points of corrupt insides and only a few have the true motive for these feelings. You are fortunate—difficult as it may seem. Someday, Chris, probably a long time from right now, you are going to do something great for this world. You know it. Rare persons like you do.

P.P.S. If you get the chance get ahold of Rachmaninoff's Concerto #3, listen to the Van Cliburn edition of the record. The beginning of the ending climax is excellent—much like a person discovering himself and feeling and seeing a rise in self-expressions, satisfaction, etc. Much feeling and emotion—well worth listening to.

A.

Letter from Glenda to Chris.

June, 1962

Dear Chrisco,

Graduation is a milestone in your life on the road to happiness. There are several branches in the road. If your decision is to take the branch called "opportunity" you will become a success in most everything you do.

You have now graduated and have hundreds of new and different opportunities.

You know that special wishes will be with you all the way.

I'm sure you know how I feel about you and that you are the most wonderful boy I've ever met and the one I have the most faith in.

You've made this last half year the most wonderful in high school and I hope that even though you're finished at Glenbard and are leaving Glen Ellyn, you won't forget the people who remain here and who are sincerely praying for you and thinking of you.

With all my love and hopes,
Glenda

Letter from Anne to Chris.

July 12, 1962

Dear Chris,

Here I am, supposedly busily working at my desk, but for a change, I have all of my work caught up (almost, that is). Your letter meant very much to me and I have wanted to answer you as soon as I could. But didn't want to do so in one of those hurried manners and so waited til I had some time to think as I wrote.

43

Even when I think, it is hard to find the right words to express how I feel about all that you wrote. I have heard it said that there are those times when only the face or heart can express what words can never say, and I almost believe that this is one of those times. But words are so needed to satisfy my desire to tell you how proud I am of you, that I am trying hard to collect my emotions into written thought.

Last spring while at school my room-mate for next year and I decided to go to the Presbyterian church and hear the minister there. Both of us had heard that his sermons were excellent and really left one with something to think about. It so happened that the Sunday we attended he spoke on social pressures in our society and how we forget to be the real self and instead try to do what we think others will find most acceptable in us, whether it is the right thing to do or not. It was a most wonderful sermon and gave me a *lot* to think about. He has his sermons typed up for the congregation because so many people want to take them home and give them to others or re-read them themselves. I picked up a copy of this sermon and have kept it put away. After I read your letter I thought, how true that sermon really was. Here is someone, you, who has done as few do and that is really admit out loud and to themselves their motive for living as they had. I am sending you a copy of the sermon 'cause I thought you might like to read it.

That part in you which I really liked has truly grown bigger and better as you said, Chris. This means so much to me and makes me so happy that little lumps of happiness swell in the back of my throat leaving me just bursting with a good feeling, but also quite speechless. It also did something else, Chris. I almost think you credit me with too much good, but you shouldn't because I, like so many, forget the real person that I could be and am meant to be, and become rather careless in thought, valuing some of the wrong things in life. As I read what you had said, I cried inside bcause I could see myself in so many of the instances. It made me snap up so fast and really take stock of what I was forgetting. So, in all sincerity, Chris, I owe you a tremendous Thank You!

Hey, excuse me for one momento, OK? I have to go get some files.

There is something else about your letter that means a great deal to me, and that is the complete sincerity with which you wrote. One just does not often see sincerity like that. Thank you, Chris, for trusting me enough to be so honest about yourself and thoughts.

It sounds like you have a girl who is terrific in all the important ways. You can really have so many fun times with a person like that. And they are times, like you say, so wonderfully fun that afterwards a smile just finds its way to your face and inner self for no other reason than that you are truly satisfied with the self that you become when with this person and the happiness you seem to find together in the simple and plain and wonderful things in life. I am most happy for you, Chris, and I do hope that everything continues to go well for both of you.

There is one thing which somewhat disturbed me about your letter, and that was that you are still trying to preserve your enthusiasm. Chris, please don't lose this asset of yours. A great thing about you was that you seemed to have a zest for living every day and an ability to realize your faults. I will grant you, there are a lot of reasons for depression. But we cannot let them become the destruction of our happiness and enthusiasm. I don't think I was put here to see and understand as best I can all around me, only to become blind with happiness and enthusiasm. I hope you undersand how I mean this, Chris, because that terrific laugh and smile of yours is too great to lose.

Chris, you have discovered for yourself, by yourself, and with yourself, *life*—its good, its bad, its sorrow and joys. Of course, there is going to be more as you grow older, because there will be more for you to meet and to cope with. But, because now you have learned the real way to cross each problem, all problems in the future will be so much easier to iron out and understand. Because you have discovered where life really can be found and where you should belong in it, you have a fortune so great in your hands that you must never lose sight of it. Instead try and spread it to others that they may understand. I am not going to mean I have been everywhere and done everything in what I am going to say, but rather tell you something which I have noticed in the places I have been and the things I have done. College is truly an education, an education of not only academics, but of life itself. Moving is the same. Both I have experienced in the last year. And in doing both I have met many people our age and much older. And I have been fortunate enough to get to know more than the face of each person. I have been fortunate enough to know their ideas, worries, solutions, etc. concerning life. And it is through what I learned from this that I can honestly say to you that you have a fortune, because Chris, out of all those people, older and younger, there are perhaps three who will admit to themselves, let alone others, where their mistakes have been, who will benefit by realizing them, and who will try to improve. There are perhaps three who make an honest attempt at understanding life and finding and enjoying those characteristics in it that make it so warm and satisfying. Yes, Chris! You do have a life!

I do hope that I don't sound square as hell, so to speak (amen), but you know me by now and square as hell or not, it is me.

Hey, what are your plans for next year? School or work? Whatever, would like to know. When you get the chance do let me hear from you, it is something I look forward to much. Guess I should really end this

45

cause I have some dictation that must be done; I am working as a secretary in an insurance company—much fun—but work.

Be good and do write soon.

Most sincerely,
Anne

July, 1962

As I placed a piece of cherry pie before each member of the family at the end of dinner, I was amused to see that Chris made his usual quick check to see if anyone got a bigger piece than he. He still cared at age eighteen!

"Good dinner, Mama," Art commented, finishing the pie and pushing his chair from the table. He was making a get-away before we got into another serious conversation. Or should I say argument? I had to admit the talk had been especially vigorous tonight. Tim was home from college, full of new ideas, everyone was talking at once—I was as excited as the kids. Of course, Jeff, being six years younger than Chris, always felt that no one listened to *him* at these family discussions. Art always felt we were laboring points, and found them rather tiresome as a rule. But Tim, Chris, and I loved them. No one ever ended up angry. Tonight the discussion had centered around communism.

"Everyone's a little pinko in college," Art had said. "Even I was." We all laughed at the idea—Art had voted nothing but straight Republican since he had first registered.

The doorbell rang. It was Pat O'Donnell who had come for Tim. "Try to keep out of the police department!" I called after Tim. We all liked to kid Tim about the time he and Pat had stolen some hubcaps years ago and received a stern lecture from the police chief. "You boys are lucky you got caught. The next time, you might have taken the whole car, and then you'd really be in trouble." It was Tim's only misdemeanor so far—at least that we knew about. Chris, on the other hand, had had those several brushes with the authorities, the worse of which was selling beer to minors when he was only a minor himself and then lying about where he got it.

Jeff wandered off to do his homework, and Chris lingered on at the table. He often stayed on.

"I got a letter from Anne today."

"I thought that was her writing on the envelope. I wish I'd met her before she moved away. Will she be coming for a visit?"

He lit a cigarette before answering. "I don't know. I suppose it sounds crazy, but I hope not."

"Chris! It sure does sound crazy. You really like Anne. Why, I thought you felt she is one of the real people as you call them."

"That's just the trouble. I—well, I feel sorta uncomfortable with her. See, she thinks I'm a good guy." He was slumped down in his chair with the dog's head on his knee.

"Well, you *are* a good guy!"

"Listen to my Ma talking! Just like the murderer's old lady—'Why, he was always a good boy!'" He snorted.

"Come on, Chris, you *are* a good guy. Oh sure, you're difficult, you're a darned adolescent, you argue over everything, but underneath you're really okay. You know, I've been really pleased with the way you've been improving. You used to be so self-centered, but lately you've been taking such an interest in others. Look at all you've done for Glenda, trying to help her get her problems straightened out. And Joanie Kelly! No one ever took any interest in that poor kid before. Her mother says you're really helping her believe a little in herself."

"Well, Ma, the trouble is everyone builds up that stuff so much. It makes me feel nervous. They think I'm better than I am. God, I have some really rotten thoughts about shooting people down."

"Chris, everyone has some rotten thoughts. You have so little patience with yourself. Who are you to think you should have no faults? What do you think life is all about? Isn't it for growing? If we were so perfect we wouldn't have to be here."

"Well, I try to let people know I'm not perfect, but they even think I'm perfect in my imperfections—that is, that I'm so *honest*. It bothers me like hell that they keep being so thrilled with me. Even Joey Hornbeck. He's a great guy. I really like him. Yet I don't want to be with him much because I'm afraid he'll stop liking me, that he'll find out what I really am."

There he was, handsome, charming, intelligent, with lots of friends—and unhappy. "Chris, what the heck are they going to find out? You tell it all, as you say. What is left to find out?"

"Maybe I'm afraid they'll find out I'm not happy. I keep feeling that everyone needs me to be happy! I guess I do a good job of acting like I am! And they all want me to keep them cheered up!"

"I think I know how you feel," I nodded. "I have some of that trouble myself. People will say, 'You always seem to enjoy life so much!' Then I feel that when I'm with them I have to enjoy, enjoy! Funny thing is, I usually do. But before I see them, I wonder if I can live up to my reputation. Oh well, it's better than having a reputation for being nasty!"

Chris laughed. "Yes, like Myrtle! She has to be nasty all the time, poor lady. Oh well, Ma, don't worry about me." He got up and put his hand under my chin, giving me one of his half smiles.

47

"I'm not worried, Chris. You're going to come out okay. You should have seen me at eighteen. Moody and unpredictable." I made a face. "I was at least thirty before the pieces of the puzzle of me began to fall into place. Only then could I begin to understand myself."

August, 1962

He took a trip over to the Mississippi River without any money except for gas to see if he could live off the land on grasses and berries. He was not successful, and he got food from a family that befriended him. They loved him.

PART 4
1962-1966

Fall, Winter, 1962

Note from Chris's Baby Book. September, 1962

Chris is off to Cornell University. I dread to see him go, yet am happy he has developed enough to be on his own. We know he'll do well—he's a mighty good guy, with the ability to be kind and interested in the other fellow.

Written on flylead of *The Perennial Philosophy* by Aldous Huxley. For Chris from Lee.

September 13, 1962

Dear Chris:

Today you leave for college. It makes me happy to give you this book which has meant so much to me. When you feel the need of spiritual refreshment, you will find that it has all the answers.

It came into my life at a time when my need was great, and was invaluable in helping me to tie up the many loose ends in my thinking. So it is perhaps the most important book in my life (though without Horney's books to help me, I might never have understood it so well); and I'll never be without a copy.

Love,
Mom

Letter from Chris to family.

Sunday, September 1962

Hi,

Well, things are rather hectic these beginning days at Cornell University. My trunk hasn't arrived yet, by the way, and if it isn't in by tomorrow I'll have to start checking things out. We're running around doing every-

51

thing from pictures to meetings with counselors to mixers and picnics and the sweat running from my underarms is superfluous.* My room-mates are two entirely different guys. One is an out-going guy who feels he must become friends with everybody. Last summer he and a friend travelled all over Europe working their way. The other room-mate, on the other hand, is a farm boy who has little urge to put himself out in the company of others and, I'm sure, is finding these first few days very hectic. At any rate, neither is my idea of an ideal friend, but for superficial talk they'll do. Last night I came across a great big Italian boy and his room-mate whom I took to, right off, and I seem to see a budding relationship. By the way, he's a psychology major.

The over-night produced no great friendships. The only two people I met that I enjoyed to any extent were upper classmen, one a girl and one a boy. The girl I rode to the forest with and she was an ideal person with great interest and charm. I was really impressed, and had she not been a senior I would have been quite interested in forming a more intimate relationship. Yesterday Prof. Simpson said she had been written up in *Post* magazine in the "People on the Way Up" section. Funny how these really outstanding people show themselves immediately. Prof. Simpson is a good but busy man. He knows both Sherm Fisher and Glen Ellyn because of an ornithologist who lived there. I'll write later when I've met my professors and classes have started. I'm looking forward to becoming interested in classes and buckling down to study.

Love,
Chris

Letter from Chris to Family.

Thursday, September 1962

Dear Mom, Dad and Jeff,

I've now met most of my professors, the chemistry prof. looking most promising. I can tell now that studying is going to be of utmost importance for good grades. The social life around here is mighty wearing, constantly having to put yourself out at picnics, breakfasts, dances, open-houses, convocations. I find it hard to be myself too much, constantly having to give and discuss mediocrities and make new friends. I've met a good looking girl of the rebellious nature and I'm going out with her twice this weekend. She's got something on the ball and enjoys talking to me and

---

*He had a problem with excess perspiration when nervous.

getting things off her chest. After this weekend there will be no more free dances though.

This brings me to money. I'm down to $10.00 and still have $2.50 worth of paperbacks to buy, $1.50 worth of manila envelopes and drawing paper. I've had to buy lab. glasses and an apron, my food up until today when the meals started, my books which were $49.50, pay $4.00 on a yearbook, plus lab kits, plus many other expenses which I can't remember, but which mount up. I'm going to need $18.00 to buy a ticket worth $64.00 for football games, basketball games, baseball games, wrestling, LaCrosse, soccer and many other events (50 altogether). But if all I go to are the football games and one basketball game I'll have made what I spent. I'm convinced one needs one of these tickets. So if you could send $20.00 that would finish off expenses. I know it's all a lot of money, but there's nothing I can do to help it.

Well, to get back to pleasanter things, I've gotten to know this guy, Tom, real well and he's really a funny guy. He's not too dedicated to studies or other people but he's helped to cheer up some rather harsh times. I miss home quite a bit, both you and Glenda, but I'm making the adjustment.

I have two eight o'clock classes and three labs of 3 hrs each, but I'm very happy with my schedule. My classes stop at 11 a.m. on Friday and don't resume until 10 a.m. Monday leaving the weekend clear for studying and recreation.

Well, I really ought to go up and get a reserved book at Mann library now which we're supposed to study for Cons. so I'll close.

Looking forward to seeing you again, even though it's only been a week!

Love,
Chris

Letter from Chris to Family.

October 19, 1962

Dear Mom, Dad, Jeff,

I have no time to write, but I want to tell you about some important decisions. First of all, conservation is no major for me, it deals with hunting and fishing and has a complete coldness of thought towards animals and the managing of little animal lives. You know also that there are two contradicting aspects to me—one, which was the strongest in me for a long time, was the urge to get out away from people and live simply, which was what conservation, naturalist or any other such fields would have given me. The other aspect, which has now gained priority, was the liking and wishing to work with people. As you said before, and as I now firmly believe, one is never happy until he is serving people in a universal, loving way. I also feel that I've been given a gift, the family which I was born into, which has given me a wonderful understanding and feel for life and I naturally have the ability to talk to people in a comfortable, easy way. Keeping all this in mind, I've been seriously considering changing my major to pre-med. and becoming a doctor. Of course, this would be a big change, 8 years of school and a move from ag. into the arts schools which I may not be able to do. I'm going to talk it over with Prof. Simpson pretty soon (he's my advisor) and see what he has to say.

Oh, yes, and my very pessimistic attitude on marriage is changing also. I feel very strongly now that I could be happily married to someone with whom I had a basic sharing of major ideas. I can feel myself becoming more versatile, more adaptable, which was what I wasn't before and which made the thought of sharing a life with someone almost unthinkable. Also, I'd love to bring up some kids, to be able to start from scratch with them and give them an understanding such as I have. In fact, I almost feel that is a duty. By the way, don't worry, I'm not planning on getting married for a long time yet! But my almost obstinate attitude towards the idea is changing or has changed. Well, enough said there.

Dad, send me addresses of the letter-writers to fraternities and I'll be glad to send them a little note. It is good to have those recommendations and thanks a lot for having them written. Fraternities don't start rushing until a week before the semester ends and in all this meantime we are not allowed to talk about fraternities to any fraternity member.

There's a bus home Thanksgiving for $32.00 round trip. By the way, if I'm to take it I'd have to have a reservation in as quick as possible; so send money as soon as possible if you want me to take it.

Well, Jeff, I haven't had too much time to say much to you before, but I hope you're getting the grades you want. According to my calculations you should be moving into the new school very soon, but of course, those things don't always come out as planned. What did you think of the Dodgers-Giants playoff! That was pretty disheartening to the Dodgers. Just think, if you were a loyal Dodger fan. And for crying out loud, what happened to Floyd Patterson? I saw the fight on TV and he didn't get touched. Well, maybe Dad got a good look at it. He must have flipped when it ended so quick. Sports are the only news I can keep up with around here. I didn't even know that they shot another man into orbit until 4 days after it happened. I listen to the radio very infrequently because of the time element. If you think yu've got it hard in seventh grade wait till you get to college and learn about Phytomastiginas and Psubshell pi antilonding. It's enough to drive you bats.

Well, new girl friend, Betty, and I think an awful lot of each other. I can't remember what I last wrote you about her, but though we have some pretty rocky times caused by the unwillingness to change in various ways, we know each other very well and I feel very close to her. We've gotten a lot accomplished in a month, about a hundred times better than 99% of the people who know each other until they die! I did need someone to talk to, and I feel she was a kind of Godsend. Of course, this serious stuff is all new to her and at times I'm sure it seems probably to her like more than she can handle or wants to. But she's doing well for a beginner.

Prelim time (this week) is just about unbearable. There's a mountain of facts to be memorized for those tests and I feel like screaming at times.

By the way, my money isn't holding out too well, laundry and food, and dates and hundreds of unexpected things (lost all my keys; new dorm keys cost $1.00), but I still have $18.00 left. If I get too pinched I'll let you know though.

Altogether, I'm having a wonderful time!

Love,
Chris

Letter from Chris to family.

November, 1962

Hi,

Sorry I haven't written before this but time really does fly and I have someone to talk to and complain to right here so I'm not driven to write. If I make the switch to Arts school it is a rather complicated process which I'll have to go through next year. I'll tell you about that when I get home.

I arrive in Chicago early Wednesday morning, leaving here at 7:00 Tuesday night by the way. I'll have my midterm grades by then. Comparatively, I'm doing real well in school but my average is $C+$, the way I figure it. I've got a B in Bot. and Chem. and C's in all the rest. But, like I said, compared to the other guys I'm doing very well. And I feel like I'm using the majority of my potential.

Well, I do have a lot of things to discuss but I will wait to get home to say them. I'm looking forward to seeing you all very much and seeing everyone else, too, (big man home from college) especially Glenda, to whom I have very many things to say. I guess I never told you much about that situation, but I told her about Betty a week after I met her, and since explained many things to her in numerous letters. Well, all this is stuff I want to talk about when I get home.

See you soon and looking forward to it.

Love,
Chris

Christmas Season, 1962

Betty came for a visit. Her shyness was unbelievable. If one of us, young or old, caught her in a room alone, she darted out like a rabbit. We tried hard to win her and failed.

I worried about the relationship. They had their own little safe world. Chris, who had always had so many friends, now had only one. He had grown dependent on her and she on him. It did not seem healthy. Chris was tender with her, helped her try to analyze her problems.

Betty wrote a note to Lee when she left. She told, among other things, of how much she appreciated what Lee had given Chris, and what he, in turn, had given her.

Winter, Spring, 1963

Letter from Chris (back at Cornell) to family.

January, 1963

Dear Folks,

We had a good trip back; in fact it was the high point of the vacation, I'd say. We had a terrible time with all the luggage in Chicago, on the way, and here, but it was the kind that was fun because of its absurdity. The bus ride itself was the most fun I've had in a long time. Both our spirits hit a high point at the same time, which is a fairly unusual circumstance for us. We discussed innumerable topics and we had a wonderful time just curling up and falling asleep.

By the way, I thought you might be interested in the fact that I am now in Arts and Sciences and am soon to become a zoology major! I had a hectic interview with a quite unfriendly dean who was about as responsive as an insecure girl meeting a fellow's folks for a few days. After telling me Arts students needed 3 years of a language when I'd only had two, and that I was going to major in the subject which I'd received the lowest grade in, he suddenly announced that he'd take a chance and let me in. (I think I fast-talked him; I even made him smile for a split second.) Well, I lose three hours of credit that I earned, one hour for orientation that is purely an agricultural subject and two for conservation that just won't do me any good because it is two hours, not three. I now have quite a range of choice as to what I will take.

Mrs. Hubell* has invited me to stay for a couple of days between terms.

*Betty's mother

56

(We have four days together—actually, we have 14 but the last ten are donated to rush.) Jan. 22 is the start of finals. I'd be going, probably, Jan. 27. Round trip tickets are $13.50. If you think this is pushing things a little, I understand, but Betty is anxious for me to meet her friends and show me a few of her sights.

I was very interested to hear your comments on Betty's note. No, I didn't read it, nor was it my suggestion that she write it, although she told me she wanted to and I told her that if one feels like doing something and that it would be good, one ought to do it. We've discussed what I feel are weaknesses in her. She no longer gets upset when I bring them up. I tell her about my weaknesses.

I got the two packages okay. Thanks a lot. Also thanks for having us around for four days. I never fully told you all my reasons for it. Betty had a tendency to blame her problems on Cornell surroundings. She thought that people were looking at her because they were sexually interested, and the loudness, swearing, etc., that you run across in large groups of kids made her feel uneasy, etc. Putting her into different surroundings helped make her see that this wasn't the reason at all, it helped her to admit more, which was what I hoped it would do, although I knew it was trying for you. My other reason was that Cornell forces you into little habits. It is a small life, actually with much less freedom than you have at home. To break from these habits for a period helps one to realize what they are and gives a realization of life much larger than the one that you fall into, when you do the same things day in and day out. In other words, when you do the same thing day in and day out, the details of them become more important until they seem to be the whole world. A breaking away from these habits and details brings one to the realization that life is much larger and more encompassing than the small portion that we must live in here; and that, though one may conquer most or all aspects of this small portion, one should keep in mind that it is only a small portion, and that one has not conquered life as a whole. (This applies to Betty, not me). Of course there were a few other reasons, like it would be fun to have her around, and it would give me a chance to show her off to my friends and show her what a nice house and Cadillac we own! And show my parents off to her. (I was very proud to bring her home.)

Well, that takes care of most of the news, and thanks.

Love,
Chris

February, 1963

He failed to get into the only fraternity (Tau Delt) that interested him. He had been warned that if he didn't sharpen up, get out of the flannel shirts and the field boots, give up the long hair and beard (he set the styles for the hippies to come) he might not get into a fraternity he wanted. Perhaps this was the problem. (We had never heard of this fraternity.*)

Yes, Chris had become eccentric in his dress, non-conforming. I didn't mind, I like people who have the guts to be different.

He began to get a few boy friends. That was reassuring.

Leaning over backward not to encourage dependence, I never called him up, and I seldom wrote him. But *he* called, and there would be long conversations. Dad would try to get us to hang up, but you can't shut off a guy who needs you. And he did, he needed to talk to someone who talked his language. And I knew there would be few outside of home. Didn't I have the same trouble? There are so few people who are concerned. Who think.

Letter from Chris to family.

February 15, 1963

Dear Folks,

Well, I guess the thing you'll be most interested in knowing is that I'm speaking to you as an Independent. The decision wasn't hard because after a smoker and two dinners, Tau Delt politely told me I hadn't met enough guys to get enough votes to be invited back, and I suppose it's true. The fellow that runs out of things to say after a few minutes is then rushed off to meet more people so there is no embarrasing lag in the conversation. I didn't have that trouble and met and talked to only 9 out of 72 members while I was there. I had no idea that it was the rushee's place to get around and meet more guys, but that's the way it seems to have worked out. Maybe they got mixed up thinking I'd already met lots of guys the other times. But whatever the reason, I didn't get invited back to the last dinner. It required a quick adjustment on my part because the guys I met were friends. D.K.E., Alpha Sigma Phi, and Delta Phi all invited me back, but they are just houses with real average guys out for a good time and lots of laughs and with whom I would rather not live if I had a choice. So I just turned them down and decided to try the Independent way of life this

---

*1984—Neither has the present dean at Cornell! He suggested Delta Tau Delta—but that is known as "the Delts."

next year. The reason I wanted to join a fraternity at all was to have a social life set up for me which I could go to or not go to. As an Independent, it requires pushing, making your own parties, etc., which I would have liked to avoid. I feel that we must go to college parties and associate with plenty of people because Betty's tendency is to run off into "our own little world," and just let the "big world" go without our presence. This would do her no good and a fraternity would have helped me out with this problem. Well, it just requires a little extra effort. If it doesn't work out I can rush again next year (heaven forbid!). I did have some very interesting conversations and made some firm friends, and in this way had better luck than most of the guys who pledged. (54% went fraternity this year.) Well, Saturday I start looking for a room with a guy I met in the fall and enjoy very much, Tom Deanett; I couldn't ask for more in a room-mate and he will be a pleasure.

Will let you know how we come out. Hope all's well there.

Love,
Chris

Letter from Chris to family.

Spring, 1963

Hi,

Well, I'll unload the news. We picked up an apartment for five men finally. That also means we picked up three room-mates, all of whom are really good guys. The apartment is 8 minutes walk from the campus, takes up the whole second floor of a house, and has three single and one double study-bedrooms, a living room, kitchen and naturally a john. It will be really nice to fix it up with curtains and other little things and I'm looking forward to it very much. By the way, it costs forty-five dollars a month for September through June and we have to pay for the first month before we leave school. Bus fare home will be twenty-one dollars. It's hard to cash checks for over twenty dollars around here, so if possible could you make three checks for twenty dollars and one for six. I guess that will finish up the money transactions for one year!

I guess I never told you what my mid-term average was: 83. The chem. prelim I was worried about I did flunk, but so did everyone else and my grade was 10 points better than the average, so I guess there's no problem there. We just finished the last "round" of prelims and I got a 91 (A) in psych., 90 (A) in zo., 86 (B) in chem. and 83 (B) in botany, so they came out pretty well. Next year I have to get started on a language so I picked Russian. I also have to take physics to become a zoology major, and I'll be taking philosphy and genetics. It will probably be quite a bit harder than this year was.

Betty and I are still getting along fine. Now that it is nice on Saturday, we've been trying to do a lot of interesting things. Last week we went to an old quarry and searched for fossils. We found quite a few rather interesting ones, had a good picnic, found a rabbit skull in perfect condition, tadpole for which we are now equipping a small aquarium, and many other interesting things. Other times we have found and identified many wildflowers and have been enjoying our Saturday "vacations" very much. It's wonderful territory around here.

Finals are in two and one-half weeks, then I finish around the second or third of June. I suppose you'd have written if I'd gotten any returns on jobs. Well, maybe it's still too early.

Well, that's the important news from this front. How are things at the other side? Actually, it won't be too long before I'll be home again for good. Time sure flies around here. According to my calculations the new house should be pretty well underway by the time I'm home. Don't forget that I'll be quite a bit of help now with my newly acquired knowledge of conservation, botany and zoology. Why we'll have the best garden in town by merely taking into consideration day length, annual precipitation, humidity, altitude, soil content, drainage, etc. Yes sir, big man home from college! Freshman year, no less.

Mom, don't forget those ceramic polar bears you're going to make. They will really delight Betty. I'm sure of that. And by the way, Happy Mother's Day, Mother! Thanks for the extra five dollars, by the way. As usual it came in very handy! We've seen a lot of really good movies lately, the caliber seems to be rising. The latest ones we've seen have really been "deep" and thought-provoking. Well, this is just to say that the money hasn't been wasted. Thanks for everything. I don't know if you can tell, but I'm feeling pretty good!

Love,
Chris

Summer, Fall, 1963

During the summer Chris worked in an amusement park.

Every night he wrote Betty long letters.

Then suddenly the romance crashed. Betty had become involved with another man. Chris had always demanded that she be honest with him. Now she was, and he could not take it.

He was devastated.

Betty wrote some letters to Chris expressing her misery over Chris's letters which evidently had indicated that their relationship was greatly harmed. She emphasized that what Chris had given her had been wonderful, that he had not wasted his time, that he had not failed.

September, 1963

After the summer at home, I took him to the bus station to go back to school. As he got out of the car, he said, "So long, Mom. It's sure been great to be home and get a shot in the arm so I can go back and face the world."

Letter from Chris (back at Cornell) to family.

October 1, 1963

Dear Folks,

I got all the money, etc. and all the trunks and things so there is no problem along that line. It's been a lonely and disheartening first week, which seemed like a month. The trouble? Nothing much goes good. One room-mate didn't show, although through great effort we did get another. Tom has hardly been here at all because he has been helping out his sister (pregnant). Roy Kramer is a farmer from upstate New York, and the guy who didn't show up is also a farmer. At any rate Roy is a hard worker and a pretty good person, but to the others he looks uninteresting because he isn't a "slick" New Yorker. It's depressing to watch and a great complication to keep everyone reasonably happy.

Betty has been a thorn in my side. I saw her a couple of nights ago and rode around in my car and had a really great time. But I talked to her again last night and we got to the problem at hand. We talked about an hour, the last half of it being a battle. I tried my hardest to understand, be cautious, but things were so unreasonable and my emotions are still so tied up with her that I couldn't be "detached" and we argued like cats and dogs. The frustrating thing is that my ideas don't count with her anymore because I was too honest. I have admitted that I have been oppressive in putting my ideas across and that sometimes on the very things I have been oppressive about I have been wrong on, and that I have been pretty confused on sex and sometimes its role. So any arguments, no matter how good, fall on deaf ears. At any rate, it all hasn't made me happier.

College kids are cruel, cold, know-it-alls to a large extent, and it gets mighty depressing. But I'll spring back and find some warm friends pretty quickly. These are the reasons I need a girl. Almost for an escape. If I do

61

get a girl, though, she will only be an escape once a weekend at the most. None look too interesting. My confidence is not at its peak either.

Well, that's the story. My classes I enjoy very much. And I'm sure the only room-mate who enjoys all the others' company and vice-versa. Activities start next week and perhaps some amount of settling will come with them.

Dad, I presume you are now at home after your sub-total gastrectomy and I hope you're feeling pretty decent. Here's hoping now that you are rid of the ulcer problem you have gotten rid of all alimentary problems. So long now.

Love,
Chris

Letter to Chris from Lee.

October 6, 1963

Dear Chris:

Just got your letter a few minutes ago. Have been wondering about you and whether things were looking up, but I guess not *too*—so I typed the enclosed from James Agee for you. This may not seem like something to cheer a guy up, but it will remind you that sensitive, spiritual type people always have a struggle before they get organized.

Sometimes they never do get organized. James Agee never did, and died at only forty-five without having written more than three books. *Yet*, in spite of the fact that he was so miserable, the greatness of him gets at his readers. He was great—but not great enough to learn the self-negation to which he refers. As I have told you, I feel a great rapport with him. If he were not dead, I would most certainly try to know him. I felt the same way about the writer Thomas Wolfe, but he was also dead before I read his books.

This excerpt from Agee could very well have been written by me at age twenty-five, except for a couple of lines. I doubt that the words "self-negation" would have been used by me at all. I think that whenever I heard such words, I *didn't* hear them. It was about five or six years later that I was ready to listen—after I had learned to be myself a bit. After all, one can hardly think about giving up oneself if one does not yet know what one is. Also, I was never troubled by the apathy he refers to—but that really doesn't mean much. Or maybe it does. Both his apathy and my phobias, etc., were incapacitating, neurotic symptoms, and therefore similar. But perhaps the fact that his symptom was apathy and mine phobias was due to some little basic difference between us. That little difference

62

was the cause of his never becoming adjusted, and my *becoming* adjusted compared, that is, to other people and compared to what I was.

The reasons I typed it for you are what I said in the last line of the first paragraph, and that it does sound so much like me at 25, and is meant to encourage you because you will see that it does not sound in the least like me now. True, one has never completely arrived, but I do feel I know in what direction I'm going, and I find it a joyful road, even the bad parts, for one reason or another (though I'll fight like a dog to keep the bad parts out!).

I kind of hate to write about the deeper things—there are always semantic problems even with one's own family—because the written word is so, well, blunt, compared to conversation, which involves gestures, facial expressions, etc., which can change the whole meaning.

About Betty, I do wish you did not have that problem to add to your complications. You are a good guy, and through all your fumbling and emotionalism this fact shines through for anyone who wants to see it. To me it seems she is seeing what she wants to see because she wishes to reject you. She wishes to reject you probably because she chooses to be what she is. In short, she wishes not to change. Her wish not to change is worth more to her than the good friendship you have to offer. Confusion, oppressiveness, etc., do not blot out the bright light of friendship. A true friend of yours would look right through them.

I don't think you are anywhere nearly as confused as Agee, or as I was. But it is true that you have still to find out some things for yourself. Your relationship with Betty has been a good education in your self-understanding. And too, you are not quite ready to give up hating, that is, to begin to try. You wish to hang onto your ways for a little while longer.

Oh dear—if I have said anything that sounds wrong, it is just that it is on paper—if you were here, you would understand.

Anyway, I hope by now you are getting more of a feeling of "belonging" where you are. Since girls are so important to you—as escapes without which you feel you can't get along—it's too bad you are at Cornell where there are comparatively few girls. You should be some place like Northwestern where there are a lot more to pick from!

To sum up, I wish *I* had run into someone like you when *I* was in school! For all my neurotic problems, I wouldn't have fought you, I would have looked right past your weaknesses. And if you weren't so neurotically in need of a girl, you would probably forget Betty.

Again, things look so harsh on paper.

By the way, please don't quote me!

Dad is feeling better and stronger every day. He dictates *exactly* what he wants to eat each meal, and it had better be right! He spends part of each day at the new house directing the workmen. Actually, it is nice for him that he has this mild activity.

Jeff is up for treasurer of 8th; was co-chairman of mag. drive; is captain of his room's touch football team (and has been commended by the teacher); is the room's student council rep. A real big shot. It must be his deep voice.

Have heard nothing from Tim for two weeks.* He's pretty worried about some comprehensive tests he has to take, you remember. Hope he'll pick up some satisfactory friends.

I'm still trying to get permission for us four women to present our case** at the big state conservation board meeting concerning Dr. James. Have had a long 'phone conversation, since talking with you, with the chairman's assistant who tried to mow me down—called me "Honey"—what a guy. Tomorrow our state senator, who wrote a bang-up letter for us (which has been ignored) is going into action on the 'phone. One thing is sure—we intend to be *heard*—*some* place. And it is obvious that they are scared to death of us. This thing has gone way beyond Dr. James, who's become a symbol. The meeting is next week. Wonder if we'll be there?***

How did you come out on the D.J. test, and the singing?

Yesterday I had fun painting an idyllic scene—lovely brook, willows, beautiful ducks. Then along came the farmer, talked at length about the wonderful eating qualities of these ducks—not greasy, etc.—and said a man was coming after them next week. Ah me. It was like the time I painted the pigeons flying around a cupola while a rifleman decided to shoot some of them. I see there is a move to rid N.Y. City of several million pigeons (one of the best parts of the city) because in their droppings is a fungus that has supposedly caused two deaths from some form of meningitis. It is interesting that human life is held so dear, while animal life is looked upon as just plain nothing.

Well, about the college kids, and then I must stop (Grandpa and Aunt Ethel are coming!). Remember that they are cruel, cold know-it-alls because they are really pretty darned afraid they don't know anything at all. Try to concentrate on what you can give to them rather than what you can get from them. In other words, there is no time like the present to get into the loving bit. They may seem not to give a darn about warmth, but they do. Just think of what most of them have had to defend themselves against. As Kierkegaard said, in effect, it can be tremendously exciting to find good in someone—*some* good, be it ever so small. And then if you just can't find any, it's fun to forgive. Love has all the answers.

---

*Tim was at the state university working for his Master's.
**I was deeply involved in the fight against the indiscrimate use of DDT and other chlorinated hydrocarbon pesticides.
***We were!

Yes, I know you have to find out the desirability of self-negation for yourself. But others can be a great help. *I know.*

If I've said anything that doesn't seem to add up, don't hold it against me. I can explain!

Love,

M.

P.S. (On envelope) Your garden is keeping us well supplied with great tomatoes and wondrous flowers.

Letters of James Agee to Father Flye. George Braziller, Inc.

". . . . I am in most possible kinds of pain, mental and spiritual, that is, and the trouble revolves chiefly around the simple-sounding problem how to become what I wish I could when I can't. That, however, is fierce and complicated enough to keep me balancing over suicide as you might lean out over the edge of a high building, as far as you could and keep from falling but with no special or constant desire not to fall. It works many ways: one is apathy, or a sort of leady, heavy silt that, always by nature a part of my blood, becomes thicker and thicker, and I less pleasant and less bearable to live with, or to live within. Another is that without guidance, balance, coordination, my ideas and impressions and desires, which are much larger than I can begin to get to paper, are loose in my brains like wild beasts of assorted sizes and ferocities, not devouring each other, but in the process tearing the zoo to parts . . . The wise answer of course would be that there is only one coordinator and guide, and that he is come at through self-negation. But: that can mean nothing to me until or unless I learn it for myself. Without scrupulousness, I am damned forever; and my base, if I ever find it, must be of my own finding and understanding or it is no sort of base at all. Well, it cannot be solved. Not at any rate in process of this rotten letter. I can I think quite surely promise you that I shall not suicide. Also be sure I am sorry and ashamed for this letter, in every way but one, that being that between friends even the lowest cowardliness is not to be shut away and grinned about, if worse come to worst. Aside from all these things, there is much to enjoy and more to be glad for than I deserve, and I know it, but they are mostly, by my own difficulty, out of my reach."

From *Letters to Father Flye*, by James Agee. Permission granted by David McDowell, Trustee, the James Agee Trust.

65

Letter from Chris to family.

Hi Population,

Well, things are very bright right now and have been for quite awhile. Before I say anything else let me first thank you for the wonderful warm letter I got from you, Mom. It bolstered me a lot and reminded me of the friends I have, and the worth I can be, and my garden. This may sound a little strange and isn't the greatest vote for my emotional stability or adjustment, but the letter came just before I had to go to a class and I had no time to read it; but I read the outside about the tomatoes and flowers, and I knew what else would be in the letter when I opened it; and I had a terrific struggle restraining tears as I walked to class. They were the most joyful, sympathetic tears I ever restrained. Maybe I should say what I mean by sympathetic. The letter gave me the power to step away from myself, sort of like an outsider looking in at the situation at hand and being able to muster a few sympathetic tears for the guy and his problems; the same sympathetic tears I restrain when I am aware of someone else who is undergoing problems. But since the reception of your letter I have been quite a bit more equipped to handle problems, and am now a lot happier person than I was and worth a little more to his surroundings.

I enjoy the guys I live with a tremendous amount. There are three guys from upstairs and five on our floor, all of whom are very good friends. The five below us are just acquaintances, by their choice. There is never one night that passes when there aren't from 2 to 8 guys in our living room til 2 or 3 in the morning in bull sessions ranging from light to deep discussions, everyone contributing to all types. This room is painted purple with bright red window trimming, and 3 red lights on one side, two blue on the other, our "mood lights." In this atmosphere we hold our discussions, sometimes very potent, over a beer or two. Mel, the senior whom we got as a replacement for the guy who didn't show, is a very good friend. He put together a "washtub bass" and we take time out every now and then to sing a few songs with my guitar and the bass. Our favorite is "Summertime." Mel is going to get married in Denver, during February intersession, and he asked me to be an usher. I accepted. I can ride out and back with one of his friends, so I thought I better give you pre-warning. Needless to say, we're going to have to find another room-mate for second semester, and we're going to miss Mel a lot. We put together an intramural football team and won the Independent league, so now we are in the finals. Three wins and we're university champs—fat chance.

As far as girls go, I haven't gone out on one date, though I've had two dates which have been broken for one reason or another. I've found a girl who looks interesting to me in my Russian class, but I have procrastinated asking her out for many reasons. But I'm going to pretty soon, because she's the only girl I've met up here lately that radiates. Betty, of course, has completely alienated herself from me. A fact which gave me much torture for awhile, but now gives me little or none.

These last two weeks have been my first round of prelims. In physics I got a 75, but that was 14 over the class average, so with a curve to 70, it should be an 84. I got a 95 back today on the Russian prelim which made my spirits soar a little, even though the class average was a very high 80. Very few times do you find a class average that high around here, which is proof of the smartness of people taking Russian. I took a plant breeding prelim today which I think I did pretty well on, but we'll see. I got an 83 on . . . (rest of letter missing).

Winter, Spring, 1964

Letter to Lee from Chris.

January 1964

Hi Mom,

Almost happy birthday time again! I guess the time for you goes pretty fast. Well, your present this year is the same as last year, a few kind words and a sincere smile. It's too bad your birthday comes on the last day before finals start, because this week is a hectic one with all the finishing touches having to be put on the semester—final lab, practicals, papers, etc., and studying for finals. I am not able to just sit back and think up something original. I enjoy doing that but put together business and inhibition and it doesn't get done. Well, happy birthday at any rate, Ma. And maybe someday—

I came out with a fairly lucky break the other night. We cleared everything out of the living room and held a series of wrestling matches, referee and all. I beat two guys; one in my weight group and one in a higher group—a big guy—Ken—190 lbs. Well, it was a good match, but my foot went through the window. (It was really a rough match and Ken spun me right over. Don't worry, there was hardly any chance of it happening!) Well, no injuries at all, but there will be very little wrestling for awhile.

Right now, our living room looks real good, our rug just got here, and with the curtains and the fairly decent paint job, it looks all right. Also have our collection of beer bottles and cans in the corner, a pyramid 10 stories high of cans surrounded by bottles, but it's only ⅔ done.

I've cut my smoking down to less than 10 a day, allotting myself six, but usually going somewhat over that mark, natch.

Psychologically, I rise and fall periodically, but generally with a higher average than I had the first term! I'm enjoying lots of things, even talking about mediocre things for a period of time, an accomplishment believe it or not!

The tape recorder has been used pretty close to incessantly since it got here, and everyone is taking a lot of enjoyment from it. I wonder how long it will last? We've all taken a lot of time out with it, recording our singing, languages, and general discussions and jokes.

Gradewise I'm averaging 82½ with all but the finals to go. They worry me as usual.

Dad sent me an accident form to fill out for the car I backed into and his letter was extremely abrupt, his disgust showing through. Then he wrote again after I answered it and it was a warm letter. Something bothers me quite deeply about our relationship and I can't quite put my finger on it. It's more than just like or dislike and I hadn't ever felt it before the argument over Christmas. My attitude toward him has suddenly become businesslike, bargaining. Fewer emotional involvements is the characterization of it. I doubt that he could say very much now that could hurt. Along with this has come a more intensive speculation of his ultimatum, that of taking his guff and his money, both or neither. Well, I want to be honest to you. I've spent a couple of nights pondering it, and it remains a true temptation—to support myself. I doubt that I will decide to do it ever, but the reasons I won't are only because I think it might mean a lot to you if I didn't, and it might mean a lot to Dad if I didn't, more than he realizes.

I'm afraid part of my reason would be revenge, never a good reason, of course. But I've calculated the money aspects, and I'm sure I could make it in that way. I doubt that that has much to do with my reluctance at all. Well, I thought I ought to just tell you my thoughts on this.

I'm off to Denver on the 4th and back on the 9th. I'm not going to ask for any extra money, but just make the trip as cheaply as I can. I will need my brown shoes, which I left at home, and a new pair of black shoes, as the ones I have now have just about had it. So what you can do is mail a pair of black shoes, 12 C, from Giesche's, and the brown shoes I left, or else money, ($15) to buy black shoes with. At any rate, I need them before the fourth. That's about all, unless you feel like sending my Bob Dylan record up too!

If you're pondering over my birthday at all, here are some suggestions I just thought of.

1. A harmonica with a finger press to change keys. (Crescent Music store has them for around $8.00).
2. A harmonica holder for around the neck so I can play both harmonica and guitar together. The big one wouldn't fit, so you could get an F and a C harmonica that would sell for about $2.00 apiece. You could order them from the same store. I really enjoy the little harmonica I bought.

Well, that's about all I can think up for now. I hope you and Dad are still on peaceful terms, if for no other reason than to have a pleasant celebration.

I just thought of a problem. Parts of this letter will make Dad pretty hostile I'm sure so I'd better copy over the parts that won't and send them too.* If you want Dad to see this I don't care, though in my judgment I wonder if it would be too wise. I'll let you make the decision at any rate without forcing it on you.

I hope you've got most of the house out of the way by now!

Love,
Chris

Letter to Chris from Lee.

January 27, 1964

Dear Chris:

I called the music shop about the harmonica. They have them from $7.50 to $20.00. I ordered the $20.00 one. The man said he could get a holder that would fit. I assume that is o.k.?

Ordered the picnic outfit from Fields, a $17.00 one. Think since you are being an usher, you should be giving as nice a gift as this. Sent, or rather am sending today, your brown shoes, and Dad is mailing you a check for $50.00, to cover new black shoes, and to give you some expense money for your trip. We didn't know just what to send you, not knowing just what you have from what you made, etc.

About going on your own, I am sure that in so doing you would find that you were unable to force any kind of a show-down, or that any good would come of it as far as your relationship with Dad is concerned. Truly, I believe that he has become resigned to things the way they are, and that would not make a dent in him. Perhaps something would, under some circumstances, but I feel sure from what he's said, that would not be it.

---

*Which he did.

As I said, I feel your reasons for thinking these thoughts are many, covering many different facets of your personality. Only you would be able to unearth them all, and even you could not if you had neurotic reasons for not wishing to do so. To me, your wish to make things hard for yourself, with the thought that actually for you it would be easier, because of your particular needs, sounds as if you are attempting to put yourself through some sort of penance, or self-mortification, with the hope that it would bring you more quickly to a spiritual goal you would like to reach by bringing about what Aldous Huxley (and Agee, remember?) calls "self-naughting." It is true that self-naughting is a desirable aim, but only so that one may better become part of the Whole. To the extent there is self, there cannot be the One working through one. However, I am wondering if this being on your own would really help you to get rid of self. Read the chapter on mortification in *The Perennial Philosophy.** I'll just quote a couple of things here from it. On page 98, from St. Teresa, "Once, when I was grumbling over being obliged to eat meat and do no penance, I heard it said that sometimes there was more of self-love than desire of penance to such sorrow." And on page 101, last paragraph, in Huxley's words, "To sum up, that mortification is the best which results in the elimination of self-will, self-interest, self-centered thinking, wishing and imagining. Extreme physical austerities are not likely to achieve this kind of mortification. But the acceptance of what happens to us (apart, of course, from our own sins) in the course of daily living is likely to produce this result."

You said you don't know what to do to change. Well, you could start alerting yourself to every envious thought you have, examine the reasons for having it, and little by little you could, *if you truly desired* to do so, eliminate this selfish practice which keeps you from self-eliminating. You are aware enough of what should be your goals to know what you are doing to prevent yourself from reaching them. It is not that you don't know what to do, it is that, as I said, you do not want to *enough*. I myself work on eliminating these bad habits of self a great deal of the time, yet there are a couple of people who annoy me so much by their sanctimoniousness, that I indulge myself in hostile thoughts about them, and I enjoy the hostile thoughts. I also dislike having them a great deal. But I am not ready to give them up. However, they are not a very important part of my life, and I am not suffering very much over them. But you are—you're suffering a great deal.

Suffering comes from separation. Separation from the One. Nothing else. You have enough desire not to want to be separate so that you suffer greatly over your selfishness. The only way to get over your suffering is

*Published by Harper and Brothers, New York.

to keep trying to eliminate self. Do read *The Perennial Philosophy*—it made things clear to me, and has sustained me many times. Don't say, "I'm not a good reader." That's usually what you say when I suggest you read something. To become a good reader, read! (To become loving, love!).

I wish you were closer so that from time to time we could talk when you are feeling too much alone and disturbed.

Just remember above all, spiritual freedom is not easily won. Getting it is HELL! But it's HEAVEN when you get it. There are, as I said, plateaus. One makes a big step and feels great. Then one practices. Then there comes a time for another step. Every step is thrilling. Without suffering, man would never advance. Earthly being that he is, he could never be lured except by a desire to stop suffering—that is, until he comes closer to becoming part of the One. When he comes closer, he can be lured by the joy and comparative peace he feels, and he wants more and more to become part of God; not because he does not want to suffer but because he is convinced that God, not self, is all that really counts.

Just be sure that whatever you decide to do, you are not doing it just to avoid changing. As neurotics do with guilt feelings—they have the guilt feelings instead of changing. Just be sure you are not making a change in your material circumstances to avoid making a change in your thinking. One thing you said sticks with me. You said if you were working your way, you would *not* be one of the others that you do not like, one of the "spongers," one of the "useless." But isn't it better to be not one of them in a more important way—not be one of them because they are hostile and you are not?

Harder, yes—much, much harder. As they said of Jesus, he was in the world but not of it. You also said that if you were on your own, you wouldn't have to keep proving you were different—with boots, beards, shirts out, etc. But again, if you should grow in spirituality, people would know you were different. Your added warmth would shine like a neon sign—your warmth without strings, without hope of reward, *any* reward.

Well, these are just *my* thoughts. It is you who will have to make the decisions. You know that I believe in your great spiritual potential in *this* life-time. By what road you will come to that potential I cannot know.

I suppose your analyzed friend is telling you this is all caused by your guilt feeling due to your hostility toward Dad because of your Oedipus, natch! At least he keeps you remembering that many of our most important drives are subtle in the way they come to our conscious minds.

Chin up! We're here to suffer! We'd *never* grow or give up self if we did not suffer. Hurray for suffering! I mean it. *Let's get on with the business!* Things may be tough, but let's grow with them. (Remember during our stressful times when I used to say that *all the time*?) May I be

71

forgiven my weakness in hoping that you will soon reach a plateau of peace!
You may not agree with any of what I say here! And that's o.k.!
I think of you.

Love,
M.

Have fun going to Denver.

Postcard from Chris to family from Denver, Colorado. February, 1964

Hi folks,

I'm having a really good time at this point, but yesterday was a small amount of misery before I met everyone! It took about 38 hours of pure driving to get here. We drove into the mountains yesterday and they are just great. Today we're cutting down to Colorado Springs.

So long,

Chris

Letter from Chris to family (back at Cornell).

February, 1964

Hi folks,

I had a pretty happy birthday altogether! I'm planning to cut my two classes tomorrow so I can take tonight off and write a few letters that ought to be written for a final birthday present to myself.

The harmonica was (is) great. It's got a wonderful sound to it and it's going to be a lot of good time to learn to play it "reasonably well." (This phrase means to me, what "poorly" means to other people.) At any rate, it will provide a lot of enjoyment for me I know, because so many times I like to just sit back or lie back and play "old favorites" to myself. This one is good enough to make even the poorest players sound like they know something about what they are doing!

All the other presents were an extreme enjoyment to open and to be watched opened by those in attendance. I think I detected a few pangs of jealousy here and there, but everyone enjoyed them pretty much. The smoking dog made a big hit as well as the mints, which are no longer present. When I pulled the necklace out, the saying that went with it sent a few quick "emotional chills" over me.* I was also pleased to see Kierkegaard, as I feel that very soon I'm going to start reading a lot. Eating is such an "indelicacy" around our place, that the various foods may look a little out of place . . . as Brian hauls out his hunk of chuck steak and

---

*A verse from Edwin Markham;
  He drew a circle and shut me out—

Ned's slurping spaghetti out of the can, I'll be aristocratically and daintily masticating my caviar and crackers.

One of the guys brought home a cake and candles and we had a little cake and beer for the celebration, and it was at this time that I first used the beer cup you also sent. It was't till a while later that I figured out it was an egg cup—but no harm done. I haven't had a good old boiled egg in a long time.

I'm not sure whose idea the beatle bonnet was, as Mom's handwriting was with it, but it looks like something Dad dreamed up; it's really a scream! I wore it up to my philosophy class, I figured that would be an appropriate place for it if anywhere, and it raised quite a ruckus. I haven't quite gotten up the courage to wear the snoot suit, but soon. (As far as the beatle bonnets go, we're thinking of getting some more somewhere and using them as our intramural team uniform.)

I've had a couple of interesting experiences lately. I got myself slightly involved with a senior girl in high school, first of all, but have gotten myself out of it, a fact that I'm rather proud of. She's a farm girl who aspires to "leave the farm and enter the big world." I only went out with her twice and found myself falling into "dependent love" with her after many hours of discussion and laughing. Well, I told her what was happening and why it was not good for me at this time to have such a relationship, and after many hours or so I believe she realized why. I know it would have been another "Betty" relationship, and that's one thing I know is not best right now. But I'm not shutting her out completely. I will write some letters, and if I feel strength enough, I'll go out with her once in awhile. She did not, however, share the idea that such a relationship would be in any way bad for her! It's funny, but in a large way, I'm dependent upon experiences such as this; they make it easier to have confidence when you're facing people. I guess maybe the final goal is not to have to have any props such as this.

The second experience was a dream I had, directly before the second date with this girl. I was in the library and I just sort of conked out while studying and woke up having had a rather traumatic dream centered around this girl. The dream was completely Freudian, if one wanted to interpret it this way—complete with symbols. I would like to say at this time, that the dream could also, I am sure, be interpreted in 9000 other ways if one

Heretic, rebel, a thing to flout.

But love and I had the wit to win:
We drew a circle that took him in.
From *Outwitted,* published by Doubleday, N.Y., N.Y. Copyright expired.

wanted. This also brings up another point that is coming into my life right now.

The subject is open-mindedness. So far, this semester, I've talked long and hard with a variety of people, all of whom are intelligent and most of whom are people I consider to be "good." The distinctive thing about most of them, or rather, the uniting thing, is that they all believe in something which is guiding their life. Of course, each thinks his own belief is best—because he's realizing "success" in life, and knows there is better to come as he keeps working. For Brian it is Freud; for Ned, the Jewish religion, etc. What I'm trying to get at is that it doesn't matter really what you believe, as long as it's something. And then, if you're naturally a "good guy" the "good deeds" will come naturally. The "good guys" who don't believe in something go through all life tormented. It seems that a belief serves as a foundation upon which and from which the rest is built. And if the rest is to be solid it has to be a good firm foundation. Well, to make this story short, I no longer believe your way, Mom, which has now become my way, is the only correct way.* It is just one of 10,000 ways, all of which are correct. I still believe in the Self and spiritual evolution, etc., but I don't believe my way is the only way that's right, and I'm getting more and more not even to care that it's not.

What I have now completely incorporated into my beliefs is the belief that I'm right, but so is everybody else who gets himself together and out in life with malice toward none. And I'm convinced that a guy can do it with Freud, or a religion, or other things. By incorporating this belief, I've cut down a lot of the frustrations I've felt so many times in arguments or discussions with people. And the only changes it has made in me are that I don't feel so frustrated, and that I don't feel I'm going against a religious doctrine admitting that my dream might have been Freudian—as it might have for all I really know; and I've come to believe that Freud's theory did include love, in that it was conceived to help people who were disturbed, and that it has helped many people I am sure, to lead a happy, more loving existence. So three cheers for Freud, and three cheers for "our side," because they both serve as strong foundations for good guys. Good guys are good guys no matter how they arrive at it.

This portion is being written a week after the last part you just finished reading. After I finished writing that (on my birthday) I came home, and when I walked in there was everybody standing around two more gigantic cakes, one from you and one that Tom and his sister made for me at her apartment. Both had twenty candles, to bring my total to 60 that I blew out. I'll have to admit that it was very exciting! I really got a kick out of it.

---

*I always told him I believed there were many pathways.

Last night I took my first prelim. of the semester and I think it turned out pretty good. I finally got rid of my cast today, but it will still be a month before I can use the hand much.* Right now I'm losing a layer of skin that was under it. This equalled out the sizes of the two arms, the left always had been a little smaller from the operation I had on it.**

For the last four days we've had 55-60° weather and everyone's been touched with spring fever. It's very funny how a bright, warm day with little streams of water running along can lift the spirit and ease pressures!

The other day I got up with an overwhelming compulsion to grow a pair of side burns, at which I am now engaged. I never had a really good pair of them! And along the same general lines, motorcycles are appearing during this good weather we've been having, and I'm sorry to report that I still have a great urge to own one of my own for awhile—long enough to find out that it won't help me solve any problems at least.

Things are pretty cheerful altogether.

From the sound of it you had a good stay in Florida. Did Jeff throw any parties while you were gone? I imagine Mom enjoyed the trip as a rest from "house-making."*** By the way, what made you decide on getting a landscaper? Or was that always the plan? It seems that you must be planning on quite a bit for the price! Are you going to have the yard sodded?

By the way, we finally came up with a room-mate. I haven't met him yet as he's moving in sometime this week. So we all had to pay an extra ten dollars for last month which is already taken care of. I'm enclosing the bill from the Triangle Book Store for books. I had another from the campus book store for only $3.00 which I've already paid.

Love,
Chris

March - June, 1964

One of his apartment-mates was in analysis, Freudian style. In talking with him, Chris heard more and more about Oedipus complexes, and though he did not say so, chances are he thought he might have such a complex. I myself thought he might. (Yet he had such important girl friends.) I think it was probably along about this time that he told us he thought it might be a good idea if he went to a psychiatrist. We encouraged

*He had broken his hand in a fight with a fellow worker in the Willard Straight dining hall who was always bragging about scoring with girls.

**The operation was for his shoulder which was prone to dislocate.

***We had moved into our newly built house the previous December.

75

him to do so if he felt this would be helpful; but we never heard any more about it. Since we never received any bills for such a venture, we knew that he had not even gone once. I personally was disappointed.

Chris tried to throw off his old beliefs in love and concern. That was o.k. Hadn't I always told the boys that my ideas worked for me, they were what I believed, but that when they grew up, they might think very differently? It seemed that Chris was indeed apparently changing. He dropped all ideas of morality, science was everything, nothing mattered but what could be proved in the laboratory. All right, so he was getting his own ideas. But he pounded away at me, I was to change my ideas, too.

Chris had always been close to me. We had talked so much, shared so much, we were so much alike, in so many ways. But now he was going into Freudian concepts. And he went on arguing with me about my own beliefs, as if he were forced to try to make me change along with himself. It almost seemed as if he would *have* to make me change as a sort of o.k. to his changing—as if otherwise he couldn't really change after all, if I did not have the same beliefs.

From then on, it seemed as if I could do nothing right, even my cooking which he had always loved was wrong. Everything his father did was right, while before *it* had all been wrong. He could no longer kiss me hello or goodbye, except sometimes with some flip remarks to make a joke out of it.

I heard about the gorge at Cornell, into which many had fallen to their deaths. And strangely, I worried. I was afraid of Chris's impulsiveness, especially after he saw a man thrown down the gorge by a car that hit him; I was afraid of Chris's extreme sensitivity, his growing intolerance.

Summer, Fall, 1964

June, 1964

As soon as Chris got home from school, he and his father bought a second-hand Harley motorcycle for him. This was very upsetting to me. I was very much against motorcycles. It seems that his father had promised him one, without consulting me. (I suspected that his father wanted to ride it a little himself to satisfy an old desire.)

September, 1964

I worried about Chris the whole summer as he rode his motorcycle back and forth to his work in a greenhouse which was in another town.

Fortunately (as far as *I* was concerned), the motorcycle turned out to be very much second-hand, and Chris spent most of his free time working on it. Consequently, at the end of the summer, he consented to sell it. But not before he had lots of pictures taken of himself sitting on the Harley in his motorcycle jacket (which I had bought him in a weak moment at a church rummage sale, before he'd even had the cycle). He had several of them enlarged, and was very proud of them.

We then bought him a second-hand car (which also turned out to be a lemon!) to drive back to school.

Letter to Chris from Glenda, just married in Texas.

September 21, 1964

Dear Chrisco,

Well, things are finally beginning to settle down and get organized now in the ol' home-sweet-home.

Needless to say I was more than shocked when I heard your voice on the 'phone that night and to say the least, very happy that you cared enough to make such a long trip to be at our wedding.

As you obviously figured, I think the aquarium is great. I can't wait to get it fixed up. I hope someday to bring our bird down here.* Natasha is taking good care of him for me. It was nice not to get a practical gift! Believe me we have everything and more than we need to set up house.

I was sorry you didn't have a good opportunity to get to know Jerry. He is a wonderful person and I am extremely happy for the first time in a long time.

Well, Chrisco, I have a lot of things on my mind to talk to you about but this is neither the time nor the place.

I received a letter from Gen today who said she was told you had quit school.** I hope with all I am worth that this isn't true. Chris, please, if for no one else, for yourself, don't do anything foolish. You've got too much goodness and love to offer to people who need it to waste it. Remember how you told me to look for the good things in people, to overlook the bad, and to help them develop into good human beings. It doesn't sound like you're doing a very good job of it by being pretty much a "loner." It's true one can find great comfort and love and joy in small things, like a flower, a feather, a bird, a star—but one needs more than that. You have certainly found the peace in the nature side of life—show it to others and likewise let them show you the human side without your becoming depressed and at odds with yourself and them.

---

*A white parakeet he had given her when he left for Cornell.
**No basis for this that family knows.

You used to contradict yourself by saying people had much goodness inside themselves and yet you would get in a crowd and see only the bad.

Be true to yourself and what you really believe, Chrisco. Don't let yourself become so depressed by outward appearances. All people need a leader and right now the leaders aren't doing a good job. You can.

I have a cross around my neck which I wear constantly. As you know, it symbolizes a truly good person—Jesus Christ.

You were well on your way, Chrisco, and I have great and complete faith that you will continue upward.

If no one else, you put me on my feet and I know you can do it for others.

Thank you for everything, Chrisco. And that "everything" takes in a lot.

I've found my happiness. I hope to God you find yours. (After all, I have a half dollar which is no good without the other half.)

With love,

Glenda

P.S. Look who's lecturing. P.P.S. Jerry said to thank you for him.

Letter from Lee to neighbor.

October 26, 1964

Dear Mrs. Warner:

I found the literature which you left in the door, and looked it over. Jeffrey told me that you mentioned to him that you would be coming over some time soon.

Mrs. Warner, it is not easy to have to say this, but nevertheless I must: please do not come. At least, do not come prepared to minister to me as a Jehovah's Witness. If you wish to come and visit me just as a friend, you are welcome.

Over the years, I have spent quite a good deal of time listening to one or another Jehovah's Witness, and I have looked over quite a bit of the literature. Because I have my own way of life, my own kind of dedication to what I feel to be Truth, my time is very carefully budgeted. I feel that I have spent as much time as I care to spend on the beliefs of Jehovah's Witnesses. I appreciate your efforts in my behalf and your interest in your fellow-man, and it was for this reason that I listened to the extent that I have—that, and the fact that I am always interested in all religions, and believe that every one of them at the base is quite a bit like all the rest and all contain at least some elements of truth.

Even now I can hear you saying that yours in the only way, because it is based on the Bible, the word of God, and that your interpretation is the one true interpretation. Mrs. Warner, that is your privilege to believe, and

I respect your right to your beliefs, and I admire you for doing your best to live by them. But while I see much Truth in what you believe, I also see intolerance—an intolerance which is inevitable in any religion which is considered by its followers to be the only way.

So please, consider that you have done the best you can for me, and allow me to pursue my purposes, even as I allow you to pursue yours. I am just as dedicated to my beliefs as you are to yours. My whole life is being lived in an effort to come closer to the true brotherhood in which I believe. I am not saying that you are wrong in what you believe, though I will say that it is my feeling that your insistance that yours is the only complete belief is not right. However, I recognize that, having the belief that you do, you have no other choice.

This tolerance that I feel for all religions—this belief that I have that all are working toward a common goal—is the very essence of my spiritual attitude. As I told you once before, I believe that *all* will be saved, that all will reach perfection by spiritual evolution. In this, I feel quite sure that I shall never change, and that no matter how long you talked to me, I would feel just the same in this matter.

Thank you again for your interest, but take your message to others who will benefit more from it, who may very likely be longing for it because they have no religion at all. Don't waste it on me. I already have a belief, and I am already dedicated. I am, in fact, no more available for your belief than you are for mine. As you can see, I am making no attempts to win *you* over to *mine*. You have found your answer and you are happy in it. I have found mine, and I am happy, too. Let us, then, each go her own way.

Sincerely,
Lee Jens

Letter from Lee to Tim and Chris.

December 1, 1964

Dear Tim and Chris:

This is a sad day. Suki* died this morning. Ever since you left,** he had gone downhill, in spite of further feedings of glucose and various other helps from the doctor in Lombard.

On Sunday I was able to catch a specimen (this was the last time he ever urinated), and I am grateful that I did because now we know that it *was* his kidneys. Dr. Farrell said that even with deteriorated kidneys, an

*Our Seal Point Siamese cat, aged 13½ years.
**Chris and Tim had been home for Thanksgiving.

79

animal can do quite well with what is left until he has some other problem—infection, or the like. Evidently, Suki's teeth were that other problem—or perhaps he was having constipation problems that were not evident. (I had not seen him straining at all, and with the box right there in the family room could keep pretty good track of him.) We'll never know, but about a month ago his coat began to look spiky. (I gave him a laxative at that time.)

Last night I slept on the davenport and set the alarm every hour so that I could try to gradually get some sugar water or eggnog into him in the tiniest amounts without his throwing it up. So twelve times all told he was picked up and held close while I fed him and innumerable other times he was stroked by each of us. He had not talked to us at all for quite awhile. Once on Sunday he tried to answer me, but it was so weak. Monday eve (last night) Jeffrey felt that Suki's little moans were answering him; and during the night every time I picked him up, he would make some sad little moans, as if trying to tell me that he was so, so tired.

Actually, this process is self-poisoning, and he was like someone drugged though he was at least semi-conscious. He apparently felt no pain, and by five o'clock this morning I could see that trying to feed him any more was useless. He could barely swallow, and his mouth began to hang open. For the next three hours, his breathing became less and less, his heart fainter and fainter. He passed away just as Jeffrey was to leave for school.

I had planned to dash over to Aurora to get my monthly allergy shot while Dad was going to stay with Suki. I followed through with that plan, though I was looking pretty seedy. Dad prepared the grave while I was gone and put Suki in the wooden box that he had picked up yesterday after being positive he was dead (rigor mortis). When I came home two hours later, we buried him under one of the wild black cherries north of the house, right close to where I planted the wild flowers. I read the first few verses of the 139th Psalm (as usual for our funerals) while Dad pulled in the dirt.

We are all quite shaken. He has been a part of our family for a long time. He was not anyone's favorite cat, but I'm sure we all loved him. He wasn't the brightest or the most interesting, but I think we could say he was the nicest. Just a real good Joe. A little mixed up on sex, but that was our fault, not his, for altering him.

We are grateful that he had no pain, and that he died at home. It didn't work out that way with Chica and Yaki.* It was awfully hard to have to watch his life slowly ebbing away, to think at times that he was already gone. But it was heartwarming to be able to send him out with lots of love. I hope he realized it, and we are sure he did. Dad said he didn't

---

*Dog and cat.

want our pets to die anywhere but at home, where they are most secure, and commented on how hard it was to go and bring Chica home. It does seem the right way. Of course, when it is as in the case of Yaki, who had been operated on, the pet must be in the hospital. But I have always wished that Chica had been home where she belonged. Now that I have seen how they give those feedings—with a syringe, intramuscularly, instead of intravenously—I think there was no reason she could not have been at home.

I am glad that you both got to see Suki again, just the day before he died.

It was great to see you both again, and am looking forward to more of the same at Christmas.

Love,
"M"

Letter from Chris to family.

December, 1964

Howdy,

I suppose by now you've all become pretty well adjusted to the loss of old Suki. I'll have to admit I felt real sorry when I got your letter, and it will seem so peculiar not to come home to a "full house." It's funny the shock one feels when one reads of a death of a fellow whose been with you awhile. It just goes to show that we are all of the "same thing" no matter what's said of animals by others, and no matter what is believed about origins of goodness, etc. It does please me a lot that he waited for us to get home, and that I was able to add a little extra maybe to the end of his life. Very few cats have lived a life as plush as Suki did. Well, it's time for another generation to move in I guess. I wonder how much the other cats will notice his loss, or already have?

I very much enjoyed my last visit home; the conversations we had; Alistair Sommer, poet and publisher, the sickness of Suki; all have put very different thoughts into my mind than I have ever experienced before. I'm not sure whether things are clearing up or becoming confused now, but I do know my insight into things in general took a long awaited advance, the vacation precipitating it. I will be very interested in discussing things with you all again (that, of course, includes Tim) and am looking forward to Christmas vacation more than ever. I'll be home next Sunday, or late Saturday.

The book of poems Alistair presented to me I've found extremely intriguing. There are some very good things in it, which have had great meaning for me. (As you can probably guess, form has not been too important to me—it is meaning.) I'm going to bring it home again and show you a couple of poems in it that have really moved or gotten to me. I've tried

81

writing a few myself, which are so bad I'd be embarrassed to show anybody. It's harder than it seems. I think it's because things that would be in a poem are vague, anyway, and it takes just the right combination of words to express a feeling so that it *is* that feeling. Perhaps that's what "form" in poetry helps do. If it is, then I am, after all, interested in form. Well, school's floating along not good, not too bad. My efforts are not producing so well as they have in the past. I'll probably do a fair amount of studying over Christmas. I'll see you then. God bless you all, and God bless Suki.

Love,

Chris

P.S. Enclosed are the bills I told you about Thanksgiving. They want the money. Money reminds me, I need a cheap pair of skis, ski boots, poles and bindings for (can you guess?) skiing. It's far too expensive without your own equipment. Think I can get the works, or most all of it, for $25 to $40. This will be a good Christmas present. But I doubt that you can find any. Second hand skiing equipment is hard to come by. I'll look around up here and back home and try to dig some up. At any rate will use Grandma's check for this, okay? The boots are least important, cheap to rent. I can also think of some albums I'd like, etc. We can get them when I get home. Better wait till I get home for presents in general, I guess. I'm sorry, last minute shopping. It'll work out. See you soon.

Winter, Spring, 1965

Letter from Chris to family (written on birthday card to Lee).

January, 1965

I hope this gets there sometime around the right day! Don't worry though, I haven't forgotten. I just was waiting for enough time to write something worthwhile. I just finished up the Lab exam in Chem. and yesterday in comp. anat. and am now awaiting my last quiz (makeup) in Chem..

It's an interesting time of the year!! In my psych. reading I've come across some "revolutionary" ideas. A guy named Mowrer came up with ideas concerning the relation of id (primitive drives), ego (conscious), and superego (conscience). Freud says a neurotic has an "over-learned" super ego, that the superego has learned too well its job and hence incoming impulses from the id cause anxiety in the individual. Mowrer, however, saw and has developed a theory around the fact that the superego is under-learned in neurotics. Example: child born is all id—wants all satisfaction, is not requested to give and does not give anything. The older he grows, socialization begins and becomes more prominent. Every child rebels

82

against having to give, being "forced" into some responsibilities. This is the negativism stage, supposedly well observed (age 2-6). If a child doesn't get out of this stage (learn a strong enough superego) he can become a criminal (strong id, weak superego), or a neurotic (superego still a little weak). Hence a neurotic can't move backward (strong enough superego won't let him). Can't move forward (id hasn't been subdued enough and is still too strong) and can't stay in the same place (miserable because of conflicting id and superego). This means the neurotic is frustrated at every turn and must try to run away, etc. At any rate, if you're looking for an environmental approach to psychology, this is a lot more sensible than Freud.

Second big discovery was exactly what behavorists you've heard me mention before are doing. Their hypothesis is that if these neurotic behaviors are learned, then they can be unlearned by simple laws of learning. Ex: Woman with lots of tics was cured of tics by making her practice and use them constantly while she was in therapy. There is a law of learning that says, if a behavior is practiced and worked on constantly or enough times, it will disappear. This is technically called reactive inhibition and commonly called getting tired of doing something. In other words, they figured that the entire personality didn't need to be uprooted. They've reported great success and no conversions to other forms of neurotic behavior.

Now I know this will sound absurd to you, but none the less, looking at psychology in a naive way, this is what I'd consider the "common sense" way to get rid of a behavior. Well, this is all just to say that I'm sure I'm no Freudian right now, as these two things show they are both radically different from anything Freud came up with; that anyone else has come up with, as a matter of fact. These types of things do a lot for my "open-mindedness" as they have uprooted, or at least shown that they could uproot, parts of Freud's theory that I did believe for awhile. So there is a full card to make just that one point.

I got an 88 back on a chem. prelim.—highest grade so far this semester. Finally!

I've been enjoying myself in various ways. To revert back to psychology, I've always been a somewhat "cycloid" personality hitting highs and lows. The difference between now and last year is that my lows are now normal and my highs continue. In other words I'm moving from manic-depressive to just manic!

Well, there's not much more to report. Brian is leaving in 10 days for the army band. I don't know if I ever told you he's quite a clarinet player. He's first chair in the Cornell band, and it's quite an honor to get into the Army Band. They are the ones you see on Ed Sullivan, etc. It's a big thing for him!

My friend Ned is sick again in the clinic just in time for finals. It's a trick he's pulled twice before, and now that he's had a fair amount of psychology courses, he's recognized "the conversion reaction." I talked to him on the 'phone last night, and he said he ought to write a paper of exactly how it felt. He said he could "feel" himself converting his final exam anxieties and other worries into a headache and then a fever. It's so foolish, though, because you just end up with more trouble than you started with! He'll soon be out to face makeups, etc.!

Well, Happy Birthday! I hope Claude, old black cat, is still doing fine. I'm looking forward to seeing him this spring!

Love,
Chris

Sketch written by Chris for English 206, January, 1965

THE HARDEST 'PHONE CALL IN THE WORLD

Now the seconds tick away, quickly forming minutes, forming hours, time unrealized, unknown. Now the time has come; further delay would be sure defeat, as schedules must be kept and life must proceed in order. Now a somewhat numbed and cooled, hard and dampened hand disturbs the peaceful immobility and slowly finds its way toward the cold and black receiver, almost unknown to its insensible owner. Now its slender fingers bend around the wretched thing and leave a trace of perspiration as they soon envelop all the danger that's forewarned by its grave blackness and compulsive buzzing whenever it's disturbed. Now the buzzing threat comes closer, and grows louder, forcing full recognition of its presence and of the fear that it evokes, 'til its maximum is reached. Now a thousand lights are flashing, now a wheel spins 'round and 'round. Now a spark hurtles through the darkness. Now a raspy clanging ringing overwhelms and then retreats.

In the silence there is peace, peace of being at one with oneself. There is no intruder, no environment, only peace and eternal, timeless silence. Thoughts and ideas run wild and free, there is no one to please, there is no obligation, there is no right or wrong, no future or past. Only the endless "now" which knows or understands nothing of what can and inevitably will happen. In a moment of silence time ceases altogether and only wondrous things happen. A moment of silence is eternity.

Now a shot rings through the silence, causing startling, screaming, stabbing pain. Overpowering fear and fever, trembling, fierce and ceaseless sweat overcome the slight semblance of order that existed before. Now as if the devil turns angel and raindrops turn to rays of sun, that bleak and cold and black receiver delicately sings, "Hello." Now the forces start to gather, slowly order is restored. Panic dissipates for tension, tension disappears for joy. Now the 'phone sits harmlessly, now all the rooms are filled with light. Now another asks, "What happened?"

"Wow," I say, "I've got a date!"

Early 1965

Karen came into his life, only briefly, but so importantly. It was his short time with her that seemed to start his seeing himself darkly. Though he was able to respond with vigor to *her* warmth, as the relationship progressed, he saw himself as selfish in his reaction to her.

It was probably a process that started with his failure with Betty. Now he *contrasted* himself to Karen, instead of finding himself like her, as I feel he might have done a couple of years before. Far from being the strong one in this relationship (as he had been in his other relationships with girls), in his own eyes, he was a follower, or even worshipper. He saw her as a lover of mankind. He saw himself as inferior. While before (and with good reason), he had seen himself as quite loving, he now saw himself as quite unloving.

In his usual way of being too vigorous, he was ruthless with himself. The picture he drew of himself was not accurate. While he was not as loving as he had perhaps pictured himself before, by the same token, he was not as unloving as he now saw himself. In truth, he was both loving and unloving, as we all are in one degree or another. But he was different from most in that he wanted so passionately to be more loving than he was. And he was angry with himself for not being fully loving.

Paper for English written by Chris, February 15, 1965

ON SECOND THOUGHT

He just met her yesterday. He had seen her many times before, since she was in one of his labs, and he'd had ample chance to allow a rather ill impression of her to precipitate. It was not, however, crystallized well enough so that he wasn't still a bit curious and somewhat respectful toward her ready laughter and efficiency, exemplified by her fine grades, and in her learning the multitude of details that he himself had so often found exasperating. She was awfully tall, taller than himself and most others in the class, and from the distance at which he had seen her, he'd observed a long, thin face and a boyish physique, a fact which he generalized to her personality. He attributed to her a sort of masculine aggressiveness, which had been partially reinforced by his few observations. These factors had predisposed him to dislike her since he had never appreciated these types of characteristics in any girl. But the factors which took advantage of this predisposition and drove him to the actual feelings of dislike which he harbored against her were much more obscure, and he had only a vague knowledge that they even, in truth, did exist. For instance he had often felt small hostile impulses when he heard her laughing as she so frequently did with other members of the class. Other times he had felt slight waves of resentment at the other forms of attention she often received from their classmates. He attributed these feelings to the fact that he never did like the way aggressive girls acted, and that they didn't deserve to be made over as much as she was being made over. He also blamed much of his annoyance on the fact that her gaiety and laughter were disrupting to those trying to work alone and quietly. He had felt twinges of anger when she had come back with consistently higher marks than his own, and for the most part blamed those on his belief that this type of person always gets good grades. He'd had intimations that possibly these feelings were in some way not justified, but he'd quickly pushed them out of his mind or rationalized them in a way concordant with his set of feelings about her.

And thus he had continued for three months up until yesterday with vague curiosity about her, but mainly feeling a degree of hostility and resentment toward her.

Then yesterday that all changed. Yesterday he'd been working on some minute detail in a specimen, when she'd come up and asked him a question about it. He had answered and they had talked a moment. He'd asked her what she was interested in and she'd told him she wanted to be a doctor. He'd expressed some interest in this, for he too was planning to become a doctor, and he'd asked what kind of a doctor she wanted to be.

It was then that it happened! It was then that her blue eyes seemed softened and penetrated him through and through. It was then that her entire face appeared mellow, and its delicate tenderness beamed warmth and interest, forcing the traces of his hostility to dissipate and to turn inward, turn to shame for the jealousy he now so fully recognized that he had entertained up to then. It was then she gently replied, "I want to be a good doctor."

Paper written for English by Chris, February, 1965.

SOME HELP WITH LIVING

I want to let you in on a little book I read just yesterday, that may change my life and beliefs more than any other little factor in my life ever did before. But then, maybe it won't change me at all, since I'm almost a grown-up and my ways of thinking have been so firmly set. But I wish it would and I hope it does, because the little book holds a gold mine of universal truths. And these truths seem to be innately important and inherently present in all little kids, yet somehow are trampled out both by the speed and obligations of growing up; and by the study and growing concern for scientific ways of thinking and scientific proofs, the need for which has little by little been indoctrinated and propagandized into us all along life's path.

Let me give a quick example. How many adults do you know that ever wake up and, having jumped up and down on their bed springs a few times out of sheer excitement and joy for the new day, are literally bounced out of bed and drawn toward the front door, with as little time as possible wasted on dressing and eating; then pulled out the door and into the burst of sunshine and out-of-doors smells and right into the middle of a giant leaf pile? There are very few adults I know who would be doing that—ever. But grown-ups have words to describe this rapport with life and with being alive. If they hear another adult describe it, they call it sentimentality, or if they see a little person engaged in the act of it, they see the "spirit of youth," more commonly called plain old naivety. But the little book I'm talking about would deny these words. And I hope I'll always be able to deny them! Because people to whom these words are applied are thrilled and delighted with life. It's not the spirit of the young, but the spirit of the non-sophisticated and really alive people. The people who can walk outside at night and see all the stars as bells and fountains, ringing, laughing, singing so loudly and clearly that they are overwhelmed, these insignificant little closed off spheres, and they feel joined with the rest of the universe. Yes, when this infinite feeling that you and the rest of the universe are One slips through your consciousness and envelops your whole awareness; only then do such problems as making impressions on other people, hiding your emotions in public, or wondering whether a button-down collar would be appropriate for this occasion suddenly become omni-insignificant; and only then can you step out of yourself for a second, and look down at yourself and the milieu in which you are running around, and rear back your head and laugh and laugh that such goings-on could ever be conceived

87

of as significant. And then laugh some more as the joy of life surges through your entire body.

Well then—granted that most adults have lost something that most children have started out with; and granted that the thing is important and good if one's life is to be fulfilled happily, then it's a shame that somehow grown-ups have lost it, and in some way it should be retrieved. And indeed some grown-ups have relearned it and some never lost it at all. These are the really lucky ones, for they have met the universe's problem and have "tamed"* it, and now it is their friend and their possession. The young ones don't know the problems and therefore have tamed nothing to their knowledge, and therefore cannot understand and treasure it as can a grown-up. It is for this reason that children are prone to lose it as they mature. And it is just this understanding and treasuring of the universe that leads to a happily and efficiently fulfilled life.

So I was telling you about this book. There are a great many people, I am sure, who would read this paper and find it quite unintelligible. I'm afraid they are lost for awhile to the pleasures of living and will need much more radical help than any book can give them, even the one I'm talking about.

It is the ones to whom any part or parts of this paper give a small tingling of excitement deep down under their chests that I most hope to communicate with, and it is to them I divulge the title and the name of the author of the book which can help them to become part of the universe, rather than remain only part of the busy-bodiness of their own "little sphere." It's *The Little Prince* by Antoine de St.-Exupéry.**

Letter from Chris to Tim.

February 1965

Dear Tim,

It was nice to get a letter from you, I was interested to hear what you wrote. I knew someone would write soon but I wasn't sure which one of us it would be. I've sat down several times to start but something came up always, so scattered through my notebook are several nearly blank pages with "Dear Tim" at the top.

I don't particularly envy your position in life right now. You're now going out to see what all these years of training—at home and in these infernal schools—is all about, and how well you can apply it to the world

---

*St. Exupéry's word
**Given to him by Karen who wrote on the flyleaf, "I think perhaps—this is my most favorite of books—and you know—I believe what it says—and seek what it promises." Karen, March 2, 1965

at large. I hope the experience isn't too traumatic, i.e., application isn't too hard. I've still got at least several years before I have any worrying to do, but every now and then, when I realize that I'm more than halfway toward seeing if I fit in the world at large, I get vague feelings of expectancy, coupled with abdominal flutterings. This is all to say, I know somewhat what you must be feeling now as you compose various letters to "supers" and get answers back. I know that it's somewhat of a bitch.

It will be interesting to see where you start out teaching. I was interested in the fact that you preferred the midwest to start out. It's been my own experience that there are four groups of people in the U.S. to make a broad, and almost totally invalid statement; midwesterners, people from the coasts, southerners and farmers. Of those four types, I get along with, or understand, midwesterners best of all I think, and if I get a chance to go to medical school, I think I'll choose a midwestern one for those very reasons. This is all baloney, to some degree, since people are very similar from all over, but there are atmospheres about large groups of each of these types of people which are recognizable. The midwestern atmosphere I join in with most fully, or feel most rapport for. Enough of this——

I'm doing fine myself. A tremendously easy schedule which leaves me plenty of free time and no pressure, and all interesting courses. I think my feeling must be correlated somewhat to this because I can't remember being so contented or just plain happy ever before. There are a couple, *one especially*, of girls who have been looking better and better to me in these periods of good feelings. As I was working up in the anatomy lab. yesterday Karen appeared out of nowhere with a big box of brownies that she gave me, then disappeared as quickly. We've talked only a little, but I know, and she evidently feels something too, that we're going to hit it off. At any rate this is in the process of developing!

Tim, I have done quite a little thinking and reading since I last saw the family and I think, for the present at least, the best possible thing anyone can do is to learn to radiate warmth. Maybe it's because of some universal good, or maybe it's because this is the only way that we can survive together—doing things for others, which, when done right seems to necessitate having that feeling called warmth behind it. Whatever is said, though, one just has to admit that if everyone had this built-in good to a sufficient degree, there just would hardly be any more crises in the world. But the main reason (main because there's no way to put enough of the warmth into everybody) is to follow the warmth road rather than the self-interest road, because of the fact that it works so much better. The warmer the person, the more people like him, the richer and more satisfying his friendship, the more people have trouble arguing against him and degrading his arguments. Mom never agreed with this, and I don't think you did either;* but it's been a fact I recognize to the fullest degree by direct observation, especially in these last few unpressured weeks when everything has been optimistic for being "warm." I have been warm during this time, and the rewards have been so great that I have had to realize warmth is the best way of life! Let me just enumerate some of the rewards I've received in the last 3 weeks.

1. I was a great hit with both my roommates' families when I met them all, something I wanted to happen very much.

2. I have 4 prospective girls who have become "victims" of my warmth.

3. Both my room-mates have responded to my warmth by becoming deeper and closer friends than ever they were before.

4. Everybody I seem to be coming in contact with, both formally and informally, is paying more attention to me and seems to enjoy me. These are primary rewards. The secondary rewards are:

5. My mind has come to very great peace with itself right now.

6. I feel no need for sloppy dressing, etc. to attract attention to me anymore.

7. There is no telling how much other people are benefitting from my warmth, both mentally and physically; although I know of some cases where it has greatly affected some people!

I have written these rewards (and these are certainly not all of them) in a purposely egotistical way to make my point. I'm sure you recognize quite easily that these definitely are things that happen when someone is warm. Well, the egotistical way I've written them is to demonstrate more fully why I will continue, or rather, try to be a warm person. If the rewards I mentioned didn't occur, if none of those things did happen, obviously and a priori; I would give up trying to be warm as a way of adjustment, or at least, being warm as a way of adjustment would not have as great a significance to me as it now does have. So this basic fact we agree on—the best way of life is warmth. The questions of why warmth works so well, and why things are this way or that way have only philosophical value, and time spent on them is not of the greatest significance, nor is there any need for hostilities about them for they have very little practical value. But the great and practical truth, that the best way of life is to be warm, we're in full agreement on and it is for this reason I understood your letter and I'm rooting for the things you're trying to do. I can see that if you master them you can only end up happy in the end, though the reasons

---

*I did not agree because I thought he was using "warmth" to get rewards (as he here indicates). And I believed—do believe—that true warmth does not look for rewards; it exists for the joy of itself.

90

for this final happiness we may differ on, a fact of no significance obviously. So let's bury all the hatchets on philosophical matters and get on with the good friendship we've been covering over by fool arguments for quite awhile. Enough of this——

In exactly 45 minutes I'm going to go barge in on that girl's lab, like she did yesterday with the brownies, and give her an official comparative anatomy bracelet that I cooked up yesterday. It's a foolish 10¢ bracelet onto which I wired some vertebrae so they hang off it like charms. She should get a kick out of that, and I should be going out with her pretty soon!

I heard Richard Alpert speak on L.S.D. the other day. He's the man (one of them) who got thrown out of Harvard for "unscientific use" of L.S.D. and for giving it to graduate students which he had said he wouldn't. He's also one of those who went to Mexico, the Caribbeans, etc., trying to find a place to use the stuff. As you probably remember, I did a paper on L.S.D. which really aroused my interest in it, as I read very much about it at that time. However, everything I read about it was biased on the scientific side, so to speak, in that nothing was mentioned of religious experiences and all phenomena were explained in psychological terms. L.S.D. is used fairly commonly in experimental psychiatry because of its "mind-loosening" power. They think it is dreaming while being conscious and some think it simulates a psychosis closely enough that investigation of it may disclose a biological cause of psychosis. So hearing Alpert was my first real encounter with the religious side of L.S.D. and it was an experience. His talk was moving, mainly because of what he represents.

Tim—it's been 9 days since the part of the letter you just read was written and a lot has changed. The girl hit the spot.*

Tim—when I get a chance I have some amazing books to prescribe for you! For right now, *Of Human Bondage*—Somerset Maugham**; and *The Little Prince*—Antoine de St. Exupéry***. Tim, read *The Little Prince*—86 pages of the most meaning I've ever had in my life. It holds the key to the "Land of the Mushrooms."****

Love,
Chris

Notes by Chris. March, 1965.

It is at certain very special times that I begin to understand some of the abstract phrases that have been thrown at me ever since I began to hear

---

*Karen
**The Modern Library, Random House, New York
***Harcourt, Brace and World, N.Y.
****An ideal place imagined by Karen and Chris.

and think—self-realization or self-actualization, love thy neighbor as thy-self, unselfishness and goodness, etc. I don't know what makes these times occur.

My feeling at a time like this resembles the feeling that follows when something quite important has come out perfectly. It's a feeling of lessening fears, of exhilaration and confidence mixed with a much more than usual abundance of empathy, with love for other persons which extends to everyone so that even enemies become lovable. It is now that self sacrifices most readily occur and material losses seem so minuscule.

I'm running, flying, spinning through the environment, laughing always inwardly, and free from inhibitions. I'm enjoying life up to the hilt.

Letter from Chris to Karen.

March, 1965

Hi Angel,*

I've got a little load of things on my mind so I may as well sit down and pull out another all-nighter and tell you things that I want you to know and I want you to remember about me when you've gone** and when neither of us are that much a part of each other's life anymore. I'm just going to shoot off and try to tell you honestly and with the affection I feel for you about what's going on behind those eyes that you were curious about the other night.

I'm going to start with the subject that is most interesting, or at least most on my mind; and then I want to work into other things that I've tried to tell you before but I'm afraid I wasn't all that articulate!

So I start with your date Friday. The first thing I can say about my reactions is that it made me do a lot of thinking real quick! My first reaction, interestingly enough, was relief, because the build-up you gave it about guilt and other things made me get real scared. When I heard that all it was was a date for Friday I felt quick relief, for I naturally had fears of the worst! Such things flashed through my mind as, "She's making love to Chuck on the side." So I felt that quick relief before I felt that rise-up of hostility that inevitably had to come. That came almost immediately and my heart dropped a few notches. It is still down there and I think it's there to stay, because the real situation sort of interrupted the fairy tale for now. There is a fairy tale that goes with boys and girls, you know, it's the one about finding the right person along life's path, and there is

---

*Chris called three of his girl friends "Angel."
**She was going to India.

true love forever more. Most people are pretty much aware of that one, and most try to talk themselves into it some time or other. But every now and then it seems to happen really. I think that the movie *West Side Story* showed this fairy tale the best I ever saw it, and that movie helped me become part of the fairy tale. Before I saw it I had chortled and chided so many times at the idea of "the one true love of my life," etc., because I knew there were lots of people I could love and because I knew that most people that talked about that sort of thing were just kidding themselves into something. But Mmmmmmmmmmmmm! *West Side Story*, and the fairy tale, came alive for me.

Angel, I've felt special things for you. But you see? I'm not looking for a girl. I haven't even been trying in the least to find girl-friends. Sometimes I went out because I sort of wanted to dance, but that's about all. But see, you sort of popped along, and we had birthdays on the same day, which made us of magic, and all of a sudden—Karen—I just kissed a girl named Karen! And you showed me the Land of the Mushrooms and St. Exupéry, a land that I've been so close to, but never would have discovered on my own. And a land I needed and need so much! You not only showed me this land, but you did it with little mannerisms and with such a beautiful face, that I saw you with a pounding heart. And then when you said the nicest things that anyone has ever told me in my life, I broke into this funny sort of fairy tale, the kind in *West Side Story*. But it wasn't a "marrying" kind of fairy tale or a "lived happily now" kind. I've been in the Land of the Mushrooms quite a few times since I saw you the first time. And it's such a happy land, where Grecian candymakers and homemade corsages come alive! Sure, I knew we were through in two months, and I knew that there were many years of schools and grades between me and marriage so things like that could never even enter my head. So they didn't and I've just been enjoying the Land of the Mushrooms and enjoying someone to share it with!

But *see*, it's not really a fairy tale, but reality. Old *West Side Story*, Humph! Maria was the tender and sweet little woman in that fairy tale. But she, she didn't go out with anyone other than Tony. I've got to sort of laugh at what it would have done to the fairy tale in that movie if somewhere in it they had stuck in a section where Maria came to Tony and told him she was going to go out with the leader of the Jets because she had been sort of sleepy and she was so happy and flattered when he called. I think maybe if they had put something like that in *West Side Story* it wouldn't even have won a single Academy Award. Well, it looks like old Chris's fairy tale won't be winning any Academy Awards! That's the thing that hurt just a little, Angel, and has lowered my heart a few notches. The ending of a fairy tale, and taking the book and closing it, and getting back to what's really going on out there where fairy tales don't really exist—that's sad.

But, you know this is the important thing you have helped me with. I've gotten little feelings that if I look at everything right I can make all life a fairy tale, where everything that happens is significant and beautiful in its own right. Where each person is a new and wonderful mystery and adventure. This is what I think you and St. Exupéry both have done, and this is what I'm getting closer to understanding and accepting for my own. I'm not too far away right now! It's a wonderful place where hurts and sadnesses are deep as deep can be, but then along hops an Alice in Wonderland type of rabbit, with all its mystery and adventure, and it is not long that the hurt must just be put aside in order that that rabbit be followed to the Land of the Mushrooms and, sure, pretty soon the rabbit will hurt you again, but along comes another rabbit and a whole new Adventure. The important thing is not to let the "Baobabs"* get too great a foothold. Follow those good, good rabbits! Well, Angel, that's the life I'm just setting foot on, and that's because of you and a few other good people in my past, but *you* especially. And do you know what I'm going to do about your date Friday night? I'm going to feel bad and jealous because the rabbit, and the Land of Mushrooms I've just been in, hurt me a little. This phase of the fairy tale had a gargoyle in it, ordered there by the Wicked Witch of the West! But I'm watching the "Baobabs" closely. And there'll soon be a new adventure, a new rabbit! Do you understand that, Angel? Maybe the new rabbit will be Saturday night when I go out with you. Maybe it will be new adventures with you. But then, maybe I'll still feel hurt, and maybe I'll just let it wreck the evening! You can't tell about these things! I hope I've pulled up "Baobabs" by then, though. Because already I'm anxious for some more adventures. You know, you've sure given me a lot of adventures!

This all bears on the last thing I want to say to you about what happens in 8 weeks. But first I want to tell you what I just discovered. Forty minutes of a class just went by, and I've been so busy writing I didn't even notice! The reason is because I'm in the middle of an adventure right now.

In eight weeks, you told me, you were afraid that there might be regrets. But now I'm going to tell you what I've tried to tell you so many times, but every time it comes out sounding terrible and you get a little mad. I'll have a lot of regrets and bad feelings and I'll feel a loss when you're gone. But don't you see, I have *The Little Prince* and it's signed by you and I have all the adventures you've given me. So I won't feel bad! I'll be going out to face new adventures, new rabbits will be rushing by and all the time

---

*From *The Little Prince*

94

I'll think of a wonderful girl gone away and feel the loss. But you can't wipe out *The Little Prince*, and therefore I won't feel bad. Every now and then when the mail comes, I'll go on a new adventure with you!

Love,
Chris

Paper written for English by Chris. Spring, 1965.

ON SELF-CONSCIOUSNESS

How often I have sat and wondered at myself and become angered and frustrated with myself, that somehow, in various given sets of circumstances, my pulse quickens, my hands become lost for things to do, my throat dries and thickens, and the glands beneath my arms begin a ceaseless production of perspiration for which there is absolutely no voluntary control. But worse yet, worse by far and away, and the crux of the entire problem, indeed that which makes this a problem at all is the desensitizing effect on the mind and its perceptions, the loss of honesty, the evocation of inappropriate response, the surrender of precise control over one's thoughts and behavior.

There are so many factors about my self-consciousness that have passed through my mind. How did it get there, why is it there now, is any of it legitimate? But most important and compelling, how can one rid himself of it?

Of one fact I am certain—in every situation in which this syndrome emerges, be it an interview, or job application, or meeting a new person, or being in some new situation, the fear (that is, self-conciousness) is unnecessary; and, in fact, a hindrance to the fulfillment of the goals for which I have gotten myself into the situation. Self-consciousness never leaves a good impression, and the simple irony is that most situations which elicit it are precisely those in which a good impression would have been desired and treasured. There is no doubt in my mind that these feelings are a special case of fear, just simple fear.

Heaven knows what roots it has within my framework nor does that particularly matter to me. I do know that I am a reasonable man and that in most of the situations which elicit self-consciousness within me, the fears I have are unreasonable. The fears I feel, however, do seem to center around one central factor—fear of rejection. Whether I shall be rejected from a job for which I am applying, or rejected as a human being by some new person I am meeting, these differences matter not at all. I have

95

somewhere learned to fear rejection.* This is so unreasonable! So childish! And, yes, so humorous. But it's such a millstone to drag all the time, and I hate the inaction and apathy for which it is responsible. I am writing this for my benefit and for the benefit of others who feel the chains, wrapped in which they have lost out on and been forced to abandon much of life's offerings. I have had the luck and pleasure to experience a release from these chains, due to fortunate circumstances, for short periods of time, and I want to describe some of these offerings and joys that life can hold when the bog of self-conciousness has been drained. I then want to describe and recommend my way of overcoming this foolish millstone, so simple, and yet so hard to discover and put to use.

I have been amazed at the artistry in all human beings. I only discovered it a short while ago, while I had lifted my self-consciousness and while looking out from under that screen of distortion I saw another person, whom I had just met as he really was. I saw the trace of a smile, barely perceptible, that in normal circumstances I would have been incapable of seeing and which gave me great pleasure to discover. I noticed the small scar on his chin, and I pondered what it might have meant to him—had he hated it and tried to cover it when he met new girls; or had he been proud of it because he thought it made him look rugged and tough; or had he never much bothered with it? All these questions, and more, became important little adventures to me, and I listened to what he said carefully to gather clues to their answers. I became involved in the wonderland of this person. I saw his dreams, felt his sorrows, became a part of his fairy tales and joys. We only talked a little about the orphanage he'd once lived in, and how he was trying to win a girl right now. But I saw his eyes squint a little when he talked of the orphanage and twinkle when he talked of the girl and I was in his world. I was a part of his world. I had known him for years. I had only talked to him for half an hour.

All this because I had dispersed self-conciousness for a time. No acts, no defenses, no inappropriate responses—all caused by fear. Now there were no fears. I just honestly reacted to him, and his reception of me was good. We shared rapport. But I had experienced something I had barely realized before. I had seen a new joy in my old world. The joy of seeing beauty in a person because I was not on my guard.

And how had I achieved it? I just vowed for awhile not to let my opinion of myself rise and fall with what other people think.

---

*As far as I know, this was a newly developed fear. He had always been popular with his peers, *and* other age groups; always managed to get most of the things he went after.

Letter to himself written by Chris, Spring 1965.

A letter to myself, attempting to uncover roots of some personality traits in myself that I find highly disagreeable, and wish to be rid of, with suggestions on how to rid myself of them.

It's time I start trying a little harder on being what I think about all the time. There's nothing hopeless about it, but somehow I get those hopeless feelings, and then I start procrastinating about trying again.

I vary from being extremely ill-at-ease with people to not ill-at-ease at all, depending on what has just happened in my most recent life. The tiniest factor can make me feel very good and change my feelings with other people almost completely. But then the tiniest factor can throw me right back into doubts and ill-at-ease feelings. My ill-at-ease feelings I know are caused almost entirely by my aspirations and self-images.

I seem to want to impress everyone I meet as being a great guy, from gas station owners to professors. And, when I think I don't, my opinion of myself drops. So my feelings upon leaving them are either that hopelessness if I feel I didn't impress them; or exhilaration, if I did. So my opinion of myself rises very high or falls very low according to what others are thinking about me.

My wish to impress all people has caused an extreme change of character with the different types of people I've dealt with. My speaking becomes sort of tough with a not-give-a-damn air about it when I am with a person I think will be impressed with me in that way. When I'm with a person who's interested in the social whirl, I let him know "I've been around. I know the score." When I am with a remote, indifferent person I act like he does. I become warm and helpful and "good" with people whom I think will be impressed by my goodness. But, it is the good that I most want to be, and I'd like to be that way with everyone. I'd like to be spontaneous, enjoy life and all its little pleasures, love people, and mostly get over this fool self-conciousness or ill-at-easeness. This *good* way is my *main* self-image.

My "I've been around" self-image makes me lie and say I've done things I haven't done, or makes me exaggerate the things I *have* done. It also makes me feel inadequate and embarrassed when people ask me if I know him or her, or if I know about this party or if I have heard of this place when I haven't.

It makes me mad when I hear about someone who is doing something well that is part of one of my self-images.

I have fears and inhibitions about doing something new or learning new things such as dance steps or going to work camp. Because these things would be new to me, I'd have a problem with my "I've been around" self-image. They would cause me to be embarrassed and ill-at-ease with whomever I met and had to talk with before I was really into the new thing. While I was just starting on whatever it was I'd feel anger at anyone who called me on something that pointed up my inexperience or ineptness. This is what causes my life to be small to some degree; because I fear new things, I stick to old patterns of life at which I have been adept. This explains why, after I have been on a new thing for awhile, fears of it go away. But fears are immediately reinitiated whenever a new situation pops up. Last night when George told me to do the job just a little differently, I felt very sensitive about it though I know I'm good at this job, I'm a hard worker, I know what I'm doing, I'm experienced.

I feel I can explain almost all of my peculiarities and personality at this time by these main self-images: "I'm tough and I've been around"; "I don't need anybody"; "I'm good." These account for the various acts that I put on with people. Because these are conflicting self-images, they often throw me into problems due to the fact that when I am one, I can't be any of the others.

Just off-hand it seems to me the best way to rid myself of these problems is to rid myself of the conflicting images and make one new self-image which I will follow. This won't be an entirely new self-image, but would consist of parts of all these images I have mentioned plus a few more that have been less significant. For instance, part of the self-image would be *to be interesting* which has remnants of "I've been around," but there are ways to be interesting even if you haven't been around and I must use these. I must learn not to be "tough" but "rugged." Being rugged fits better with being good. I must be a "good guy" as in the movies. Billy Budd is the fulfillment of the ideal male role partially because of the fact that good people are also strong.

To fulfill this self-image calls for facing a lot of things head on. Then fighting them dead. I must learn to admit that I am not a know-it-all, and that there are lots of things in which I am not a know-it-all and haven't been around. These I must not be afraid to tell anybody. I must speak honestly and spontaneously to everybody about things that I am now afraid to do. Take Al R. for example, I must tell him my exact situation about parties of Independents. It would erase any future embarrassment and I should definitely not be embarrassed to tell him that I just don't go to Independent parties and don't know much about them. (I just had a twinge of nervousness in writing that because it is a fact that in this world people who have connections are somewhat prized.)

I recognize that Al thinks I am a connection to Independent parties and life which he evidently thinks are pretty hot. I am interested in not alienating Al's affection for similar reasons (he's my connection to many people).

98

And besides I like to be a connection for people. Therefore, I lie and take on airs that "I've been around" and that I know about the big Independent parties. So how to remedy a situation like this? Admit to Al that I don't know much about Independent social life. Or get interested and start going to Independent parties and become what my self-image says I am. Then I'm fulfilled in every way. I then would have gone to the parties. I then would be a real connection for Al. I then could be honest to Al. I then could drop all my airs to Al and ask him for favors, too. So it seems the best thing is to do the things I want to do, and if I don't want to do things, admit it always. Also admit if I want to but haven't yet, and if I don't want to. If these simple honesties could be followed to the letter, the end of troubles would soon be in sight. I think one of the reasons for not doing these things honestly is that I'm afraid I won't be able to get important people to like me. Even a gas station attendant can be important because he can give my girl the impression that I get around. Hence almost everybody is important to me. But with these lies I avoid people so they won't figure out the act. This is why I hate to see people the second time after meeting them the first time and having made a good impression on them. So they won't figure out the act, and so I am still that important person. And this is why I'm not afraid again to see someone with whom I have been honest. I would like to be always an honest person.

Until I have become a loving and accomplished person who has been around and *who can be with kings and not forget the common ways** there will be people I can't impress if I am honest and I must admit that and not worry about it all. People are not failures if they cannot do things. But people are failures who try to do them when they haven't got the stuff right now. The idea is to drop the pretenses, lose a few "important people," then work at becoming the new self-image. I can't have it all at once though, and I know that all the guff is still right there in my mind. Luckily, I'm now a junior in college and I can start making some decisions about what to do with life. I will start to do things that fulfill my self-image. I must definitely quit pretending!

Finally try this. I worry many times when I'm excited because it feels and maybe is the same feeling as being ill-at-ease. However, try not worrying about that. I have proved to myself that some of my "trends" were normal! Therefore, don't worry about these. I feel excited about going to see my girl. Don't worry about it. There's a good chance Ghandi would too!

---

*As: Idea expressed in *If* by Rudyard Kipling.

Paper by Chris for English, Spring 1965.

I was all set to write a paper for English today about a certain photograph hanging in the Willard Straight Hall Art Room when I was quite suddenly sidetracked by an extraordinary little book that so warmed my heart and overwhelmed my insignificant self that I was forced to abandon my first idea. I must now tell you and myself about this strange little book which has so suddenly and radically expanded my trivial perceptions into a system so large that I can only recognize and describe it as the universe. And so, the only term I can apply to it, and feel some safety in applying it, is the term "universal."

And yet tomorrow (I know because it's happened before) will bring back a return of the old system, where fears of what impression I made on that person and what grade I will make on this test, take precedence over the realizations that these are ridiculously insignificant problems, and in fact, are not even worth the time to formulate.

Yes, suddenly sometime during my sleep tonight "my little sphere" will again differentiate itself from the universe in which it has been immersed for a brief interlude. Suddenly it will become the grain of sand, not a part of the beach, but the one that has rolled into an ant's nest and has concerned the members of the colony for a long period of time.

This is what will happen, but for tonight my heart prays, leaps and begs to keep these universal beauties that have now welled up so prominent in the big sphere. I can't explain how even writing this paper seems humorously meaningless, and yet I want to record it quickly and effectively for tomorrow I know how important it will be to me when I have again descended into my little sphere.

The name of the book is *The Little Prince*. It is by Antoine de St.-Exupéry.

Letter written by Chris to family.

Spring, 1965

Dear Folks,

I think now would be a good time to write a little letter. I got your letter about Grandpa and I felt bad about his passing. I've thought about him several times since you wrote, and I wrote a paper for English based on his death, or maybe his life, the part of which I was involved. It's funny actually how many sentimental feelings I have felt about his loss; and, Dad, I know you must have felt many more. You knew him for a long, long time.

I'm doing well still. Our spring vacation ends today and everyone will be coming back. I have been back for two days, as Montreal was very cold and there was little to do. We had all our good times travelling. We hitchhiked up and slept in the Watertown jail, then coming back we stayed there again for two nights. I met a guy who was an ex-guitar player, and now just a sort of bum, so we went and rented a guitar from a pawn shop and I had brought my little harmonica along with me. He showed me some new things to do with it and altogether we made some interesting music. He was a very good guitar player. That's why we stayed in Watertown for two days instead of one. I think that's probably the most fun he's had in many years. That was about the main thing that happened. For the most part we were cold and miserable, but in its own way even that was fun. I missed coming home, and have felt quite a few "nostalgia waves" for not coming home for the regular spring visit. I will be there for two or three nights at the beginning of summer and two or three weeks at the end. You know? If I didn't have that to rely on, I think I'd be a scared rabbit right now.

I have to take the medical school boards May 1st, and it's how I do on them that determines how I do on getting into medical school. They are four hours, and I don't relish the idea of them. By the way, they cost $15 which I will pay. I must, I am afraid, also join a fraternity for $25. It is Alpha Epsilon Delta, the international premedical honor society, and from what I can gather it is good to have it on your record when you apply to med. school. I'm going to look into it a little more, but the chances are good that I should join. I'll pay that too, if I do. I also just shelled out $12 for a new coat, as my old green one lost a tail. I also just paid $5.50 for two new headlights (I was driving with only one for a month, until the other one went out.) And I paid $15.50 for my books. That all adds up to $73. I have made $63 at the Straight. So I will let you know if I get the bite too bad.

I'm going to try and write you a letter every two weeks that is not real long. I think if I set up a sort of schedule, I'll be able to get everything done better. I made a tentative schedule up and discovered that with four hours a night for studying, one hour for reading Russian, one hour for reading good books, one hour for practicing the guitar, five hours for work, six hours for sleep, and four hours for classes with an extra hour thrown in for walking and waking up and washing and eating, that leaves one hour a day for such miscellaneous things as writing letters, talking to friends, reading newspapers, etc. Busy day.

Well, that's about all I can think of for now. By the way, that guitar practice and Russian reading are something new I'm going to incorporate into my schedule. I figure if I put in an hour a day for a long time I will be able to become pretty good finally. It seems a shame that after I put in so much work on Russian if I don't keep it up, I'll just forget it all. So I'm going to try it. 'Bye now.

Love,
Chris

Part of a letter from Chris to Jeff. Spring, 1965

Jeff,

I just got back from a rousing trip to Montreal. I went with a friend but he had some girl-friend problems and was feeling so bad that he wasn't much fun. So I spent three days amusing myself and trying to think of things to do. I met a good guitar player. I wrote a lot of notes, etc. and we lived (slept) at the Salvation Army. A very productive thing that came out of it were the notes I got on a bum named Morrie who sort of got to like me. He didn't speak much English but he had many ways of expressing himself and we became friends for the while I was there. That is their life. Rotten filthy underwear, if any at all, 3 pr. of pants to keep warm and to cover the holes of the other pairs, and mainly because it's easiest to carry pants that way. Begging a dime and scrounging the streets for cigarette butts which are dumped into a sack and the tobacco collected, rewrapped in newspaper and smoked. Quite a life! I was glad to get back here because of those guys. . . .

(Rest of letter lost.)

Notes on a scrap of paper written by Chris, April 1965.

. . . there is a little showy psychology teacher in all of us, and a hard motorcycle bum in the most sophisticated of us; a hermit in the loudest of us and a politician in the quietest of us. It's true I don't want to be any of these and in order to be none of these I must be all of them at the same time. I have just spent some time with bums and wanted to be one very much. I wanted them to accept me as one. But they wouldn't and you know why. It's because I wasn't one. To become one I had to be an unsensing, unfeeling, poor emotionless bastard that had no college or be able to act like I'd had none. I had to become inhuman. This I couldn't do. The same was required of me when I owned motorcycle boots and a big old Harley, the same was required when I was . . . the hard tough guy and the beatnik, etc., etc. By Jesus, why is it so hard to be oneself? To be clean and unhindered by these fool acts. To be blessed with innocence of motive, guilelessness of intent. Sure, that sounds pedantic. Maybe it

102

is. Maybe that's the act that I was trying to put on right there. Maybe so, but what's yours, pal? . . .

(The rest of these notes not found.)

Note on back of Easter card from Chris to Jeff. Spring, 1965

Hi Jeff,

I hope you have a joyous one-man basket and egg hunt. According to my calculations, you'll still be looking for the basket by the time I get home for summer, if things go as well as they usually do. Mom was always very proud of her ability to hide Easter baskets, so I still might find it before you! Make an egg for Dad from me that says "To the bald eagle." Yuh! Yuh! And make one to yourself from me that says, "To Fats Jens." Well, at any rate you can make one to Molly Cat for me. I've got to go study for a prelim. tomorrow so take it easy, future "Oscar Robertson of Glen Ellyn!" I'll see you in about a month and a half or two and don't take any wooden nickels.

Love,
Chris

Letter from Chris to Tim.

April, 1965

Dear Tim:

Here is the letter I started about a month ago.* I know I'll never get much more written on it because there is just too much more that has and will happen that I am too dumbfounded to write anything. The girl, Karen, is still all mine, which makes everything look rosier. This girl has the "milk of human goodness" in her, and can and does show it to everybody. And when I am with her, and now even when I'm not with her, I feel "goodness," and I feel "love" and all the things that I've argued against. I cannot possibly argue against these at this time, nor do I want, nor care for any scientific explanation of love.** You see, this girl serves as a sort of guru for me in one way, and she's a fairy tale in another and makes life for herself and me a fairy tale. You know, sometimes we cut out of studying and go to the Land of Mushrooms. But we really go! And I love the Land of Mushrooms. It's the same land I was in when I was much younger. Remember those football games and marshmallow roasts in front

---

*Do not have the letter to which he refers.

**For awhile he argued against anything that could not be proved in a laboratory.

103

of 251 Forest? I was in the Land of the Mushrooms then. Thank God, I found it again, before it was lost, Tim. This I'm sure of—I would soon have been lost had not someone from the Land of the Mushrooms come along in time. I'm on the right road now, Tim. It's a matter of ploughing through now. Answer soon, Tim. Sooner than I did.

Love,
Chris

P.S. Don't let all this stuff scare you. I feel happy is all.

Paper written by Chris for English, Spring, 1965.

OFF TO THE ENCHANTED FOREST

The day was sunny and just warm enough that when one took off his jacket, there was no chill, no discomfort. Rather it was the kind of day when one takes off his coat and experiences an inexorable sense of freedom and totality of mind and body, unequalled in any other season. It is the kind of day when the sparrows maintain a background of brash, insistent scolding as their young ones spill from their nests and try their wings for the first time, and in the distance can be distinguished the sweet "Phoee-bee" of the chicadee, while nearer by the full rich crescendo of the warbler warms the spirit. As I walked along toward my apartment, I saw the children laughing and shouting and speeding about on their bicycles playing follow the leader, while another group was playing softball on the playground. This was a day to be outside, a day which calls to those who must sit inside, the trees and flowers becoming sirens, enticing those who have obligations to meet and a paper to write to throw them to the winds and be off to the green sweet outdoors. Thus I determined to visit my forest, which I have come to call the "Enchanted Forest."

So I was off to see if the flycatcher had built her nest down by the stream yet, and if the snow trilliums had spread their rose tinged petals to the shady forest air, and if the bumblebees were making their rounds to the wild rock bells; I wanted to check in on the hooded Jack-in-the-pulpit and make sure that the small fungus flies had come back again this year and were spending their time with this delightful clergyman; I was anxious to hear the scarlet tanager singing. And I wanted to play tag again with the beautiful, iridescently blue green tiger beetles that live along the creek and take delight in tempting any who pass by to pick them up; yet scurrying off when such an attempt is made, only to reappear later and continue the game. Most of all I wanted to visit the old, lonely hemlock and see if he had any sad stories to tell.

The woodland proved no disappointment. As I entered the forest wall, the cool, humid air of the place felt clean against my face. Excitement and adventure pulsed through my body. I have never been to the Enchanted Forest when some new discovery, a new butterfly or moth, a new bird, a new flower or salamander has not made its presence known to me. And each time the thrill of seeing something I had never before set eyes on, and watching it carefully for new habits, new designs, new ways of life has overwhelmed me and made me feel quite unimportant indeed, quite insignificant.

This time I discovered a little water snake, the kind I have seen before from a distance swimming in the stream, but had never before been able to get a close look at. He was lying in the path in a portion of the woods that lets a fair amount of light filter through the trees, and was quietly sunning himself. He was brown and had two black stripes running down his back and as I stood over him, my presence evidently came to disturb him, for he began to crawl off. I had gotten but a quick look at him so I stopped him and picked him up. He was soft and very warm from the sun, and I could feel his breathing quite distinctly, his body noticeably contracting and expanding beneath the point where I had grasped him. I looked into his round yellow eyes and saw nothing there but the fear of a small animal caught by a giant, and a wish to be allowed to go on his way. His forked reddish black tongue emerged from his mouth quite regularly, helping him to smell that which was holding him back, and to look as ferocious as possible. Altogether his mean looks didn't work, for he had one of the cutest faces of any of the snakes I had ever seen. I lowered him to the ground and released him, and watched him crawl away in the direction of the stream. And then I went on my way, happy, to see the rest of the woods and to make my visits to the Jack-in-the-pulpits and the old hemlock.

The woods is a wonderful place where one's curiosity, aesthetic needs, adventuresome spirit, sense of well-being, and "outdoors fever" can be satisfied to the fullest. It is a place of greenness, of flowers and mushrooms, and life, of sweet smells and mellow, happy sounds. Best of all it is a refuge where one may go when concerns pile one on top of the other and provides inspiration and enthusiasm to face the world happily and light of heart. These things are good for me.

Note written by Chris, Spring, 1965.

A diving beetle, for no apparent reason at all, pulls himself out of the water and lounges on a rock. The sun soon dries all traces of the pond off his wings. Still he lounges, quietly, gathering strength. Suddenly he's off, the whir of his wings faintly audible, rising into the breeze. He makes a half circle, then heads west. Soon he is gone altogether, searching and seeking new circumstances, a greener pond, a mate. So long, fellow. I could have captured you when you were so vulnerable, lying there, damp and unable to make your wings work right. I could have kept you with me always in a little container, I could have owned you. But that would not have solved the problem. No, you could soon have died, and I should not want that. You had best be gone, if you must. Others will soon come here, just as you will be arriving somewhere too. I will soon love them as I have loved you. But I will not forget you. The emotion you aroused in me, the hard time you had dragging yourself out of the water, with one of your legs missing, lost in battle somewhere in the world. These feelings are etched on my soul. Next year, when the warm winds unfreeze the ponds, I shall remember you, and weep and smile as I think of you, whom I shall never hear of again.

Miscellaneous notes by Chris, Spring, 1965.

I'm not versed very well in your world, Karen—of being friendly and interested in everything and everybody. I just know more about the world of jealousies and take advantages. I understand your world and respond to it, but try as I might, I can't seem to get myself into it.* Maybe you can help me get into it?

I'm dropping off to sleep now, slowly dropping away from conscious will, to dip into the vat of drives and impulses that make up the other part of me, the part I only know when my will is down. It must be an awful part since I seem to so thoroughly cancel it out when awake.

Things I can write about—

1. Insignificance of you, me, everything.

2. Turtles with Merry Christmas (carved in their shells). Cactus with phony flowers.

3. Good and bad—warmth or callousness—loving, not caring, hateful, etc.

4. For only a few cents additional the word "love" can be added to any of the above texts. . .

---

*Yet he was a young man with a great many interests, who had made many friends who loved him because he was so friendly and interested!

Letter from Karen to Chris.

Hello Old Man,

Suppose it's now time for me to put pen to paper and begin stringing out thought, confusion, disappointment, anger—all neatly surrounded by punctuation, and not quite so neatly ending in a funny "well there's something between us." Fine—it's there—but what in God's name is it? Don't know—simply don't know. Sometimes I don't even want to know—maybe out of being frightened by what I'll have to face. Instead—I just somehow bumble through the good days hoping they'll last—though too well aware that they won't. Instead—somehow to pass from a lovely contented warmth to a rather harsh frustrated irritation. It's not so much the bickering that is intolerable—far more painful is the aching which it leaves. You seem quite able to laugh—often louder and freer than ever—after things have been repatched, re-glued. In some ways that's justified for food does indeed taste better when your stomach is empty—even if it has been empty for only half an hour. But, you know, despite the food that's come to fill the emptiness, my stomach has this memory: see—in some ways it resents this mass of substance that takes it so much for granted that, once deposited, things have never been any different. I suppose I have what, in unanatomical terms, is called a grudge-bearing stomach. The grudge—the memory—the ache—remain. I'm not justifying it, but simply stating that it's my way and I do hold grudges, and often they complicate each other and—once again—I promise you they are very rarely forgotten.

But as we both know, the differences go deeper than that. They involve intellectual outlooks and all the rest. Look Chris, I've spent three years taking much anthro-sciences; but do you know how much I desperately want to learn more about music—about French poets—about *abstract* idea systems? Right—I love your joy over nature and your preoccupation with its complications and components. But mind you, in many respects these other things are just as important and fundamental to me, and I want to converse about them. I miss the abstract, less practical, less realistic talks and want to have that side of me drawn out and enriched. This is the greatest factor that caused me to accept the fateful Friday night excursion.

. . . We've often argued over this—you know—PLEASE stop the constant "you're just what I'm becoming." First of all, I'm not. Second of all, if that's what you want I'll write you out an outlined recipe. Third of all, Chris I don't want you to applaud me. Karen: "What is a good person?" C.Q.R. "What you are" . . .

I don't want praise from you; nor do I want you to somehow rest your head on my shoulder. Christ, Chris—how many times I've said this. I realize that you're going to receive this letter in not at all a praising state—but, regardless of what you say, it's true that you put yourself in the "before" category and me in the "after" category.

Gosh—it's late—very late and I'm tired. Really tired. And hence both impatient with you and with all the mucking about that we've done. You, my friend, have walked yourself so deep into my system that I'm just not sure that I'll ever be strong enough to accept the fact that we'd each be better off going our separate ways. Any leaving to be done is going to have to be done by you. I may drive you to it.

You know, my room is good. It's big and pink and filled with you—with your jacket, your car ticket, your letters, your corsages, your pine tree peak. I've even got this bracelet. It's made of pearls, bone, wire and sunshine—and you, too, have become part of my days. And that's much bigger than even my room. As I began, there's something there and it doesn't go away. Some of it's love, some of it's not. Sometimes I'd like you to be the father of my child. Other times I'm both sure and glad that you'll never be. Now—I just know that—well, that there are things which just must be left alone to take their own course, at their own pace.

If you feel like or want to, you can call with the certainty that I'll be waiting.

If you don't, then don't. And again, I guess, I'll be grateful because it is probably wisest.

If you don't, maybe I'll call you. Maybe I won't—that depends on how strong I am and on what I decide is the strong thing to do.

Karen

Letter from Chris to Karen.

Spring, 1965

Dear Angel,

One last letter. I didn't want to write it, I wanted to say it, so I worked real hard to get out in time, but you weren't home when I called so now I've got to write it. Letters are almost as bad as 'phone calls! Here quickly though are things I want to tell you before my defenses rise up and start defending me again. These are things I *mean*.

No. 1—I lied again. I told you I woke up too, like you, and something changed. Nothing changed with me though—see? I just lied. See, I know you pretty well, and I know pretty much what I lacked because I know pretty well what you want—need. Angel, we talked about sophistication, etc. We talked so long about all that stuff, but you know that doesn't have any bearing on what's really going on. It was nice to blame our troubles, etc., on that, but I'm afraid that it just wasn't the whole problem. The real one, the basic and fundamental one, is this—you're more sensitive than I, there can be no doubt about it. You said it before, and it's very true. You're sensitive to your own feelings and to others', too. I'm sensitive to my own feelings, but not nearly as sensitive to others' as you—this is why I could argue so well against you, because I can really know my own feelings. Very many people are neither sensitive to others' feelings or their own. This I believe—that to be kings or queens of this world we must first know ourselves—then we must come to know others.

Being sensitive to another's feelings means being his friend—means knowing yourself and what you want, and knowing him and what he wants. Knowing yourself only means you can receive, but can't give back as much in return. You were right. I haven't been a good friend. I couldn't give too much. I wasn't sensitive enough to your needs, nor really to anybody's, so I've never been a real friend.* But you have been a real friend to me and probably will continue. It hurts me somewhere down real deep when I let myself know I let you down as a friend, that makes me cry a little

So see—we talked of sophistication, etc., etc., but that wasn't the problem. You don't need a muscleman, a philosopher, or a world traveller—you just need (want) a friend. This is what you told me tonight; and this is what I knew already; I knew what I lacked and hence knew what would happen.

But here's the part I feel really bad about, Angel: I knew—I saw—what hopes and maybe expectations you had about me. I was glad you had them. I had the same ones about you and they were good and fun because they were fulfilled for me. But your hopes, your dreams—I just let them fall flat, didn't I, girl? I didn't really give that much. You got the bad end of this deal. Oh, Angel, it makes me cry to know I've been such a disappointment to a little girl just going out of the door. But you're a big girl now in a lot of ways, a pretty strong one, and you've been out of the door for a long time. So you'll just add another grudge to your stomach and say, "Life is hard." Good Lord, I'm sorry about that grudge. Try not to let it hurt bad. I would have it not be there—I put it there, though, didn't I? "Forgive them for they know not what they do."

Angel, I guess it's right. I was just an Indian from Montana, or an Algerian refugee—the pupil. Only at a certain few times did we seem to equal out or cancel out, before the inequality came back again. But maybe this will be some consolation—I think I learned this lesson well, Angel,

---

*Many would deny this! Including me. I miss his friendship *so much.*

as much as I hated to admit it—because I wanted you badly and I know pupils don't get teachers—there's been a barrier for years in front of me, and I needed a kick in the pants to get me going over it. You have given it to me, because you were sensitive to me, and I lose you because I was insensitive to you; but I win in the long run, see? And Angel—Godspeed on your search for a friend—I can tell you now it's a wonderful thing to have one.

Well, a lot of pipe-dreams came to an end. I guess we *were* just a lot of pipe-dreams after all. For me there were other dreams too—ones that will come true someday, not just pipe-dreams. But I want to say this—and take it for whatever it's worth to you—you have been, are, and will be something special to me, extra-special. You've given me hope and faith in myself but, more important, in people I have condemned, which in actuality was everybody. You've given me courage to test my insecurities in reality. For these things which you possess, and which you have helped enrich in me, I love you. There are no ties or bonds for that statement. I found a rose in the weedpatch and smelled its beauty and caressed it, and suddenly the whole weedpatch broke into blossom. It doesn't matter what's said or what's done for nobody can take away the fact of what happened and the effects it had. But I know it's time to leave the rose alone now, before I bruise it any further. I feel joy and sorrow in leaving.

Every now and then, when I get to feeling a certain way, I'm going to make you a little something or other, Angel, because I like to make things for you. There are also three or four songs which I want to give you someday and some poems I would like to share. There will be lots of things I'll want to share with you. Because you're special.

'Bye now.

Love,
C.Q.R.

Chris's notes on an envelope, Spring, 1965.

The poor guy. I'm interested that someone else realized the humor. He is trying so hard. But his hair is just too long and his levis pull in too thin against his legs, barely wide enough to go over his rawhide boots. He doesn't see that it's all wrong, what he's trying to put across; the way he dresses he's making people laugh. A little while ago there was the roar of his motorcycle that went on just a little bit too long, and I knew what would come in the door. He filled the bill to a "T." Helmet with bubble shield thrown back still on his head. And black engineer boots that were too big. I could barely hold my laughter down. Here was his big thrill since he bought a new motorcycle. Striding in the door in what he thought were cool motorcycle boots, but they were too large and too new, still had a shine. They were a dead give-away.

It's easy for me to see the acts. I see my own constantly. I've had the act above. But now, rather than fight my way out of the foolishness and try to make myself a real act as I was wont to do for years, the idea has crept into my mind of ridding myself of all acts and just being human. This, I was not long to discover, was the job of the century. Here is a row to hoe. To play an act, you merely buy the garb, make sure it's "cool" as this chap had failed to do, and then say the lines of the role in which you cast yourself. I don't care if it's motorcycle bum or philosophy teacher. It's a lot harder to be just plain human than one of them because humans have to respond appropriately. They have to be so uninvolved with themselves that they hear, see, and understand the circumstances in which they are placed, no matter what they might be. They must respond with the correct emotion. It's human to feel compassion, sympathy, warmth, anger, joy, sorrow, love and sometimes hate, liking, attraction, and humor.

But to feel these at the right time, the time that will allow communication to another human, requires the knowledge of that individual's frame of reference and requires that one not be in his own frame of reference. One must be free, free to float into the other's frame of reference. If one is a tough motorcyclist, one will miss the little child's tears, and the young boy with the limp; he will miss that boy when he falls awkwardly and flushes as he lifts himself again off the ground and prays nobody was watching. And the psychology teacher will miss the working man's repugnance for Freud and Allport and explanations of *Of Human Bondage* in terms of popular learning theory. But now let me illustrate how hard it is to rid oneself of "the act." I'm sitting, a little high, and hence less fearful than usual, here at a table all alone. But I cannot help notice the glances of people, and I am conceited and happy they are watching me, and that I am giving a little grimace, a little smirk, a little wince to convey to them that I am filled with emotion. It is true, I am filled with emotion. But it is happiness. I am trying to give the impression of a poor, hardened sympathetic soul who is trying to get along in this world. It is true that sometimes I am. But not tonight. I'm a little lonely but very happy and well and that's the way I feel.

Why do I act to show them differently? In my act I've missed that one of those girls is lonely, and wouldn't mind dancing. In my act I've shut myself off from humaneness and humanity and yet I can scarcely overcome it. I want people to think I am what I am pretending to be.

(Something missing here. Notes continue on a coupon.)

. . . when we both will listen to Peter, Paul and Mary sing it we both

111

will weep. But when it comes to out and out face-to-face contact, the acts move in and there will be no weepinig. There will be petty hostilities, rivalries, envies, joys, likes, but there will be *no weeping*. Because petty things are all that can result from acts. When two acts face on to each other, great pettiness and no more is the sum. It happens every time. Because human emotion is absent to a large degree. Humaneness is not its rule. The rule has become: don't tread on the sacred act.

(Another note, at a different time)
And I had clambered up to the heights by means of my new wings, with leaps and bounds yet, being there, found myself in solitude and hate. And being a young and sensitive bird, with wings not strong enough to keep me aloft, found no help, but only a vacuum, something that was below me, pulling me down.

From Chris's notebook, Spring, 1965.

Why, hello little kitty, small object of the night. What is your wish? You're begging for my love? Don't bother. There's so little love in the world. You, a mere cat, can scarcely expect to receive any at all. So I'll leave you in your misery and go satisfy some of my needs. What's this . . . you're following me. You mustn't follow me, put your faith in me, for I will only disappoint you. After all, I'm only human. Get away kitty, scram, beat it. I have important things to do. Go away, leave before—before—go ahead, Chris, it's the truth—before you discover that I too am just another heartless human, possibly worse than the others. It's hard to face the facts. Go ahead, love me. Probably you'll get a kick in the mouth for it. But possibly you may light a spark which I'll pass on to somebody else. You've helped me kitty.

Another note.

Ah, this breeze is wonderful. It serves to blow away one's cares, one's fears, one's self, leaving an empty space into which one's buried soul may emerge and express itself. This shows there is something in humans other than self; something that's good; something that matters a lot; something that's possibly the most important thing in the world, in the universe—goodness, love, peace, God.

Paper written by Chris for English, Spring, 1965.

A GREAT AND POSSIBLY IRREVERSIBLE LOSS

I have felt awfully bad about something for a long time now. I don't know quite how else to express it except by just sort of starting and then letting it run free until I feel satisfied that I have expressed it.

I can remember when life was so tender that I used to bounce awake in the morning and after giving a few jumps up and down on the bed-spring out of sheer excitement and delight for the new day, race out of bed and down the stairs, wasting as little time as possible dressing and eating; then tumble through the door and out into the burst of sunshine and out-of-doors smells and literally breathe in life with the new-morning fresh air. I remember so plainly how dressing and eating were just things that had to be gotten out of the way, as quickly as possible, for the important and good things in life. And how well I remember such events as Christmas-time and the Christmas spirit, and my wonderment at the beauty and the pine smells and presents and people. And I was *sensitized* to life. Little things were significant. Big things were stupendous. I could really enjoy, and I could really feel.

But things change and as I remember it, it was about seventh grade that it started. What I was wearing had become important for the first time. I had blue jeans and everyone else had wash pants, and I had developed a need not to be scorned by them. So I pleaded for and received my first pair of wash pants which I donned proudly, and which made an irreversible mark on my life. It wasn't long until I began losing a lot of my spontaneity and wonderment; and personal problems, somehow created by the world, began to govern my thinking, forcing love of life out of my mind, never to appear again except in brief and punctuated interludes. And I remember so clearly the feelings I had as I rode the bus home for Christmas vacation a couple of years ago. All I could muster up was a sort of sentimentality mixed with sadness and worry over some very temporary problems. I've wished for and tried to feel the old Christmas spirit, and I have sometimes pretended very hard that I did. Too bad! That, I can definitely vouch for, was a real loss. And I have now had days where eating a good meal was the most significant thing that happened to me all day. But one of the most startling things to me is my lack of enthusiasm for getting up in the morning. There are no more bouncing bed-springs. I'm no longer thrilled and delighted by the new day. And so, little by little, drop by drop, I've watched my spontaneity, originality, zest and love for life leak away into oblivion. I've watched the angel-human that I was slowly degenerate to a sort of decrepit Scrooge-like person.* I watched this step by step take-over of my soul, and I became very afraid of it, so I fought it hard. But I lost.

It's repulsive, what the world does to its little children. A little cherub, completely spontaneous, is slowly pushed and prodded, hollowed and pitted by the pressures of this world until it is made into a doll, a mockery of what could have been produced. And that is what is so pathetic, that is what is so frustratingly disappointing. The world takes this marvelous little organism, the child, full of originality, spontaneity, wonderment, zest, truthfulness, and an ability to really enjoy, and produces an unfeeling, unoriginal manikin.

And so I ask, almost plead—what kind of a place is this? What kind of a place takes innocence and beauty and artistry, and crushes it? I want no part of it at all, and yet I've been caught. The world wants me to believe in its automatons and think they are fine and productive men. Right now I *know* that this is wrong. I believe in that fact through every part of me. And I will fight hard against the pushing of the world to make me believe the way it wants me to. But the world has power that one cannot withstand alone. And so the harder I fight, the harder it will push, until I stumble and succumb.

Then, just like my Christmas spirit and my joys of getting up early and racing outside, this last little bit of knowledge will be wiped out of me. And then when I am a perfect fit to the world's mold, it will congratulate me that I have reached maturity. And I shall agree and congratulate others that they too have reached maturity, and go out to crush any who have not.

Notes by Chris for Writing Class, Spring, 1965.

A beautiful, mournful song plays, and touches me. It tells about how hard life is. Why, why does it touch me, who has all the breaks in this world working for him; me, who was never wanting for money, for care and attention, who has beautiful dreams for the future and every means for making them come true? Why do I become saddened when I hear about the futility of it all? My life hasn't been a particularly hard road, and right now life is a bundle of rosebuds for me, it has brought me joys in the past and the promise of good things to come. Why should I agree, so emotionally, so totally, that life is not rewarding?

I have believed and preached and often felt to the depths of my creation, that all of us are brothers. Yet I find myself contemptuous of my fellow men.

---

*He did not seem this way to his family and friends who loved him greatly.

Letter from Lee to Chris.

May 2, 1965.

Dear Chris:

I have wanted to write you before, but life has been one big jam ever since Grandpa got sick—mainly because of guests—all of which has put me way behind on the hundred and one things that are just ordinary for me.

The guests included a week of Dad's family, all of whom stayed here except for Mary and Larry, who stayed at his mother's. It was a very interesting week in many ways, and I ended it up by writing a nice letter to my in-laws, to whom I said, "You have all made me feel that you really like me, and I return that affection." This is so very true. They really have shown me a great deal of warmth, every one of them, in stormy times as well as bright. Now that Grandpa is gone and we won't be getting together at his birthday time any more, we are planning, at my suggestion, to get together at one of our homes at least every two years. I have also told them that any time they want a retreat, they can have one of our upstairs rooms, no questions asked, and I'll bring up their meals. This may seem like a strange offer, but I sure could have used such a place at one time.

After the family left, Tim and a friend of his were here for several days during spring vacation. The friend was Chip from Florida, an extremely nice and responsive kid who was a great pleasure to have around. He has taken up with Lloyd and Tim since his arrival at U. of Ill. in February.

Tim has a job! It is in one of the high schools near here in which he was particularly interested. So now he can relax for awhile—till he starts worrying about the job itself! He plans not to work this summer, but will spend his time studying up on one of the courses he has to teach—a world civilization course, starting with East India, or something like that, which he has never studied: but neither has anyone else. It's a new course being taught around. In a couple of weeks he is going to go to Maryland with Dave Pullen to Por's wedding. He's lucky all his best friends have gotten married before he is on his own, so we have to buy the wedding presents!

Tim says you wrote him all about your girl*, but you have written us nothing at all about her, except that she was going away some place next year, and (to Jeff) that things were going well with her.

After Tim and Chip left, the poet Alistair moved in with a poet pal of his. He was only going to stay over the weekend, but it lengthened out to a week, and they cleaned Dad out of his Chivas Regal and his Michelob! All in all, it was quite an experience. More about that when we see you.

---

*Karen

It is getting beautiful around here, though spring is awfully slow. The lack of leaves out is making it possible to see the birds better. Among other things I have seen a bob-o-link, brown creeper, ruby-crested kinglet, golden-crowned kinglet, chipping sparrow, white-throated sparrow, hermit thrush. These are all birds I had never identified before around here. I have a scarecrow up in the cat pen, made of an old floor lamp from Kohler's, a broom stick for arms, at the ends of which dangle large pieces of foil which flutter on pieces of string. It's dressed in a raincoat of Dad's and one of his old hats. I think it is working, and it makes me feel quite confident. Probably frustrates the cats; they try to be so still crouching by the fence, and thinking, no doubt, "That damned aluminum foil!"

I have a one-woman art show at Ruth Saxon's shop, and if nothing else it sure brought a lot of publicity. It really looks good, I think. I have sold three pictures, and some of the more expensive ceramics, and have an order for another picture. I painted an abstract yesterday of a burned-out church—the church disappeared completely, but you can see the stained glass. It's not bad.

Love,
M

Letter from Tim to Chris.

May 13, 1965

Dear Chris:

I certainly enjoyed receiving and reading your letter. I wish I were as good a writer. You really have the ability to make your feelings understood on paper. I'm sure glad everything is working out so well for you (although by this time maybe things have slid a little), and you are making a good adjustment to life. You'll have to write me further about your new girl. (By the way, I might not see you if you're coming home for the first part of the summer—I might be going to Florida to a new friend's house). As far as my "love-life" goes, I have been a virtual dateless wonder since I hit graduate schoool; the academic atmosphere, the pressures, and my apathetic attitude toward girls (born of fear, of course) have all contributed to this state of (no girl) affairs. Anyway, I feel I have learned a lot about myself and people, and knowing Lloyd, of course, has been one of the most rewarding experiences of my life.

Before I go any further, I must bring you good tidings: I have finally located a job. I have just signed a contract to teach at Glenbrook North in Northbrook (about five miles west of Evanston). This is a very fine high school with modern facilities, an excellent student body (about 75% go

116

on to college), and a very fine professional staff. The salary is also about average ($5900/year). So I am really very happy with the way things have turned out on this score—Glenbrook was one of the schools I was very interested in. Of course I'll be moving out of the house into an apartment (probably in Northbrook) in August or sometime thereabouts.

As for philosophizing: while you're moving toward "my" way of thinking (or so it would seem from outward appearances), I feel I am moving toward "your side"; at least in some respects. To boil it down, concepts of soul, God, afterlife (at least as an identity) are becoming less important to me because I cannot logically and concretely prove their existence (what you have been saying all the time!). By the same token, I cannot logically prove that a soul does not exist; thus why worry about either? The important thing is—and you are seemingly approximating it presently—that we love in as detached a way as possible. Soul or no soul, human contentment can be achieved only by this course. *This* is the "Land of Mushrooms."

Have read *Of Human Bondage*, and I agree with you that it is a very excellent book. I read it over on Elmwood Drive one summer and I remember it did me a lot of good (I identified myself with Phillip). As for *The Little Prince*, I haven't gotten a chance, but Lloyd says it's good.

I think our actions in Viet Nam are atrocious, how about you? I don't expect us to get out, but it would be nice if we started living up to some other "commitments" such as the United Nations Charter. How can we expect them to negotiate while we are launching full scale air raids on their country? I don't believe Russia is going to be able to stand by and take this much longer. They have a face to save also. I am completely in agreement with Senators Church, Gruening, Morse and Aiken who, almost unsupported in Congress, have been making logical appeals for immediate halting of bombings and call for negotiation. When will people ever learn that military action never really solves problems in the end; how many world wars will it take to prove this? Now, our action is uniting the Communist bloc (which was very *dis*united) and is allowing the "hard line" elements in the Russian Government (rather than the "peaceful co-existence" people, who gather around Krushchev) to say "I told you so"; and freeze the cold war up again—even bring about a situation which threatens full-scale war. As for the "domino theory," I think it is completely fallacious—how soon would Australia, Indonesia, or the Phillipines fall to Communism if South Viet Nam went Communist? For that matter, Ho Chi Minh, the leader of North Viet Nam, hates China and Russia almost as much as the United States—he is a nationalist just like DeGaulle.

Off my soap box. I've got to go eat now, Chris. Write me when you get a chance. I'll be at home this summer, so I'll see you if you don't go on this Quaker thing.* (Which, incidentally, sounds very interesting. The Quakers are a very impressive lot. I went to one of their meetings). I'll see you then, hopefully. If not, au revoir.

Love,
Tim

A poem by Chris, Spring 1965.

There are those who scream of homosexuality,
And try to tell me that fear of loss of my genitals
Causes me my emotion.
They will chuckle at my disbelief and say,
"Tut tut, poor fellow,
You cannot know the truth, for it is hidden to you."
And they will know that they are right.
I have only this to say to them:
Open your eyes and ears, gentlemen.
Allow the choked cry of a small baby
To envelop you,
And engage all your senses,
And transform you from reasonable and sensible men
Into perceivers and sensers of the universe.
Throw off your interpretations
And systematizations and characterizations
And look at the sunset for what it is,
For its existence.
Let it capture you.
Take just one man, and do not analyze him.
Let him communicate to you
That which is important to him.
Allow him the freedom to be unique,
And marvellous in his uniqueness.
Allow yourselves this unbounded sensation . . .
Let your souls be shaken and soothed by these things.
Yes, gentlemen . . . "souls"—that word you despise so much.
Let the word "soul" have meaning to you just once.
Then come back and write of these things in your books.
Try then to connect them
To the loss of genitalia

---

*Chris went to Nova Scotia on a Cornell sociological project instead.

I've a notion—
You will be . . .
Dumbfounded.

Short paper by Chris, May, 1965.

ANALYSIS IN TERMS OF CONFLICTS

I have often been bothered when out-of-doors for the two different ways I shall describe. When I am alone, I have always liked to collect. My motives or reasons for loving woods and fields and swamps: they are fairy lands to me, with the exciting and unknown always lurking. What new and intriguing animal will suddenly come out, what new flowers? But here is where nature trips have tied in with "other people" when I was alone. I collect things and name them so I will be "an expert" on them if and when I bring someone. I want to show them I'm an expert on nature. One of my self-images is the good and great naturalist who knows the countryside like the palm of his hand. I also yearn for someone to show it to.

When I am with others in a place of nature, I resent it when they find something better than I. I love to give the impression mentioned above that I know every flower, every insect. I enjoy being outdoors much less with someone else than I do alone. Yet I long to bring a girl friend on a picnic where I know nature and names and locations or organisms. But the resenting of her "finds" and often of her knowledge; and the looking for ways to impress her all add up to not enjoying it out there. There is no room left.

The times I have enjoyed being out with others were when I was with Mom and Dad, mainly Mom, who knows much of it and introduced me to it. I consider her an expert*, and I don't try to impress her.

Letter from Chris to family.

May 1965

Dear Folks,

It's about time to write again. As you can see, the tentative schedule that I set up for myself, whereby you would be written to once every two weeks, was a bitter failure. There is so much to write about that I scarcely

---

*Actually I'm not an expert, just an enjoyer. I've always said I know a lot more about nature than the average person but very little compared to the true expert.

know where to begin, nor will I be able to elaborate fully on any of the topics. Time is important right now because I have a term paper due in a few days for which I have many, many pages of reading that I have collected over the past few weeks.

I have definitely moved into a new period of my life. I would like to explain it fully to you, first because you will probably be interested in it, second because I feel a decided need to set it all down coherently in front of myself. It has been a period so far of intense interest and enthusiasm for various things, coupled with times, not of depression, but of emotional deadness, sort of a disgust or nausea for everything. The outward indications of these two facets have been great efficiency at times, and apathy at others, though I have had to force myself to work through the apathy in order to stay above water schoolwise. As I have said though, I am not experiencing depression such as I have in the past. And I feel a great deal better more of the time than ever before. Indeed there have been times of feeling perfectly well-adjusted, and the taste of this has made me determined to get myself to that state permanently. By the way, for the psychology course I'm taking, "Theories of Personality," we had to read any book by a psychological theorist. I picked Karen Horney's* *Our Inner Conflicts*,** and went through it very carefully. I have read it thoroughly in the past, but never before with such insights as it has given me this time. This is probably coupled with my new-found sort of philosophy of anti-science— look at things for what they are right now, not for what they should be or could be, or were. This is how I have, of course, been looking at and judging myself—constantly what I should be—"idealized image."*** Horney will help me. I'm sure I'll be making very much use of her in the near future. The impact of full realization: that much of my love for people was a little bit of real love, coupled with a wish for power over them, as Horney helped me see, but which I discovered before I had gotten into her, in a discussion with a room-mate. When I then read this same conclusion in Horney, it had the effect of opening my mind to her to hear what she is actually talking about. It's funny. Before, I had always classified myself mostly as a person "moving toward people." Now I know the truth. I also realize I'm much more of detached person, a "mover away" than I had seen before. I also have found out that I'm not so bad off as I feared that I might be. Put all this together with the direction that life has now assumed for me, both because I am going about systematically getting myself organized and the fact that good things are in the future and life

---

*The psychiatric writer who was of such help to me.
**Published by W.W. Norton and Co., Inc., N.Y.
***Horney's concept.

looks pretty good. The thing I'm planning to do this summer (which I'll tell you all about a little later) and the interests and enthusiasms and projects I've newly gained such as: reading good books, learning and observing much more about nature, digging in and finding out about subjects that I've vaguely felt interested in before (but never really found out about due to laziness), not worrying about the fact that there are some people I just don't like and, in turn, putting myself more fully into relationships with people who I do have an affinity for—all these things have given me some direction. Thinking about them, and putting them into action has given me a thrill and a new delightful feeling for life and living at times. This is when I am efficient, when I am worth something to the world, when I truly love people, or at least don't hate them.

This is not the kind of exhilaration I have experienced in the past. This is a more reserved and contented type of exhilaration, a feeling of becoming rooted in this old life, though it may be a hard road; a feeling of really living, of getting at the meaning of what it is to be alive and really communicating to some people. Millions of experiences are giving me new insights every day. Well, enough of all this, let it be known that I am finding out what's going on.

Now I'll just sort of give you the most important news item. You asked about the girl, Karen. She is indeed quite a girl. Suffice it to say that she is totally uninhibited in interpersonal relations. She talks and thinks honestly of people and to people, and in her honesty there is a radiance that I have never seen matched before around here. People I introduced her to fell in love with her nearly instantly. All of them. She was in one of my labs, and as far as I could tell, everyone in there was in love with her. I saw in her a beauty that was so compelling—the beauty of honesty, of seeing through all the muddled details and ramifications of a complicated and confused situation, and expressing in the most wonderful terms and articulation what the basic problem or ground substance of the situation was. Only on occasion have I been in a conversation where I could say what I thought precisely and not become buried in all the frames of reference and considerations that are present. For her this is an everyday occurrence, indeed, she cannot do otherwise. I learned much from her about what human beings are. But, alas, I had too many inhibitions, too many needs, and they so much hindered our relationship, as they have much hindered all my relationships in truth, that they were bogging each of us down. We are now good friends, though when she is around I feel a vague rage with myself, somewhat of a frustration. I haven't gone out with her for about four weeks now but, for two months, I was having a wonderful time with her when the needs were left unprovoked and did not flare up. She gave me a look at what a fulfilled person can be. She helped me to see a little

121

of that fulfilledness in myself. What is good is that my needs were few enough so that we could share as much rapport as we did. This gave me hope and confidence that I can conquer. Just as this letter is, my talks with her were mainly about me, about what I want, etc. This couldn't be avoided, because I was the limiting factor; it was so obvious. I hate that in me which necessitates thinking about myself so much. It ruins enjoyment, enrichment that others can fulfill or evoke in me. I want to get rid of it so badly now. Because it was so clear and is so clear now, the problem of my needs and conflicts.

I guess the biggest news item of all is what I will be doing this summer. It looks as if I will be going to Nova Scotia, to a country that is in great economic and motivational depression, which Cornell anthropologists have been studying for years.* Our problem is to use our knowledge to help them gain and use knowledge and skills. This sounds a little ridiculous I guess, but they are missing the most basic of skills in living as a community, in bringing up their children, etc. Well, at any rate, one of the main aspects of it is to develop or enrich the creativity and curiosity of the kids, for they have no groups, few games, etc. or other "stimuli" that are necessary for development of even the most basic intellectual as well as motor skills. Well, enough of this scientificy talk; what I'll be doing is trying to make friends with the kids and folks; but mainly I'll be leading nature walks and nature study for the young ones. When I realized I might do this, I spoke up that I wanted to and how I thought it would fit into the program, and the "big leaders" of the program got excited about it too. So now I'm official nature guide of the crew. By the way, this isn't a mass project. Only six new people are going and two who have been there in the past. Well, the people I am going with are good.

Love,
Chris

Portion of letter from Chris to family.

May, 1965

It should be a fine summer. Just think, nature walks for little kids. I'm completely excited. I've been reading lots of little pamphlets, etc. on how to interest kids in nature, how to teach it to them. Some are very helpful, and I feel confident that I will be able to do a good job—with the kids, at least. I worry about the 'teens and adults. Sometimes I just can't get in people's frame of reference. Everyone else on the project is similarly worried; and talking with each other about it has helped build some degree

---

*As I understood it, this was a black community made up of descendents of blacks who were thrown off of slave ships because they were sick or otherwise inadequate.

of group unity and spirit among us, over what was originally there. This could be the best summer of all!

My last exam is June third or fourth. I will be bringing little home. I don't know whether my car would make the trip. I feel as if it wouldn't. But if I drove very slowly with many stops, and made a few days journey out of the trip, I think it would make it. The project isn't until the 25th or so. I have at least two weeks. I could try to sell it here, or I could store it or I could try to bring it home. It's not worth very much anymore. As I said before, the new engine was full of noises, and now that warm weather is here, it overheats very easily. It burns lots of oil. But it starts easily and quickly always! I have been grateful for that! It has served very important and necessary purposes for me here at school, ones that would have been bad for me to miss. I have been grateful for it altogether, and have loved it. Let me know what your thoughts about it have been and are now, okay?

There are millions more things to write about but I just don't have time to. I'm doing an ecology term paper on spring flowers which is great. My grades look very bad again this semester. Hope I can pull them out like last term! I am reading lots of things and finding the pleasures of it. Never really did before. MCAT (Med. Boards) were rugged, very unconfident in my performance. On long tests there are periods of time in which my mind just won't function. Happened often on that test. Premeds are very smart up here, and competition is fierce! I joined Alpha Epsilon Delta, the pre-med honorary for $25. I think it will be worth it—another thing after my name. They gave us a good steak dinner, too. Am sending suits, sweater, shirts, etc., etc. to laundry. Will probably cost about $20. If any objections let me know right away. Am getting more interested in clothes. Still dress too sloppily, however. No longer condemning "the wish for glittering things"—am now condemning only the *need* to be associated with glittering things. I've discovered it's only natural to want really nice things. What is unnatural is the *need* for them, to *have* to be surrounded by them and by people associated with them. I'm thus changing my attitude toward clothes, etc.

I must stop now. Hope all things are good there. I think of you all more often than you probably think. I will be interested in seeing the "split with the church" material. I'll bet it was exciting. I was interested, Jeff, in hearing your beliefs, stated by Mom in her last letter to me. They are much the same as my own. Goodbye, for now.

Love,
Chris

P.S. Jeff, I have a friend who calls himself an ignostic. Believes only in what can be empirically proved. He's a mess. Watch out for ignosticism.

Poem by Chris, June 1965

I was leaving the Balch Dormitories
When I thought I would make a new path,
Rather than take one of the blacktop paths.
And I thought I would run.
The person beside me thought she would too.
So we ran hand in hand through the new spring grass,
When suddenly there were hundreds of crocuses before us.
Purples and yellows.
We had to jump from island to island among them
On our tiptoes
In order not to trample them.
And near the end we had to make one long leap . . .
I still have not come down.

Summer, Fall, 1965

July, 1965

Then to Nova Scotia for the summer and living with the blacks up there, and trying out a social program for the underprivileged communities. Margie, the only white girl in Chris's community, there from Cornell too; and a relationship developed, quite a close one.

Letter from Chris to family from Nova Scotia.

July, 1965

Hi—

It's been an interesting trip so far and we made it to our final destination in great shape. Right now we're camping out by the bay (we are near the ocean—or at least an extension of it). The guitar has come in handy many times. Are ready for hootenanny sorts of things. We've gotten through about one third of the nerve-wracking meeting of new people. Tomorrow we move in with our families and start on the next phase of the project. I have had several times the old helpless feeling and wished to be done with it all and go home, but I'm getting fewer and fewer of them now, the more and more I find out what's really going on. I hope I prove adequate to the fairly high expectancy of us. I discovered, the hard way,

124

that we must keep a dignified distance from these people while still trying to maintain a rapport. We are not, so to speak, supposed to go "native," and I got bawled out for having a sword fight at the fair here with one of the kids I'll be working with this summer (in front of all the -people, parents, etc.). It seems this does not impress the parents of the kids who we're working with and who are most important. The kids of the project are interesting and fun, each in his own way, but there are still a few barriers to real rapport. However, most things look just fine.

This is a continuation, a few days later, of what I started writing. We have moved into our home now. No running water and there are outhouses, etc. There are enough kids around to really get something going all the time. We had a birthday party for one of the ladies of our community and I'm getting together a hardball team of 12-16 year olds right now to play some teams from the other communities. We're all feeling very good about things and our "peers" are telling us all the time that we're doing a good job, maybe to give us confidence, so everything looks good. One of the girls in another community broke her ankle last night and she'll have an interesting time with that I imagine. The communities have accepted us very warmly so far, and we've really been getting a kick working along with them at such things as herding cows up to the barn, painting, etc. The well water we have to drink is delicious and I have found at least one future naturalist and maybe more!

Well, there's no more time so that will have to do for now. I hope all things are well there.

Love,
Chris

P.S. There's a possibility of money trouble due to bad cars, and some other things. If it comes, I'll let you know.

September, 1965

Chris decided not to pursue a medical career. Probably one of the main reasons for this was his love for animals and his distaste for work in the laboratory. Ecology was his new choice of a career.

Margie continued to be his girl after they returned from Nova Scotia.

Letter from Karen (in India) to Chris.

September 30, 1965

Hello Fine Chris—
I trust your summer was good and that your life is happy and rich.

125

With me, life is richly exciting—sometimes infinitely difficult, other times equally beautiful—a fantastic mixture of contrast of joy and ever present movement. How to tell you of a place where the air is heavy with heat and colored with dust and filled with odors of sweets, urine, curry, and peanuts roasted. People are darkened and beautiful—thinly, gracefully, straightly built—long fingers and poised gestures. They are lovely with warm fast smiles and talking eyes. I have very much taken to the Indian sari and feel so much like a silk princess that it's marvelous. Somehow, they too, seem to enjoy it so much—the fact that I take such pleasure in their dress. Sometimes it feels painful to know such joy and for wanting so much to let it gush out—yet it must remain in its place, proper and subdued.

The India that I have so far met is colored and noisy and deliciously new and intriguing. The streets of Delhi are undisciplined and confused with countless bicycles, scooter-driven rickshaws, cows, barefoot men, push carts, and an occasional car and elephant. Horns of all types and tones are continuously sounding, sellers yelling their wares, confusion, singing and chatter, clang, sounding, sounding. There is no space for thinking, but with open arms one simply rides, engulfed, surrounded and impatient to absorb more. On the sides of the street are the ever present small shack-like wooden structures where tasty, oily, wonderfully exciting things brew in in big copper pots. The Indians love sweet things—and every cup of tea is thick with sugar and sugar and sugar. It is such fun just to stroll along stopping at each place trying something different, jab-bering and meeting people.

Well—I was just feeling good and clean and full and wanted to tell you that I've been searching for butterflies—though so far without success. I have definitely decided to go into medicine and applications are completed and the medical aptitude will be flown to Delhi.* How about you?

My warmest kindest wishes to you Sir Christopher Q—and with lots of things yet unsaid.

Karen
(still)

Letter from Karen (in India) to Chris.

November 2, 1965

Hello Sir Forest God—
(Said she with a great deal of joy underlying her anxiousness to be invited to the forest for a picnic—jelly beans and apricot brandy and vanilla

---

*She became a pediatrician.

126

wafers and chocolate from an Ithacan chocolate maker—who by the way sends chocolates all over the world.)

And how nice it is to be talking with you. Tell me how, and mostly why, was I and am I so infinitely touched by your words and your dreams and your leaves (which by the way, are dancing on my wall over my desk, with the aid of duco cement). And tell me something else—why is it that before I can even begin to settle down to my thesis and Hindi and work (which I love) and so many other unanswered letters, why am I talking with you, and why have I read your words 4 times each? I don't know—but yes, I do. You see I am clutching, but unlike any other clutching that I've ever done—rather than out of loneliness or unhappiness or lackingness—it is with a sense of fullness and involvedness with other people, and joy—it is in saying—I don't want you—nor do I want you to want me—but I like you and feel with you and have been broadened by you—and think about you and want you to like me—and I want us to be aware of our love—and love the falling in likingness and be happy and giving and feeling. Do you understand any of this? Do you understand that when I think back about you I see none of the last weeks—but only the good weeks—and want so much for you to know that for me they were so very good. Though I don't want them back, I never want to give them up, but always want to hear of mushrooms and pine trees and green lumber jackets and nice eyes. And I want to tell you things of richness and fullness and be glad in the telling, and in return will you send me stories to read at night—before I am asleep—stories and tales and rhymes. I shall work now and then write some more of India.

Today is another—it is Nov. 3 and what in my two months of intensity should I tell you about? Let me talk of the villagers. My villagers on whom I am doing my family planning research. Last week I went for the second of what were to be informal-getting-to-know-each-other visits—chances for them to become more familiar with me so when I begin my interviewing my results are likely to be more valid. Well, by some fortune, I happened to arrive at a time when all the women were together in a prayer session. Chris, there was likingness between us. I entered, and immediately people came and held my hand. I was asked in Hindi whether I would take them home with me to America; to the best of my ability I answered. Prayers went on and then stopped as I was to get a demonstration of their dancing and song. I was fascinated—and suddenly, though I was wearing a sari, it was decided that I was to be dressed in the village costume. This is a huge skirt weighing at least 10 pounds, consisting of 30 yards of material, and a shawl which covers your head. Mind you, I was dressed in the best finery of the village—a brand new costly red skirt and ribboned shawl (these women wear one skirt for a year) and my feet and ankles were covered with bangles and bracelets—around my neck they strung necklace after necklace of gold—and then they had me dance. Chris, they went wild when I started to dance. I had been watching them and sort of knew what I had to do—and felt self-conscious, but good—there was not a soul there to see me but these wonderful simple people who so desperately wanted me to dance—and so, putting my sense of self-consciousness away in my pocket—I did, and they cried with joy—and so did I. They carried me to the car—the whole village singing my praise. Never in my life have I been so touched or happy.

With much warmth,

Karen

And please tell me a story and draw for me—a sheep.*

Thanksgiving, 1965

When Chris came home for Thanksgiving, he and his father got into great dissension. Their problem was not resolved before Chris went back to school, and a number of letters passed between them before it was.

From Art to Chris at Cornell after the vigorous disagreement during Thanksgiving.

November, 1965

Chris—

While there were financially critical times during the purchase of the Company, the building of our house, etc., etc., those times are over and as of now, the payment of 2 or 3 thousand dollars a year for your support and education means almost nothing to us.

But it is apparent that dependency on me for that support means a great deal to you—all for the worse. Your need for independence causes a hostility and indifference to the most ordinary expectations we have. Our demands on you are almost nil. Your delivery of ordinary amenities is almost nil. Your assertion of dominion over my life and what is mine—fashioned in my own way—is incredible for an adult—which you are now.

I am therefore of the conviction that the best interests of all, I included, but most certainly you, call for you to take over—at least for the present—complete responsibility for yourself, your well-being by your own lights, and your future. If later you find yourself able to accept my support without all the adverse reactions to it I will gladly resume.

Therefore, starting with the end of this semester, do not look to me (nor

*Inspired by *The Little Prince*.

128

indirectly to your mother) for support of any kind. The Buick* is to be returned and will not be re-licensed for 1966. I will continue to pay your rent whether or not you live there as I believe that commitment was for a year. I will not pay any tuition or general living expenses. If you choose to go to school, it will have to be in some kind of program which you alone can support.

I don't assert righteousness in this. I only assert my right to order my own life in my own way, and to not have it interfered with by another adult without rights to interfere.

During this period of your independence I ask you not to come here. It is just too hard. Unless you can return here in the attitude of a guest then please come. You will be welcome. You will also be welcome to my full support for your further education whenever you feel ready to accept it without showing me that I'm not running your life. Believe me, that's the last thing I want to do.

Love,
Dad

Letter from Chris to Art.

December, 1965

Dear Dad,

Your letters are to the point and, as usual, coldly businesslike and matter of fact. The main or principal point I can derive from them is as follows:

Premise 1—I am dependent on you for support.

Premise 2—I have a great need for independence.

Conclusion 3—Therefore, I am hostile and indifferent to your most ordinary expectations, my "delivery of ordinary amenities is almost nil" and "I assert dominion over your life and what is yours." You find me "argumentative and hostile."

Premise one is correct, premise two is mistaken. Exactly one year and six months ago we had our last great fight, and a great deal of the reason for that battle was that I spoke sarcastically to you, the same reason for our battle this time. A small part of that former battle was also caused by my need for independence, and during the months after this battle I did a great deal of thinking about independence. I added up figures, calculated state university tuitions and so forth, and came to the conclusion that it was ridiculous to want this; I totally dropped the idea of financial independence from you. Correlated with this decision, and the fact that I was beginning to discover what makes people tick, with the aid of adolescent

---

*Chris had been given his grandfather's car.

psychology courses and so forth, I began to view you and Mom and myself and the rest of the family in new light, in a more objective light I think. Due to the contact with ideas outside our family, I was able to start seeing through many of the difficulties within the internal structure of our family, to be able to see your own points more clearly and give you full credit for them. At the same time I often began to defend you from what I felt were unjust criticisms of your behavior, and I defended you, Dad, both in your presence and in your absence; and I dropped my alliances and the biases which went with them, which had been in opposition to you for such a long time. I stopped saying bad things about you behind your back, and at the same time I began listening to the things you said, using them in my philosophy, respecting them—and I believe you recognized these things and appreciated them, for I could see it sometimes in your face. I was happy, too, happy that a semblance of a good and wholesome relationship was beginning to emerge from what had been such a long and ragged feud. And as these events occurred, I myself began to feel better about things in general, and my wish for independence from you dropped to an unequalled low. I could now start thinking more rationally about the future, stop dwelling on the independence and see exactly what interested me most, what job would be most enriching for me.

Correlated with this new objectivity and way of looking at things came a wish for more neatness, for nicer looking dress, and so forth, a getting away from the beatnik style which you have accused me now of still being. True, none of these things have become total changes yet, they've had less than a year to really get moving. However, all have definitely improved.

The other night, for just a moment and by bad impulse, a mark of my still lingering immaturity, I reverted to extreme sarcasm to make a point, rather than using the objectivity which I have tried to make my method of arguing.* It got your goat and we had a real tussle.

Because of this incident, and the false premise which you should easily have seen was false at least half a year ago (particularly when I went to Nova Scotia, thereby depending totally upon you for tuition this year), you have decided to oust me prematurely from the family.

Before concluding I would like to make a final point pertaining to my hostility and argumentativeness. Mom and Tim are of the conviction that I am argumentative and hostile because I have argued now against *them*, on your behalf for almost a good year now, trying to uphold the points you have made to me, to help them see, as I have seen, the philosophy by which you are proceeding with life, and trying to be fair to both sides of the major argument which has been present in our house, from the time

---

*Chris had been doing quite a good job with seeming objectivity.

130

of my birth. It is ironic that you should turn to them to reinforce your conviction that I am hostile and argumentative. I want to stress that I do have a fair degree of hostility; that would come out even if conditions in our family were not as strained as they are. This hostility, plus the fact that I am still growing slowly out of my immaturity, results in such things as sarcasm, chiding, and true non-called-for negativity or argumentativeness. However, I have been slowly leaving these behind, and have gotten better rather than worse, or rather than staying just the same.

This is all to say that I'm still willing to call a no-hard-feelings truce to our petty and unreal differences now, and to resume the slow process of gaining respect and warmth which we had such a good start on of late.

Love,
Chris

Letter from Chris to Art.

December 1965

Dear Dad,

I thought I'd take this chance to explain my own dilemma a bit further than we discussed it before last summer in a talk which, to this day, I value greatly. I was becoming, then, fully aware of the "power over people" side of me, the side who wants certain things, and in order to get them, exerts influence and power over people. As well as gaining what it was that I wanted when using this method, I gained also the feeling of importance, a confident sort of feeling really, and on top of that the satisfying feeling of a job well done and efficiently maneuvered. When I put this method into play where I work in Willard Straight Hall, I found that I was soon elevated to a boss position, correlated with a pay raise, which gave me satisfaction of being worthwhile, respected and fulfilled. This is a miniature example of that side of me which wants, or better, needs power over people, power to make them do a job, power which I think I have. And with the status of boss, and the symbols which go with it, I have gained approval, affection, and satisfaction.

There is another side of me that has sat in the basement of our various houses and created crystals, go-carts, beads, painted hub caps, crystal radio sets, poems, and has gotten very decent grades in school. This side of me created things that were beautiful, for no greater end than the beauty itself and the satisfaction of a job well done. This side of me has helped me gain approval, affection, and so forth, time and time again. My handmade corsages have delighted girl friends. My outstanding awards at the science fairs delighted my teachers. My good grades have brought me no end of reward. At the same time as I was creating, I was looking at what

131

others created. As I began seeing beauty in what they created, I began seeing the beauty in the people themselves. Here, I said to myself, is the hand, the arm that created this beautiful thing. How fine it is, in its own right. What do you suppose that hand and arm has been endowed with, has gone through, that lets it create like that?

At first I only looked at people in this way who had actually created objects. Then I began to generalize this to people who had created intangible things—great thoughts, political systems, and so forth. Slowly this became generalized to nearly everybody, for nearly everybody has "created" in life, a philosophy, a thought system, a way of living, a way of dealing with other people which couldn't help but be regarded as beautiful in its own right. This is generally what I see in people now. It is what I have come to see in you, in Mom, in Tim, in everyone outside our family, and it is what I have come to see in myself. To look at people as beautiful for what they are has become a point of great value to me for by means of it I have been able to ward off hurts and pains of various kinds. You see, the whole system became beautiful, all the people, all the parts of it working together, the animals, the trees, the plants, the soil, the earth, Mars, Jupiter, the sun, the solar systems, the galaxies, the universe. The interest in these things has consumed me and it is for these very reasons I chose to study ecology, the science of the system here on earth. Every time I read of a new fact, a new theory about people, or the systems, it opens up new horizons of beauty, new dimensions, new feelings of interest and intrigues. It's exciting as well as beautiful. And in searching this thing out, in looking it over, I get the feelings of inner awe and peace that make what troubles I face and have faced seem so small that I sometimes chuckle to myself.

You see, though, to look at people as beautiful, as systems intricate and intriguing does not reconcile very well with manipulating them, another side of my nature. I suppose I will always be a manipulator to some degree, and I do not think it is a bad side of me. Hence, when people stand in my way or I need something from them, I shall probably manipulate to a certain extent, though rather than basing my life upon it, I'd rather (indeed I *must*) base my life on the beauty of the system. I must say now that you yourself, being the system that you are, may think this is a bit foolish. But I can assure you that in my small experience up 'til now, I have found it richly rewarding for itself, as well as gaining me approval, affection and respect from others.

It is therefore that I have chosen ecology and it is therefore that I respect your letter as of last night. Hence, I hope you will respect my own. I don't know where you got the notion that I thought you were running my life, or that you might . . . I don't feel that you have or will run it. So you don't have to worry about that. As for my having dominion over you, I

132

don't quite see how that is possible, nor do I feel that I have any. However, if you feel that I do, it must be that, in fact, I do. A fact which previously slipped by my mind unnoticed, and for which I am sorry. I must try harder on this score not to impose my sort of life upon your life. My only other observation is that due to my love and affection for this family, I don't care to lose my membership in it and will seek to return to it as often as I wish for the affection, help and guidance it has given me in making me the beautiful thing that I am. In return I hope that it will seek to have me return as often as it wishes as a member of the family. It's not a house, nor a lot, or a man's castle that I am returning to. It's my family, my history, my shape and form, that I am returning to. My thoughts, my eccentricities are part of the other family members, and theirs are part of me. I cannot imagine returning as a guest rather than a member of the family, and shall not even try. I shall probably return for a good many years hence, as a member of the family, for Christmases, Easters, Thanksgivings, summers and shall look forward to the joking about baldheads, silly nicknames, basketball games and easter egg hunts which have thrilled me for so many years.

As far as what you do with your money, I suppose that it is up to you and Mom, and if you don't wish to finance the investigation of the beauties of the system, I suppose you don't have to, though I really would have appreciated it. I think I can maybe make out all right financially on my own, though it will be a bit slower and a bit more clumsy and a bit harder for those reasons. That is all I can say for now, with hopes that you may seek to renew our former relationship.

Love,
Chris

Letter from Art to Chris.

December, 1965

Chris—

Attached is a check for $142.00. You have quite misread my letter.

1. I didn't say you had dominion over my life—I said you assert it—arrogantly and groundlessly. Quite the reverse, you don't have dominion.

2. I didn't say and don't think I can run your life. I said you would again be welcome to my support when you accept it without feeling that I am running your life. The last thing I want to do. The fact is, I am resigning from your life.

133

Your outline of your life-style and philosophy shows interesting advances, but I fear it will not serve you well until (á la Karen Horney's "integrated personality") you can closely merge the manipulative power need with the concept of universal beauty.

As for myself, I came by your way but have, I think, substantially abandoned your concept at the tender age of 53. I think I may be gradually becoming a Catholic. If we don't (mankind that is) contain the deviltry of original sin, the movement toward universal truth and beauty is so laborious, obscure and slow as to be lost to me. Therefore I have tended over the last ten years to emphasize the "manipulative" aspect of life because the problem seems to be more one of getting on with this life right here and now in the least distractive and confused way. (The only way I could get an integrated and useful personality). Freedom ("may the best man win") and Equality ("each according to his ability and need"), both noble sentiments, not only don't mix, but are diametrically opposed; in the aggregate I think freedom yields the best result. Therefore, I carry on with my most unequal (that is to say quite superior) ability in a competitive way with a heavy sprinkling of "Christian principle" to keep my conscience (whatever the hell that is) decently clear. I try not to deliberately kick anyone in the balls.

Now back to you. I truly feel that your own advances will be hastened by complete responsibility for yourself. Certainly it is apparent that you feel no particularly strong need to manipulate me (or us). To the contrary, you show a strong need to *show* me. My own life style is not cut out for this. I find your presence here oppressive. The occasions of your visits uncomfortable. I find you argumentative and hostile.

Finally, you say that you will "seek to return—as often as I wish" to extract what you want from the family. You are quite in error. The accident of your birth and growth in this family gives you no rights except to seek friendship here. No right to my presence and company—house, lot, bed or board—only the right to be my friend and a welcome guest. Grandma has the same rights, no more.

So I hope, Chris, after a period of complete independence we will find ground for resumption of friendship. The program then will be as I previously outlined. Be prepared to leave the car here at Christmas and while finishing the semester I hope you will be able to formulate some practical plans of your own.

Love,
Dad

P.S. I acknowledge all of your fine assets as outlined and I am sure you get on well with most people. So do I.

Letter from Art to Chris.

Dear Chris—

I have greatly enjoyed our improved relationship over the last year or so which you describe and of which I have been very conscious. So when two presumably rational adult males wind up settling their "differences" by brawling, one must do something about it.

First, you are not dependent on me. You are bright, talented and on the whole an outstanding adult person, fully capable of complete independence. What we have here is a wholly artificial dependence—a major irritant in a very fundamental sense. An adult male does have a great need for the literal exercise of independence—a fact of life—all life, homo sapiens included.

I excluded brawling (at least intellectually) from my life some years ago, as a means to settle anything. Isn't it interesting that my only brawls have been with my own sons—in modern times?

So Chris, I have dealt with this in my usual pragmatic way—and to me, the only way left open to me. And it is precisely what I would do with any other person with whom, on balance, I was incompatible to the point of "brawling"—I would separate.

So what is the "bottom line" on this balance sheet? You must know what a wrench it has been for me to reach the decision about you that I did. But believe me, Chris, it was a decision. I am not practising brinkmanship and I am not negotiating with you—nor am I calling a "truce" as you put it. I am simply reversing my decision because I think you want me to, and because about 48% of me didn't want to make the break in the first place.

But you will be required to accept these fundamental truths of the situation: That you are an independent able adult male; that your wholly artificial dependence on me brings you to me—into my life—to the place where I am, and where I live; that you cannot be there with equal rights to decide and govern; that you actually do not have any inherent "right" to be there (that ended when you became a man); and finally that you will join me in laboring mightily to keep us away from ever again having to deal with things on the ultimate terms. I feel quite sure that this dialogue will be of great service to us both in the future development of our relationship.

> Love,
> Dad

Letter from Karen to Chris (from India).

December 11, 1965

Dear Chris,

And please don't be so self-conscious. I just want to know of your thoughts—and days and imagination. There's no question of burdening or silence or the in-between. There's simply no question. None at all. Such questions just don't exist. And I am sorry that there is pain within you now and hope that it works itself out soon with learning, growth and awareness—which I guess is the reason it has come. Pain is like that. Sometimes it lasts just for minutes—other times it fills hours. But even worse is when it lies just below the surface—gnawing—emptying—disenchanting. So please hurry, feel better and send me bubbles, stars and munchkins, and oatmeal cookies which are my very most favorites.

Delhi is cold now and tea and fire are delicious. It's strange, for with December and coldness, my mind has been flooded with Christmas carols for there is nothing else to remind me of Christmas but these hosts of songs which pass gushing through my mind.

December 14, 1965

Somehow on December 14, nothing was written—but the date is now December 27 and I am south in Kerafa traveling for 14 days of Christmas vacation. We are going by plane, bus, train and the weather in contrast to Delhi is hot, and tiring and bug-filled. But the land is green and farmed and country-filled, with spices and south Indian color schemes, and new smells and new sounds of a language unknown to me. The people are dark-skinned and barefoot and mysterious for I can't talk to them. Instead we look at each other, and stall, and signal, and wonder. I am full of new tastes and tales and adventures, and expectant—for I don't know what the next 14 days will bring. I never know, even in Delhi (where I stay in one place), what is to come. But now it's as if I'm chasing it—swarmed with newness and other people and possibilities—and here I am not yet sure about yesterday's yearnings and actions, having to cope with a vast array which have without introduction—come! And I don't know which to choose, Cornell or Columbia—and my poor Daddy is so beside himself with joy,* that he, too, doesn't know what to advise me.

Warmly,
Karen

---

*Her father is a doctor and no doubt happy she was planning to be one.

136

Letter from Chris to family.*

December 1965

Dear Folks:

I thought I'd better drop a quick line to let you know I'd be home by late Saturday or early Sunday morning. Extremely busy for the last two weeks, culminating with the last of five hourly examinations tomorrow and two papers. Have been averaging 8 hours of studying a day, often 12-14 on days before the tests. Much more reading this term than ever before, and I am such a slow reader (but comprehensive). I will see you then around the 20th. I trust things are well with you all.

Love,
Chris

Winter, Spring, 1966

From Art to Chris at Cornell written soon after Margie had a natural abortion so that marriage was not immediately important.

January 17, 1966

Dear Chris:

I am dropping you this line hurriedly before departing for Los Angeles and San Francisco where I will be all week.

It seems to me, Chris, that I have a right to the minimum expectation of a complete additional discussion with you before you carry on your plans any further.

Naturally, I regard you as fully capable of running your own life in your own way and are fully capable of making your own decisions about what you are to do: but I feel, also, that as your father I am entitled to a thorough-going discussion before you reach a final position of commitment.

If it is inconvenient for you, or you do not plan on coming home between semesters, I would make a one day round trip to Syracuse to meet you and you could drive up from Ithaca. This would be practical and reasonably convenient for both of us.**

I, and I am sure the rest of the family, could doubtless get to be quite

---

*This letter arrived shortly after the 'phone call from Chris telling us that Margie was pregnant by him. Margie visited us during Christmas vacation. We liked her, but we felt very sad that Chris was now planning to get married long before he had wanted to.

**This meeting was not necessary, since Chris and Margie decided not to marry at that time. Margie continued to be Chris's girl.

fond of Margie, but things having come to where they are, I would at least like to know that you are considering many things that may have occurred to me at my age that might not yet have occurred to you; in any event it would seem reasonable to postpone final action until you have at least completed this year's school work. Certainly, a decision to go ahead at this time for reasons which are purely transitory or a matter of convenience or inconvenience should not finally guide such a serious decision as you are contemplating. Please let me hear back from you. I intend to keep in touch with Mom by telephone from the west coast.

Love,
Dad

Letter from Karen (in India) to Chris.

February, 1966

Hello Dear Chris Q—

Somehow you always come at the right time—and the joy and magic that you create with your arrival I welcome and relish. And though the days have passed full and vibrant—forming my humanity—touching my soul—laughing and tearful—and touched with the holiness and mysticism which is increasingly seeping into my consciousness; though my patterns of reacting and brooding thoughts have been colored and exercised without your presence and even without your memories—somehow deep and far within me there is a source of bubbles—of such specialness and fondness that I marvel over their existence. These have been given by you. It's strange because there really are not memories of you in my days. For life and its objects are too different here—and there is not even one of our mutual experiences or haunts to bring you back. Yet, of a sudden, you yourself come—through pencil-labored words on clean careful paper written out of your notebook—with your eyes and teeth and sounds. It's nice, really nice!

And so—I spend my days—everywhere speaking Hindi—and everywhere being watched and stared at. You know that in America I am considered tall. Well, you should see me compared to the Indians! Lacking all the sophistication and manner which come along with education and money they are simple, often greedy, but uncluttered by formalities as we know them—and simply alive, hungry, staring, surprised, pushing, open, badly clothed and beautifully colored and faced. And really Chris—life is so special and magic ripe—taking on new meanings and associations and I learn and know it better.

So love to you,
Karen

138

Letter from Chris to family.

Dear Folks,

I'm still recovering from the whirlwind of the past months—whew! It's funny what being busy does for a person. I've been very busy many times, and I've noted it each and every time. It makes me full of energy, content, sort of happy-go-lucky, and impatient, but in a much more good humored way than the way in which I usually get impatient.

The next semester has already begun today, and looks to be a good one. It's the last one around here, and of that I'm fairly glad. I'm very tired of assignments and piling information into my head on often-times irrelevant subjects (irrelevant to the purposes I'm "differentiating towards"). But one must take the good with the bad, and there has been much good.

I have very mixed emotions about graduate school. There's one reason I can seem to isolate, and only one reason why I would like to go at this time. Quite simply it is because I love to dig deep into things that interest me and I would say that ecology is one of my main interests, if not *the* main interest. The peculiar thing is that the kind of ecology that interests me most is not really the kind they teach. For instance, I happened on some books by a Frenchman named Fabré and he was the kind of ecologist I would most aspire to be. He would sit, oftentimes in his own back yard and watch ants, weevils, beetles, spiders—he would watch them for hours, days, weeks, recording every action, interaction, interrelationship that occurred between them and among them. Then he would interfere in their lives in small ways—block a tunnel, put food in the middle of some water, etc.—and he would watch which one would do what. And when he was done recording, he had a complete account of the lives, both in normal times and in stress, of these little organisms, more thorough than any usual observer: and more astounding than one might otherwise have believed. His records are a masterpiece of workmanship, and watchmanship, and the small beings they uncover are similar masterpieces. Somehow, in ordinary ecology, they get to talking populations and statistics and right at the peak of your interest, you suddenly couldn't care less. These are my qualms about graduate school. Will I be able to forego the theoretical and the practical in pursuit of the irrational? Enough so my interest won't be drowned? And I'm pretty sure I don't particularly want to be a professor, although I wouldn't mind teaching at all. Maybe at a small school. Maybe even at a high school!

And then, there's this dream that I can't seem to shake: a shop, a combination antique/homemade shop; I'd like to rummage around a little in the world and dig up antiques out of old people's attics, and make strange little sales, and take trips to out of the way places and see what might be found, like Fred Guy's handmade violins, and ancient kerosone lamps and cauldrons! And to turn out pottery, beautiful pottery like they used to turn out in Neolithic times, with bright stripes and designs and intriguing shapes rather than the dull pottery that seems to be the latest fad at the art shops. And to turn out ornate chairs and woodworking on my lathe and band saw and jig saw and drill press and electric sander. If I had but those few tools, I could furnish an entire mansion in less than two months (given the aid of an adequate upholsterer) with the most beautiful and magnificent furniture that I could imagine. Well, you see, this shop keeps running through my head, and I keep thinking how I've never seen anything like it before in my life.* I keep imagining what it would be like to spend the entire day creating and searching for beautiful, magnificent, quaint, pretty, handsome, high-quality, excellent, rich objects, and their makers, owners and creators. And I keep thinking how that might just be the most fulfilled and richest life of them all. But that's all right. It's a dream, maybe to be realized someday, to fall into little by little as I amass my fortunes doing my job! These may sound like sort of short-sighted aspirations, unrealistic, and even meaningless—but for me, they are not.

I'm telling you these things in hope that you'll understand about where I am in my philosophizing and about where I'm going, and I especially want you not to worry about either of those things.

I must try to do a better job explaining. I am at present integrating my life upon these (what I consider) basic premises:

1. To do things practically, not expecting that "The Lord will provide."

2. To accept all consequences of decisions. Decide, then take all rebuffs with a smile.

3. Equality is necessary and prized, insofar as equality is understood to mean that each man, and each group have the right to think or act as they will, provided their physical actions in no way hinder another individual's or group's rights. Murder is never correct unless it is to stop a physical action which is hindering another individual's rights to think and act as he wishes. As to who or what should do the stopping, the answer is anybody or anything, but if whoever decides to do the stopping makes the decision to do the stopping, he must be ready to accept the consequences of his decision; that is, he must be ready to be judged the aggressor and stopped himself if another individual or group so decides that he is the agressor, rather than the "savior." Hence, a perfect compromise between freedom and equality.

---

*These shops are quite the fad in 1986.

4. If every man were suddenly to be eradicated, not a particle of difference would there be. There is nothing good about humanity, nor bad for that matter, it just happens to be here, but

5. A human being is endowed, genetically or culturally, with a deep-rooted feeling that he must preserve himself and his species, i.e., that man is good.

6. Therefore, human beings have values, i.e., emotion, belief about what is good for man, and mankind.

7. If any belief one holds proves false or unrealized, nothing bad nor good has happened.

8. Similarly, all beliefs are correct, and all are false, that is to say, no one's beliefs are absolutely any better than anyone else's. However,

9. People believe that their own beliefs are best. (Allowing each man to march to his own drums is no way out of this. That just happens to be one's belief. That is no better belief than anyone else's, ultimately.) It is from these sorts of beliefs that my statement #4 springs. However, if my statement #4 proves unrealized or false, it will cause me no anguish, given my other beliefs. Even if this whole set of beliefs turns out to be false or unrealized, the set will still allow me to adjust to that fact smiling.

It is a new day. I never got around to finishing this set of beliefs and I don't feel like it now.

Here's what I got down on the letter before I quit, never to start again. Don't worry, I never got around to the other side of the story about how I still would like to be an ecologist, which I would. I will be writing again soon, so for now, goodbye.

Love,
Chris

P.S. Am taking a great "ecology" course now by the way. Biogeochemistry. Intriguing—origin of life on earth, evolution of atmosphere, etc. My lab project is the analysis of amino acids in meterorites to see if they possibly are residues of extra-terrestrial life!

Dad—I got your book and am reading it slowly but surely.* Very interesting! Excellence is possibly the most interesting of all the "abstract" subjects, and one that I am concerned with myself. Gardner is an old friend of Pres. Perkins at Cornell, another good mind, who himself has spoken

Excellence, by John Gardner, Harper Colophon Books

often of *Excellence* in talks on campus. Anyway, I'll be looking forward to discussing aspects of it with you!

Mom's, here's a belated birthday present.*

Love,
Chris

Letter from Chris to Tim.

March 4, 1966

Dear Tim:

I wrote the following letter just after my birthday, and I never sent it because I don't really believe the things it says. I wrote it in a certain kind of mood, a mood in which school work had piled up and I was faced with a week or better of studying very hard. But I guess I'll send it to you anyway, partly because I owe you a letter, and partly because you might as well know what I'm writing when I'm busy with homework. I do want to go to graduate school and I do want to study science; however, I don't want to ever be so busy with a job that I cannot have time for my hobbies. That's all. At school I have been too busy and I simply won't be so busy from now on—I won't do some of the extra things I've done and I won't be working anymore**—that'll make the time good.

I've sure basically been happy—haven't been depressed for a long time now, and feeling really alive when I wake up in the morning. I'm wondering if you get that invigorating feeling sometimes—thrilled feeling—and hoping you do. Talked to Mom and Dad the other day on the 'phone. Mom's such a psychologist, but oftentimes mistaken, according to my feelings. It's good to take her ideas seriously, but not as the truth always, not as gospel. I'm wondering how much you accept her diagnoses of you. She really does like to analyze people you know. Well, anyway, I just thought I'd say that most of the things she says concerning you, such as your girl problems, nervousness, etc., I don't exactly go along with. Anyway, just don't let her become gospel, but I guess that's just a warning to me really, for it's me who has allowed such a thing to happen in the past. At any rate—happy spring. I really feel you may be in the best profession of all, you've got three free months coming up soon. I'm curious, what do you plan to do with your summers?

Love,
Chris

_____

*I felt somehow amused that he had "forgotten" my birthday for the first time—I imagined it was to prove that he was independent.

**I had suggested that he stop working for the rest of the semester since he felt so pressed.

142

Letter from Chris to Tim.

Dear Tim,

I thought I'd drop you a note. Thank you for the five dollars, and nice note received some time ago from you.

Whether Margie and I ever get married depends on various things and too complicated to discuss in a letter; however, I do think you'll be interested in hearing of some of the things I've been thinking about of late.

Before starting on any of those things, however, I thought I'd mention I had a good birthday, lots of interesting little things from Mom, brownie cake from Margie, no classes! Altogether I've been living happily, if sometimes feeling some pangs of frustration at schoolwork!

I'm going to write to you some things that I guess I'll call home about later, for I guess these are things concerning the family and for which I hope to get advice soon.

The basic problem I'm dealing with right now is a sort of debating between the things that I like and the life situation which I am slowly beginning to adopt, i.e., going to graduate school, becoming a scientist, etc.

My interest in science is, so to speak, more passive than active, and entails sitting down and reading scientific journals every now and then upon subjects which have interested me. I have another great interest, which has often been mistaken for science both by me and the rest of the family, and by other people who have known me. This other interest includes enjoyment of being in such places as woods, collecting butterflies, keeping aquariums, etc. The fact is that this doesn't seem to be science at all, or at least not the science that I have met up here at Cornell. The science here is impersonal and has a direct end; that is, the purpose of advancing knowledge and the prestige of school and scientist. The science I have been interested in has no end, except to see how beautiful the colors of the wings are on the butterflies, to watch nature as she goes about making a really quite happy life for most creatures: to feel invigorated by the out-of-doors, etc. This kind of science would not go at a university. You see, it's an interest in collecting, in emotions and feelings, in searches and little adventures, and all. I've discovered I'm not interested in "university science." Since this is what my training has set me up to do, this is where the problem comes up. I think if I had my own choice, I'd throw it all up in the air after I graduate and get some job somewhere, any old job for $2.25 an hour or so; I'd probably marry Margie, who'd also work, and we'd scrimp and save until we had enough money to open a shop somewhere, then we'd open it and stock it with home-made things made of butterflies, and pressed flowers and other "scientific" things as well as about a million other things I have thought up, and Margie has, too.

There are two problems (+ more) to this sort of idea, however: first, I have a notion that Dad and Mom would be disappointed greatly.* Second: I have a notion that the army would be only too happy to see me out of school. Pffffff—3 more years of life down the drain. Money is the one great problem. I know Dad, and all of his consideration of "excellence" of late, will think I'd be making a foolish decision. The fact is, though, only when I'm making things, doing a project so to speak, am I really feeling totally fulfilled. It's always been that way and always will be I'm afraid. I also have never been able to stand the pressure of having to get things done, academic things that is, and they make me feel bitter oftentimes. To me, the type of life I very briefly outlined offers fulfillment, challenge, adventure and excitement, though it would not do so for very many other people.

Well, basically and briefly these are the things I am thinking about, and I'd be interested in hearing any comments you might have.

Seeing you and the teaching business from the inside has made me consider teaching for myself. This might be a possibility. I believe I might really enjoy teching general science in the 7th and 8th grades, or high school biology. However, I have none of the teaching requirements done, of course. I've also considered some type of "trade school" or something which might give me the opportunity of building things of wood, for a vocation. At any rate, I'm very open to any fresh ideas and rather dumbfounded right now as to what to do exactly.

Hope the teaching is going un-nervously now for you. The other day I had to give a "report" in front of class, and the dry mouth and sweat I felt gave me much misery.** I hope you don't have these problems, or if so, that you're getting over them. Anyway, I'll see you later.

Love,
Chris

---

*We suggested, "Get your Ph.D., and *then* do what you want. You'd then be trained for a career, if you decided you wanted that, after all. And probably the war would be over!"

**He had never spoken before of trouble like this. As for not being able to stand the pressure of getting academic things done, he had always pushed *himself*. We'd say, "Hey. Take it easy."

Letter from Karen to Chris.

Hello Dear Christopher Q—

Well—listen—I've suddenly decided with some madness—that I want to come home to Ithaca for the summer.

I have no choice but to return for I've got to do something on the 6 week organic chemistry.

And where will you be? And besides that—can you find me a room— big—cheap—and magic-promising.

Somehow—of all peoples—I trust your surprises, and insight into magic.

I don't know—I dread returning with such intensity—but for some reason Ithaca seems like it might offer some comfort.

So I will see you soon*—and I like you.

Karen

Spring must be come by now and I imagine your happiness.

April, 1966

And through it all, he would call up, and we'd discuss every kind of thing, far into the night sometimes. And often he'd say words to this effect, "Mom, why have I time and again hollered at you and criticized you, and treated you so badly? I love my mother. Why do I do this?" I didn't like those times, I couldn't understand them. But at least I knew that they were not caused by my not loving him, and that was a great comfort to me.**

He continued his relationship with Margie, and they seemed to have much in common. He enjoyed his current apartment-mates, especially Ralph.

Letter from Chris to family.

April, 1966

Dear Folks,

Margie and I decided to stay here for spring vacation. Not to go to Nova Scotia after all, since there are so many things that were exciting to do right here in Ithaca. I thought about coming home and a lot in me sort of

---

*He came home for the summer after graduating and did not see Karen.
**Just last year (1985), my oldest son Tim said to me, "You made some mistakes, Mom, but we always knew you loved us." Nothing he could say would be more heart-warming to me.

yearns to make the trip back, but I decided not to for several reasons: First, within a hundred miles radius of Ithaca are the finest "diamonds" (quartz crystals) in the world, the Herkimer "diamonds" and the drive to search them out is great! Second, the craftshop at the Straight is staying open all the vacation, and they have a fully equipped woodworking shop with electric tools, and I have so many projects in mind. Third, since Margie is staying if I stay, I've got a girl-friend, too. Fourth, it looks like spring's here to stay—however, in Ithaca that's subject to swift and radical changes at any time without warning. We've been keeping watch on the woods and the hepaticae have shoots up to ½ in. tall. Should flower next week, hopefully. The other night we took a small field trip with my terrestrial biology class—a marvelous and interested professor—to a swamp nearby. The spring peepers were so loud as to almost hurt our ear-drums—and the ambystoma maculatum (spotted salamanders) showed up that night as hoped for. Once a year—one or two nights of the year—they come out in the hundreds of thousands, and we hit the right night. We found one breeding milieu with perhaps 300 wiggling about in a mass—the professor was taken aback, he sort of gasped and exclaimed, "Look, look, what a lovely, beautiful sight—that's a sight of a lifetime!" He continued to watch them for the remainder of the night while the rest of us made other observations throughout the pond.

More and more I'm living in a magic world around here, and have been making new friends. People I feel warm towards and who I enjoy and have actively sought out, something I haven't done much of recently. Two of these friends are both janitors at the Straight. One is a jack-of-all-trades; he used to be an auctioneer.

It's five days later and spring vacation has started. So far everything is going on schedule except the weather. Ugh! It's snowing and cold and as far as I can see the salamanders that we saw on our field trip have got very little chance. As you have always said, Mom, God works in mysterious ways sometimes. Nature seems to defeat herself so often, but then I can't help feeling like maybe she knows what she's doing. Perhaps the salamanders were getting too plentiful. Anyway, better weather is forecasted for the end of this week, and we're planning to take a rock hunting trip Wednesday or Thursday.

We've been going to various sales and auctions lately and the last three have produced several new hand-made walking sticks and canes. I've got quite a collection around now, around 12 of them. We also have acquired two ancient oil heaters that resemble small pot bellied stoves, a couple of kerosene lamps, a mass of costume jewelry from which I have removed the "jewels" and have plans to make magic boxes with them. Margie's found a couple of old very tiny books, *Great Thoughts on Friendship*, and a tiny hymnal, so she's started an "old-tiny-book collection." I must admit that the ones she has are very "gurchy."

Margie's just finished up a new spring blouse and dress—very cute, too. She's pretty good on the sewing machine. Remember all that white leather I bought for saddlebags? Well, she's making a vest for me out of it. Not sure where I can wear it. The new chair I'm making will be pretty ornate.

Jeff, I'm sending along a couple of things that are fairly common around here. The superballs have become a sort of a fad. The glasses are pretty popular with little kids. I thought they might bring a few laughs at school.

Mom tells me you're getting pretty "crafty" too, with wood boxes. That's good. Gluing is all right if you use Elmer's, if the joints fit pretty well, and if you clamp the pieces together tightly for a half hour or so while it's drying.

The extra time, since I am now through with work, will definitely be a boon. I have enough time now to do things I like to, i.e. hobbies, which makes studying come easier. This is definitely what I need, at this time. Thanks for the extra cash and good wishes. I appreciate them and you, also, probably more than I let on. Well, I guess I'll quit writing for awhile.

Love,
Chris

Paper written by Chris for Philosophy, Spring, 1966

IS WHAT WE REALLY DESIRE ONLY HAPPINESS?

The question we are to discuss, namely "Is there, in reality, nothing desired except happiness?" is one that has given me untold frustration, for it is around this very question that my life has been shaped; and as there is the oscillation of beliefs that its answering one way or the other involves, so also has there been fluctuation in my life and it has swayed from stable to unstable. It is for these reasons that I must express some personal credos. I would rather not come to a conclusion as to whether, in fact, this question is right or wrong, but rather elaborate on the validity of asking and answering it. In doing this I'm going to try to bring out some important facts that utilitarians seem to have completely overlooked.

I'm going to be using the two terms "soul" and "machine" quite often in this paper, so I will start with definitions. When I talk of a "soul," I am speaking of the same soul that Descartes attempted to prove. It is something separate from the body, yet is always with the body in life, and exists after death. The only other alternative I can think of or conceive of

147

is that we are just machines: our thoughts, feelings, ideas all could be explained by mechanisms and science, had we more knowledge. At this point in the paper, I am looking for two categories, and the two categories I have just defined do not quite fill the necessary requirements for what I want to show. The first category I'm looking for has as its main principle, "there is a purpose in life." I will refer to this category as the "soul category" or just "soul," but only for usefulness. There is a possibility that if we do have souls, as I defined them, they go sit latent for eternity in a pit somewhere after we die. And it is also a possibility that if we are just machines, there still could be a purpose for life. None-the-less, when we think of soul, we usually think of a purpose for life, such as going to heaven or hell, being reincarnated (even this might have no purpose, and if so it would have to be classed with the other category) or any one of a number of other such theories. This is why I shall use "soul" to designate this category. Of course, the other category is that which includes as its main principle, "there is no purpose for life." This category I will refer to as the "machine category" or just "machine," but again only for usefulness. Hence, the terms "soul" and "machine" I will use interchangeably for "purpose in life" and "no purpose in life."

I still have one more term which had better also be defined, namely, "purpose in life." I mean that there is a general scheme in which our lives play a part, a scheme "much bigger than any of us" as the saying goes; as a brief example, some say we are living here to determine whether or not we go to Heaven or Hell. This is one of the "purposes in life" that I refer to.

Now I have to say this one more thing. To me these two categories encompass all possibilities. We either are here for a purpose or we aren't here for a purpose; there is no other possibility in between. If this is wrong (though I don't see how it could be, except in the possibility that some of us are here for a purpose and some aren't), then a great many more complications would arise, and things I am about to say might be false.

Conceded that there are only these two possibilities, what conclusions can we draw about happiness? If we do have souls (purpose in life), then the best thing we do, indeed the only things we do that count as worthwhile, are those things which led to the fulfillment of that purpose. That is, if the purpose is positive. (If the purpose were negative, it would be best to do things which lead away from its fulfillment). Hence, "happiness" could only be defined as that which leaves the soul in the most desirable position, be it towards fulfillment of a positive purpose, or away from fulfillment of a negative purpose. Let me give an example to help clear this up: Referring again to our Heaven and Hell example, anything that led to a soul's going to Heaven would have to be considered "happiness" for the

148

soul (and hence the individual) as it would definitely be better off than if it went to Hell for eternity. Or if there were a negative purpose, say the only alternative after death was for the soul to go to Hell, it would be best (happiest) to find any ways to avoid this. Thus we now have two happinesses, the comforts and pleasures of life, as utilitarians define happiness; and the comforts and pleasures of fulfilling the "great purpose," whatever that may be, as the soul would define them (if we have one). How does this bear on the question "Is there nothing desired but happiness?" and on the concept of utility? First of all, we do not know if we have souls or not. Secondly, if we do have souls, we do not know what the purpose is, nor even if it's positive or negative. Third, we decided that happiness could only be what puts the soul in the best position with regard to the purpose. Therefore, at this stage of our knowledge, one cannot state what happiness is or how to arrive at it, let alone form an entire way of life around it as the utilitarians would like to do.

Furthermore, anyone who thinks he knows what real happiness is, or what everyone desires most, must, in actuality, be denying the existence of the soul! Let me give an example here as this is an important point which must be understood—I know a man who believes that we have a soul, who believes the soul is constantly reincarnated, and that the purpose of each incarnation is for the soul to have new experiences. The final goal or purpose is that the soul has experienced everything possible, every grief, problem, and situation, so that at the end of its development it has a perfect knowledge and omniunderstanding of all other souls and "things."* Just assuming this is correct, then suffering would have been the best thing for a soul in one or some of its incarnations, and could and should be called, in this new and more encompassing sense, happiness. This is not the "happiness" utilitarians speak of. Theirs only includes what people think is best for them and think is most desirable. Had we greater knowledge, what people think is best and most desirable could very well change quite radically. Therefore, the utilitarian denies the soul when he maintains that happiness can be defined and lived by. Now if we knew we were just machines for sure, the utilitarians would have a very strong, almost undeniable point. Indeed, though they don't seem to realize it, all their arguments seem to be put forward only with the idea that we are machines in their minds. I'm not sure they would want the denial of the soul credited to them, and even if they did, there would be many who would not and could not accept the machine theory, hence making utilitarianism quite impractical.

---

*What he is expressing here is my belief, albeit incompletely.

Now let's go back and see exactly what I have tried to show:

A. 1. There are two possibilities in our lives—that we are here for a purpose, or that we are not.

2. If there were a purpose for life, we would have to know what the purpose is and how to fulfill it before we could say for certain what was best for us or what we desire most.

3. If there were no purpose in life, we could probably say right now what is best for us and what we desire most.

4. But at this point in our knowledge, we are uncertain which of these two are correct.

5. We can't know at this time what is best for us or most desirable to us.

B. 1. Utilitarians say they know what is best for us and what is most desirable to us.

2. But, only if there were no purpose in life could we know what was best and more desirable.

3. Utilitarians hold that there is no purpose for life.

C. .1. Utilitarians hold that there is no purpose for life.

2. A great number of people want to and do feel that there is a purpose for life.

3. Utilitarianism will not be accepted by these people. They will resent it. Therefore, it's impractical.

June, 1966

When they all graduated, they had a buffet supper in the men's apartment for their parents. Margie did a lot of the work. It was a great party. Ralph told me, "Chris has taught me a lot. I guess I would have matured without Chris, but he sure helped."

Summer, 1966

That summer at home, he asked not to work but to make furniture with his new power tools before going off to grad school, and we said o.k. He built a tool shed for us, put in a fence, made a chair and part of a corner cabinet and read a raft of really good books. Sometimes I felt in him an over-exuberance; it didn't seem real. He often laughed too much around other people. Jeff commented to me (about Chris) "What's with all the laughing?"

He helped with the new club* for persons trying to recover from mental

---

*A club which I organized for the Mental Health Association in Du Page and still direct.

problems and was a wow with our members, being his usual bubbling self, warm and interested in them all. "I just love these people," he told me.

Letter from Chris to Ned, an old apartment-mate.*

Dear Ned,

I thought it was about time to write you a little something, tell you that your warm letter made me feel fine for a few days, like I really did have a friend somewhere. And I guess maybe I still do have a few. At any rate, you've got one until you're dead.

We certainly had a good time together. I probably won't be seeing you for a long time since next year I'm heading for parts unknown, specifically Austin, Texas; and I doubt if I'll be back to New York for years. But don't forget to write once in awhile and I'll always answer, sometime or other. I want to know how you're doing, what your joys and sorrows are, how they are changing or maybe already have changed. I'll give you mine in return.

I finally graduated from Old Cornell, and like I said, I'm going to the University of Texas for grad—Zoology, what I've been most interested in. Thank God I finally gave up the notion of medical school. It really made me feel good to give up that idea. For some reason I hate the idea of medical school, the more I thought about it last year the more I got to hate it, until I finally just bagged the whole idea. I don't know exactly why I hated the idea so much but I think it had to do with becoming a little more honest with myself, if you want to know.

I guess Ralph may have told you most of the story about my girl. If he didn't, give him a ring and tell him to tell you the whole story. Anyway, things have been up and down with Margie and me, but I sure do think a lot of her. She is coming to Texas too, and will try to get a job teaching somewhere near Austin. Hope she can. There's nothing like having a lot of money floating around, and a girl, and the thought that you're doing something worthwhile to make you feel tops. Should be a good four years, but somehow it all still makes me nervous.

I bought this machine for one hundred eighty dollars—had a hell of a time getting it home—it's a combination lathe, drill press, table saw, jig saw, you name it. Anyway I snuck it home and down into the basement

*Art, Jeff and I were in Europe. Chris, by his own choice, did not go. When he wrote this letter, he was evidently feeling lonely at home by himself. Most of his old friends were not home.

before Dad had a chance to blow his stack, and I'm learning how to use the thing now. I had the help of a cabinet maker who doubled as a janitor at the Straight, and he gave me a place to work while it was at school. I've already made a couple of chairs, boxes, etc. and they look pretty nice.

Anyway, hell, I just wanted to say hello, let you know I wasn't dead after all, and let you know that as far as I'm concerned, we're buddies 'til doomsday. I really missed you this past year, all the crapping around about girls, bowling discussions and all. Well, see you in about ten years.

Chris

Partial letter from Margie to Chris, from Texas   Summer, 1966

. . . All the plants down here are different. . . . That should be a whole new outlook on botany for you. It's as though they are attuned to a different circuit—a different life-force, I guess. And I'm sure that's exactly what it is. I feel different here, because of so many external factors—weather, geog., etc., sun hot and ever beating down.

. . . I have figured out partially, anyway, what is wrong with me. It suddenly hit me in the depths of crying despair one night. I should hate—I do hate—and can hardly allow the thought of your setting me free. You see it is because I don't feel that I have ever loved anyone except you.

The worst feeling—I can't get over how stripped naked I feel about this—is that I don't think anyone but you has ever loved me—and that is one fact I cling to dearly. The good old reliable home is a haven because of its extreme familiarity. Things done there are so inborn and almost instinctual that it is a completely mechanical existence to stay there. No new words are said, no revelations of love, dearness, just brown and grey familiarity.

I want to be important and to have some tender fuss made over me. I must be loved. And I've tried in all the wrong ways. Made some very stupid mistakes—old boy friends, dates, telling too much to "friends."

I want to be fussy over you, or whomever it is, too. Anyway you have fulfilled and surpassed all my expectations about being fussed over. I didn't know I could be worth all the attention.

I have written fast so that I could keep ideas coming. There are many more, but I am exhausted—please forgive me that.

I don't wish you to take anything I've said as an ultimatum or demand. I'm mulling these things over—sort of testing the beliefs I have not yet formalized into concreteness. It is beginning at the practical and working back to the philosophical I guess.

I am doing some of my best ever at will power—self-determination and all those other sterling virtues forced upon one by the demands of sinking or swimming along in the heartless crowds.

Please write and don't have any more qualms—feel free—free to do whatever you want and decide to do. I want you to feel free and happy. The sadness I feel sometimes is for myself—for emotional ties and dependency and loving someone. But I shall love again—perhaps you—in a way more fulfilling and promising to you than anything before. I like to hope for that.

Love,
Margie

Note: Margie got a teaching job in a small Texas town.

PART 5
1966-1967

Fall, Winter, 1966

September, 1966

When Chris left for grad school at U. of Texas, I said, "I hope you *will* write the club,* they'd all love to hear from you." He lashed back at me, "Don't tell me the ways I ought to be nice to others!" I was hurt, very hurt. I should have been bigger, I should have stood it. But I was hurt, I could not deny it. I went to some envelope stuffing and busied myself. Finally he said, "Well, I've got to go. Aren't you going to make it pleasant?" And I said, "You seem determined that nothing between us will be pleasant."

And he left for the U. of Texas, a place where I hated to see him go because a desperate young man had shot up the campus from the tower just the month before, killing several; I felt the vibrations must be bad. But they had a good ecology department.

Perhaps if the draft hadn't been breathing down his neck, he would never have kept up with science, but become an antique dealer and maker of furniture as he thought he might like to do. But who knows? Another what-if.

Letter from Chris (now in Austin, Texas to attend U. of Texas graduate school) to family.

September, 1966

Dear Folks,

Well, slowly but surely things are taking shape; I have discussed courses, etc., with two professors so far and I am beginning to get some idea of the life of the graduate student. It doesn't look like it will be too hard, and I have a fair degree of confidence, though I wish I knew how to keep

*The one for persons with mental problems.

157

my mouth moist and my hands from shaking when I talk with the professors. For some reason this all means far too much to me, but I am slowly getting over it, I believe.

I haven't yet had a decent conversation with anyone, but I'm coming closer and closer, and I expect soon I will be integrated into the system and have friends.

All in all, things look hopeful and interesting and I am very much looking forward to getting all these preliminaries done with, and get on to the important things.

I'm afraid money is sort of vexing me. They don't seem to like to charge things down here very well. They do it sort of grudgingly. Anyway, I can't get a phone until I have a $35 deposit for it, and for some reason my car battery went completely to pot, and I need a new one, I imagine. Anyway, that's something I'll have to work on today. There are a series of Lab fees I will have to be paying, a car permit, books, and so forth. All these things are separate, can't be paid by one check, and at the same time, so it would be most handy if you would send about four blank checks, made out to me if you would feel safer that way, to cover all these preliminary items.

Well, that's about it. Classes start Monday so I have a lot of time on my hands for now. Interestingly enough, I'm hungry most of the time, and I've been having to eat four meals a day to quench my appetite.

Love,
Chris

Letter from Chris to family.

Sunday, October 1966

Dear Folks,

I probably shouldn't take time to write much but I thought you'd be interested in what all is going on—many things!

Right now I'm a student in "Animal Ecology" in the Zoology Dept. here, and have sort of become associated with Dr. Megan, since his interests are the ones most closely associated with mine. (I told them I'd like to go into a forest and find out everything about it.) His lines of interest are community structure, and his experiments now are making ponds and watching everything that comes into them while measuring chemical changes, etc. in the ponds; in other words, watching the birth of a community in a brand new habitat.

1. Not really overwhelmed by Dr. Megan (tho' nice) for various reasons (too complex to bother with).

158

2. Animal ecology requires the sacrifice of many animals—I'm feeling ever more strongly against this.

3. It is the field studies, not the lab, that I love the most.

4. There is a seemingly wonderful man who is a plant ecologist in the botany dept.

5. Plant studies are more conducive to field work than animals.

6. In general I'm more "enchanted" by plants than animals.

Conclusion: switch to plant ecology. Problem: I've had only one course in elementary botany, much "wasted" time in the past in zoology.

I will go to see Dr. McAllister (plant ecologist) and find out what he thinks of chances and what complications a switch might entail.* These thoughts, then, are occupying my mind a great deal. I'm feeling happy, tho, sometimes hilariously so. Have made several friends, not tremendously close, yet, but potentially so, finding classes interesting, etc. Problem, however; I dislike selfish competition, and superficiality as always, and dislike the pressures which tend to push one towards being a selfish competitor and superficial. Should I ever come to feel that I was too weak to keep these two intruders (temptations) from corroding me, I would drop out of what I was doing, and seek strength. I hope that this won't ever be, yet I catch myself every now and then failing.

Perhaps you understand nothing of what I just said, and perhaps you only think you do, yet are putting wrong interpretations on it; or perhaps you understand fully what I've just said. I can't go into more detail and clear up shady points because not enough time. Sometime I will explain—later. I believe in things now very strongly as opposed to past times and have a strong and rigorous set of values. If I find myself in a life-situation diametrically opposed to those values, I couldn't rationalize and let the values slip a little, I would merely have to leave the situation, at least for awhile.

Don't worry if some of this sounds as if I'm leaving graduate school, I haven't any inclination to do so yet—but the possibility is present, that's all.

So far I have dug several ponds, completed two papers, taken a most wonderful weekend field trip to the coast. Saw flocks of pelicans and great blue herons fishing in salt marshes; have run into both a rattle snake and water moccasin; and am thoroughly delighted and thrilled with Texas and all its offerings, even the snakes of which I have no fear anymore (unless alone!). Know all the vegetation (at least a lot of it) that dominates Texas,

---

*Did not switch.

159

and in general am getting along easily, often excitingly. Well that's an outline for the time being.

Love,
Chris

Letter from Chris to Tim when Tim and Debbie became engaged.

November, 1966

Dear Tim,

I must admit that such announcements leave one sort of speechless, or breathless; but this one, being sort of special you know, left me speechless *and* breathless and smiling inwardly to myself and outwardly at everyone around me.

Well, I only wanted to write and tell you of how the wind made the leaves laugh after I read your letter; and if you want to, you can have my approval, and you can give my love to my new sister, too.

At the risk of seeming maudlin, a tear for you and Debbie.

Love,
Chris

Letter from Chris to family.

November, 1966

Hi—

It's too late to write much. I thought I'd send you this little "story" about strawberry mites*—sort of fascinating in a way, I think, and certainly instructive from several viewpoints.

Things certainly move quickly around here, but in a way it's rather exciting, very exciting at times, and very interesting too. I'm learning about populations, plants, invertebrates, natural selection and I'm in a research course; I probably told you—the pond project. Spend approximately 20 hours per week identifying protozoa and algae which have made their way into our sterile ponds. The little beasts are nearly as amazing as the big ones.

I'm afraid I have become the owner of a small animal, "Benjamin"—a puppy, or at least "half a dog"—about 4 mos. old, who was on the way to the humane society. I really feel sort of depressed about it, as I certainly can't give him the life he should have, for I'm not even here most of the

---

*Not found

day. But he's got a fenced-in yard, if small, to run in, and I get him out at night all right, so he's not too bad off. I also have a fairly reliable "baby sitter" who takes him when I won't be here for extended times, like field trips, etc. I only wonder what in the world I'll do with him at Christmas-time.*

Well, aside from all this, things are going smoothly, and I'm in general feeling thrilled. Hope things are all good with you. Some news about Tim! I felt very pleased indeed.

I discovered a strange thing about myself, and every day it becomes more obvious to me—that is my lack of facility with words in discussion**—probably also in writing—so lately I've been taking the dictionary and picking out words, trying to think of synonyms quickly. It annoys me how slowly I am able to do so, much more slowly than most, I believe. So this is my extracurricular activity now and in a way, very exciting itself, for listening and speaking and reading have all taken on new depth and meaning for me, a new richness, and at the same time giving me something much needed. Well, goodbye, now.

Love,
Chris

Christmas, 1966

And by Christmas time he was quite depressed; didn't like the prof he was working under, felt the prof wasn't real and warm.

Letter from Chris to Ned.

December 1966

Hello, Ned,

How's the "kid"? Still a romantic I suppose. I played pool for the first time since junior year at Cornell. My God, I was worse than I was then, same with bowling and basketball, but my smoke rings are improving! Did you go back to Cornell? I'm at the University of Texas, graduate school of Zoology and with a lot of qualms as to whether this is where I want to be—got a lot of new dreams and good ideas, you see, and I'm itching to be on with them.

---

*Naturally he brought him home!
**We had never noticed this problem.

Anyway, I hope the world looks good to you. I really think it *is* good.

Chris

Best wishes for a Happy New Year!

Winter, Spring, Summer, 1967

January, 1967

With the help of the botanist prof, something better was worked out and he seemed to be enjoying his study of life in temporary pools, and the roaming over the Texas countryside with his dog, Benjamin, (who could run like any pedigreed greyhound). He spoke of his fear of his teachers, of talking to them and expressing himself, and he went to the school psychiatrist who asked him what was wrong. Chris wasn't sure. Trouble with school? No, he was doing well. With his family? No, he was improving in that. What then? Well, just this business about being uneasy to talk in class or to professors. But that is natural, most people are afraid, you'll get over that. And the psychiatrist sent him off.

Letter from Chris to family.

January, 1967

Dear Folks,

Amazing things are going on around here so I thought I'd slow down a bit and write.

First, it sure was good to hear that Tim and Debbie seem to be conquering the tribulations and that at least the discussions with the parents are more out in the open. To me, this is the biggest breakthrough—better to have all cards on the table than to get things distorted, through the grapevine.

I talked for a long time with Dr. McAllister (the one I like best), and decided for a good number of reasons that things are okay enough where I am now. For the most part, with his help, I decided that most of my discontent stemmed not so much from Dr. Megan, but from myself letting Dr. Megan be my "boss" rather than my teacher. It's true that I've been feeling like a pawn, a sort of laborer or employee, and that I wasn't really in control of what I was doing around here. Dr. McAllister suggested, after learning about me through a series of marvelous questions, that all I needed was to become less involved with Dr. Megan's research and start putting together some pieces for a project of my own for my Master's thesis. He then gave me a few helpful suggestions about how to go about

162

this and before I knew it, everything looked delightful again. You see, if I'd continued as I have been, I would have ended up doing my Master's thesis on some aspect of Dr. Megan's pond project—but that in and of itself is what was mainly wrong. Now that I have my own project, I'm going to formulate my own problems, my own methods, my own equipment—and this you see, makes all the difference. I don't know what Dr. Megan's response will be, for he needs plenty of manpower on his project, but with Dr. McAllister's backing and helpful wisdom that doesn't worry me.

Now as for my project—there is a granite quarry 50 miles from Austin, on the South West side of which are depressions in the rock. These depressions fill with water after heavy rain, and in them grow a number of different organisms. One of them is a strange little plant, the pillwort, which is closely related to ferns. Fairyshrimp, protozoa, ratifers, etc., plus a good deal more plant life spring up in them. In general I'm going to try to find out what's there and why. This project is interesting from two angles—first the granite area is deep into the Edward's plateau (the Hill country) and the location is amazing—beautiful, intriguing in its barrenness, rich in armadillos; a pond nearby has beavers and ducks, and deer often drink there. When I am there I feel a sense of strangeness that I have felt in few other places.

The second aspect which makes the project rich in intrigue has to do with the pillwort that I mentioned above—for this location is the only spot in Texas in which it occurs. It also occurs in one spot only in Arkansas, Kansas, Georgia and of all places, Chile. It's abundant only along the west coast. This, therefore, is a rather strange plant! Reading up on it has been like digging through a treasure chest, or putting clues together to solve a mystery—and it was chiefly this that my life down here lacked.

Ben and I had a very bad experience out there today, however; I was searching around for various depressions which might hold water after the rain, and in general orienting myself to the location. I was down in a depression and Ben was wandering about up above, out of sight. Suddenly he started barking and I heard a shot. As soon as I realized that it was a shot, I yelled, and simultaneously there was a second shot and a yelp from Ben. I scrambled up out of the depression, yelling all the while, and found a "cowboy" complete with chaps and hat, holding a gun. There was Ben, barking at him still, with blood streaming out of his hind leg. I was literally shaking with fear, rage and numerous other emotions. As it turned out, the man was from a neighboring ranch and had orders to shoot all dogs on or near their property (this was a good 1000 yards from their property), because dogs kill their sheep. When he found out that I was with Ben, he got awfully sorry he'd shot Ben, so at least he's not a total rat. Well, I got Ben to a vet and the bullet didn't do much harm—it went right through his upper thigh, though, and he's got an awfully sore leg. I told the people who ran the gravel quarry about the fellow shooting dogs on their land, and they hadn't known anything about it before this. Anyway, I've learned one more thing about Texas ranches. Ben will be all right in a couple of weeks, according to the vet, and he cleaned the wound up well and gave him a shot.

Well, that's enough news for now, even though there is more. Hope things are fine up your way. Aside from the incident today—everything is marvellous here!

Love,
Chris

P.S. I'm going to need some extra money for a couple of reasons—the trip out to this place (about every two weeks) costs $3.00 or so of gas round trip. Also, I'm sort of making a new girl friend.* She works in the biology library, is very pleasant and is a junior here in college. Anyway she is going to cost me a few more dollars a week probably. So if you add about $10 per paycheck more, it will help. Thanks. (I don't plan on getting very serious with her—I just seem to enjoy her company—sort of a platonic feeling.)

Note from Karen, back in New York, to Chris.

January 15, 1967

Christopher O—Christopher—
Where are you now—
and how?
Won't you ever come—or just write—
And let me hear your voice
and tone—and days—
I still have a most precious treasure—
and on special days—one can notice—
that on my ears a pair of purple hearts have nested.
They reminisce and pondering ask their ears
Where is he—the little prince—and—how

Lovingly,
Karen

---

*Heard no more of her.

164

March, 1967

Margie passed out of his life suddenly and married someone else on short notice, a couple of months or so after visiting us during Christmas vacation and riding back to Texas with Chris.

Strangely, about a month before we got an announcement of Margie's marriage (out of the blue), Margie called and asked if I had heard recently from Chris. (I had just talked with him.) She said she had not been able to get him, and then said, "I was worried. You know, he's back in that small building by himself. If anything happened, no one would know." She did not mention her impending marriage to me. Had she told *him*? And had he threatened something? He never expressed *anything* about the marriage to us.

Letter from Chris in Austin to:
Local Board No. 122
Selective Service System
U.S. Post Office Building
Wheaton, Illinois

March 8, 1967

Dear Sirs:

I would like to request that this letter be included in my appeal to be reclassified 2-S, as well as made a permanent part of your record. Due to a number of failings, mistakes and inaccuracies my records with you have fallen into a good deal of confusion. The intent of this letter is to give a concise and precise enumeration of these events in order to alleviate the confusion, and in order that my request for appeal not be lost on the grounds of inaccuracies in my record.

    A. I graduated from Cornell University on 6/13/66, with a Bachelor of Arts in Zoology.

    B. During the summer of 1966 I appeared in person at the headquarters of Board 122 in the Wheaton Post Office, at which time I presented the following three items:

        1. A transcript of my grades at Cornell University

        2. A certificate of my degree and my rank in class at Cornell University.

        3. A written request that I wished to renew my deferment as student, since I was planning to attend the University of Texas as a graduate student

    C. In September, 1966, I arrived in Austin and registered with the University of Texas as a graduate student in zoology, working towards a Master's degree (and a Ph.D. in the long run).

D. I carried 15 semester hours that semester, an exceedingly heavy load for a graduate student.

E. On February 7, 1967, I registered for my second semester of graduate study, this time carrying the more normal and reasonable (for a graduate student) load of ten semester hours. This, according to the rules of the University of Texas, is an acceptable load for a full time graduate student.

F. On February 17, I received from you a questionnaire as to my doings and whereabouts, and on February 19, I received a notice that I was now classified into Class 1-A

G. On February 20, I took the following steps:

1. I wrote out a short letter of appeal, requesting classification back into Class 2-S

2. I requested the University of Texas to furnish you with a transcript of my first semester's work in graduate school here.

3. I requested the University of Texas to furnish you with Form 103 of the Selective Service System, identifying me as entered upon a full time course of instruction as a candidate for a graduate degree.

4. I requested my major professor to write a short note as to the advisability of my continued deferment.

H. These items should all be in my record at this time.

On March 7th, after talking personally with Local Board No. 122 over the 'phone, I discovered that even though I had taken all the steps outlined in "G," they still somehow had in their possession two items:

1. An affidavit from the University stating that I was not registered here.

2. Another affidavit from the University saying that I was registered here but only as a part time student taking "only" ten hours of credit.

NEITHER OF THESE AFFIDAVITS ARE CORRECT, and I have been informed by the secretaries here that the errors were made by carelessness and faulty machines.

I, therefore, on March 8, requested the University to supply you with a corrected affidavit, signed by the Director of Admissions stating that I am enrolled in the University as a full time student at this time. You should be in receipt of this by March 12th, at the latest.

I hope this outline will help to clear up all confusing matters, and I certainly am sorry it has been as complicated as it has.

Thank you for your patience.

Sincerely,
Christopher E. Jens
11-122-44-165

Letter from Karen to Chris.

April 8, 1967

Finally I have learned that April has begun and March left behind. It has been a long winter—a long tale of horror and tragedy and of a decision not to marry—a week in Anghus from which I returned brown and finally once again eager and glad for the bringings of tomorrow.

I am hard at work and some day will be a doctor and am finally sure of this—that I do want to learn to be a doctor.

Christopher—oh—Christopher—

Where are you—and do you care so very little to never let me know—nor come?

Please send me some words—and let us be friends once more.

Karen

Letter from Chris to family, written on birthday card to Art.

June, 1967

Hi,

Things are all fine here, there are many unusually interesting and happy events occurring which I won't bother to explain.

I'm working on my own research project (my ideas, my design, my initiative, etc.) for which the school is paying for most of the equipment I need (glassware, tubing, etc.). It's one of the most exciting projects I've ever had. Briefly, I'm going out and collecting various protozoan, algae, bacteria, etc., and isolating those which grow well under the conditions I can give them in the lab (low light, constant temperature, etc.). Once I have an assemblage of organisms which can grow under lab conditions, I will set up a series of laboratory "habitats" which differ from each other in one factor only (high calcium, low magnesium, etc.). Into each habitat I will inject my assemblage of organisms and keep track of which survive in which habitats. If there are differences from habitat to habitat both in numbers and/or kinds of organisms, I will then attempt to analyze by means of two species cultured under a variety of conditions, exactly why certain organisms survived in one lab habitat and not another.

For instance, did one protozoan survive in the high calcium water but not in the low calcium water because a particular bacteria that it eats cannot survive in the low calcium water, or was it more directly related to a low

167

tolerance for calcium on the part of the protozoan? In other words, I am attempting to set up ecosystems with defined components, then explain the happenings within them. It sounds very simple, yet there are no comparable studies, and "Why?" is the question I do not know the answer to. Ecology is indeed a very young science, and as such is full of very many immature ideas. To sift through the chaos for important and essential basic ideas is too much for many people (many scientists included) and I have a good ability to do so, gained from our home. I am convinced at this time that the most important single thing a person can learn in life is to take its jumble of ideas, impressions, feelings, etc., and sift them; and unbiasedly, yet very actively, make sense out of nonsense.

This takes an extremely great amount of energy and cannot be done well if a person is using a lot of his energy in rationalizing his biases or in repressing worry, or otherwise being neurotic. To sit down and keep one's mind on a single subject in an organized manner as opposed to allowing it to wander chaotically and nonsensically over whatever chain of thoughts it would follow in the absence of energy-spending restrictive forces (which can keep it channeled in on a single problem) is the difference between a person who can get something done and a person who can't. We all, of course, do some of each; it's just that some do more chaotic daydreaming, while others do more rational daydreaming about a single problem, subject, etc., and they take it all the way to its logical conclusion, whence, an answer.

Well, now you know both what I'm studying and some of the major points of my current philosophy. There probably won't be much time to talk during the wedding ceremonies* (which, by golly, I'm looking forward to), so I thought I'd write out some of it.

I'll be home, hopefully, by late Wed. or early Thursday, before July 14 unless some real complications come up, to be *best man* at Tim's wedding!

I will send you the measurements you have requested, Mom, when I obtain a tape measure.

I will soon make arrangements for coming home and let you know how it all works out. Until then, hope things are well with you all.

Love,
Christopher

---

*Tim's and Debbie's

July, 1967

On July 13 we took the 150 mile trip to Debbie's hometown, our whole family (including my mother) bouncing along Route 66, off to the wedding of Tim and Debbie. I was wedged in between Chris and Mother in the back seat.

"I wonder how her parents are going to react to Jeff's sideburns?" I said to Mother as the fields of corn flew past. "I didn't tell you that Debbie requested that Jeff cut them off because no one in Mohasset has side burns and her parents would be embarrassed. I told Deb that I absolutely would not make such a request of Jeff, that he is seventeen years old and has a right to be himself, within reason!"

"Well, I should think you could have obliged them."

"Oh, come on, Mother. They have no right to expect everyone to conform to them. No, I *will not* give in to such thinking."

Mother stared intently out the window, away from my direction, as she always did when she was annoyed with me.

Chris did applaud my stance on this matter, but in everything else, he argued the whole trip.

As we were going to our separate motel rooms, I called to Chris, "I hope you brought your new sports jacket to wear tonight at the rehearsal dinner." He flew into a rage. "Maybe I don't want to wear a sports jacket! Don't you know everyone—guys my age—might not like to wear a sports jacket?"

Art moaned, and said under his breath, "Does he have to argue about *everything?*" And I was angry that Chris was seemingly putting me in a class with Deb's family as just another conformer.

All in all, it was an enjoyable time. Art's sisters and brother were wonderful. Jean said as soon as we met, "Now, I'm going to have the pre-dinner cocktail party in my room for just our family and our friends!" We all felt very festive.

During the reception, Tim whispered to me, "What's with *Chris?* He got really goofy with Lloyd and Wilber and me over drinks after the dinner last night. He sounds like a fanatic over his new love, Scientology. He was really cramming it down our throats!"

Though *we* were all annoyed with Chris's actions, he nevertheless managed to walk off with the most charming and popular girl in the wedding party.

Letter from Chris to Jeff and family

August, 1967

H'lo Jeff (& Folks),

I thought I'd better send along a birthday note this year in contrast to years past. I figured out what makes your birthday in particular hard to remember—in the summer I don't know the date, and many times, not even the month.

I'm sending along a couple of tiles from the fireplace of an old gigantic Victorian house which is presently being torn down in Austin. It was a magnificent house to see, with stained glass windows, spiral staircase, delicate woodwork everywhere. They told me it was being torn down in accordance with the will of the old lady who had lived there and died there recently, who felt that no one but her family should live in the house; and since she was the last of her family it had to be torn down. Most everything of value, even the wood paneling, was sold at tremendous prices to treasure hunters, of which Texas seems to have as many as any other state. The fireplace from which these tiles came was in an upstairs room that contained a bed, and desk and rocking chair all of which were similarly decorated with hand carved roses; and an oriental rug for wall to wall carpeting. It was definitely the best room I've ever been in and literally reeked of strange tales and potions.

I'm not sure if you'll be back from your trip yet. Mom told me you didn't make it too far with your thumb and so took a Volks. That can be just as much fun and give you more freedom although it will keep you out of the peculiar situations which arise when one is completely dependent on strangers for his needs. I know I've enjoyed my automobile trips very much, just driving along with the radio playing and all; but one meets nobody and can get lonely. I'm wondering how you felt—let me know sometime. (One also gets lonely hitching, needless to say.)

Love,

Chris

P.S. Boy, that was some wedding! I never loved so many people so much—you, Grandma, Aunt Jean—oh, I really loved Aunt Jean! And I felt pretty much of a big shot being *best man*!

Fall, 1967

September, 1967

I asked him if he didn't want to come home for a little vacation, when he called from Texas, and he said he would. "I'd like to get out of this place for awhile. Some queer things have been happening. I've been feeling disoriented." They were chilling words. Yet, I did not really believe he wasn't making it. I still felt he was just someone having a very long adolescence.

He came home with his dog, and he seemed on the whole doing all right at school. He told us he liked what he was doing now. He asked for, and was given money to spend a few days in Indiana to collect some plant specimens for the teacher that he admired. But there were difficulties. And then there was a morning when he started in on me.

Chris sat on the barstool, facing me as I got breakfast, the cats under my feet as usual. I felt tired—it had not been one of my better nights. It seemed as if Art's light had been on half the time, showing under my door, and I wondered what his problem was. I wasn't very happy to have Chris waiting for me—he had been so disagreeable since he'd come home for this two week visit from Austin, even though we had done our best to give him a good time.

The very first full day he had been home, he had gotten very incensed. I had invited Deb and Tim over for a family dinner. "What did you do that for?" he had shouted. "I'd rather see them alone!" This was the guy who had always loved family get-togethers.

"I just thought it would be nice to have one family dinner while you're here," I answered. *Now* what was the matter with him?

"So you just thought you'd do it *your* way!"

"No, not my way," I defended my action. "*Our* way. The way we've always done. If you don't want to do it that way, I'll cancel it right now." I turned to the 'phone again, and he grabbed it out of my hand roughly, and banged it down. "You don't want me to cancel the date?" I asked. "I don't care *that* much, though it seems too bad. Jeff especially would really enjoy us all together. There's no reason you can't also see Tim and Deb alone—I know they'll want you to come up to see their apartment."

He was silent and we let it go at that. Why did he argue over every little thing? Would he *ever* get over this delayed adolescence? My God, he was 23 years old. He still seemed dissatisfied with everything I did; he was constantly trying to harass me.

I tried not to be hurt over his hostility; I kept trying to tell myself that this, too, shall pass and he'll finally grow up—but he kept at me and at me, and at me. Yet I knew—I *knew*—we were friends—basically.

And now, here he was this morning, laying for me, as I found out. He had just returned from Indiana where he had supposedly had a wonderful two days. He and his dog had romped through the wildernesses gathering the special kind of plants for the favorite professor.

I had not even got the cats fed before he started in. "I don't like the way you rejected *Walden Two*.* You read it with a closed mind."

"That isn't true. I'm tired of hearing that closed mind bit. I've made a lot of changes through the years. I couldn't have done that if I had such a closed mind."

"Oh, Mom, you know darned well you'd never accept the behaviorists. You always have to make everything much more complicated, all your belief in deep analysis, and all. . . ." He poured himself a cup of coffee, and helped himself to a doughnut.

"Put me down as a pragmatist. I know what worked for me. All those hideous weeks of standing on the 6th floor fire escape when I was your age to get over my fear of high places—yes, it worked for awhile—but I immediately developed fear of jumping in front of elevated trains. And after that man killed himself jumping from the 4th floor of the old post office rotunda, I was right back to my high-places phobia. All the hostilities that were at the basis of my phobias were still sitting there in my unconscious—until I got rid of them with my self-analysis."

He quietly dunked his doughnut, and I could almost feel his groping for another argument. Then he lashed out, "You are one of the most intolerant people I know. You tried to bring me up to be intolerant, too. Look how you have ranted about Freud, even though half the world worships him."

"Does it? From where I sit, the world is growing beyond Freud and his patriarchal biases. Again, I'm a pragmatist. It was Horney who worked for me, not Freud! But I never said that no one could be helped by Freud—like your friend Brian. Or that Freud didn't get us pointed in the right direction. What do you mean I brought you up to be intolerant?"

"You said Jesus was simply a very great man. But many think he is the only Son of God. You taught me to be intolerant of those people."

"No, I told you those people are intolerant of *me*. I include them in my 'Family of God'. They don't include me in theirs. Nor do they include followers of other world religions. I believe there are many pathways. Is that intolerant?" I knew I was talking too loud, and I lowered my voice.

---

*By B. J. Skinner, behaviorist psychologist. Macmillan.

"What I told you was that *I* believe we are *all* children of God. But I *always* said that might not be what *you* would believe."

I extricated the cats' toy mouse which had become wedged under the door and tossed it to Henry who pounced on it, hooked it, threw it, and reared on his back legs, back straight, preparing to move in for the kill. I laughed, hoping, to break Chris's mood, but he would have none of that.

I poached a couple of eggs for him, and he continued, "You have always looked for good in people, and you try to look beyond the bad. By doing that, you're promoting evil, instead of facing it. You've made me too tolerant of people, I'm tolerant of everyone's ideas, I think they are *all* right. That's why I can't make up my mind what I believe in. People who believe in the devil as king are o.k., too—we look for the good in them. Everyone's right when we look for good, and don't dwell on evil." His beautiful eyes were narrowed.

"Some good is only potential, I've said. I never said that neurotic needs are good or animal selfishness is a goal. But when I look at another human being, I like to emphasize what is good about him rather than what is bad. Say, first you accused me of intolerance, now it's too much tolerance!" I got the eggs onto pieces of toast and managed not to break them. They were perfect, thank God he couldn't complain about *them*.

But he did. "How come you didn't fry the eggs?" Even though he'd always loved them poached. Could I do *anything* right?

With his mouth full, he went on, his eyes now like flashing mirrors. "You've done all our thinking for us, got it all mapped out, made me feel I couldn't do a thing without getting your opinion, made me dependent as hell on you, made me come running home to Ma."

Now I was really getting angry. "Chris, you know how I always discouraged your running home to me even when you were a kid—I wanted you to handle your own problems out there with the kids. I wanted to give you the tools to handle your problems with people, I wanted to help you to help yourself." I was breathing fast. "You know how my mother was, always telling me what to do. I've leaned over backward trying not to tell you what to do, to let you go your own way, make your own decisions, yes, even your own mistakes."

"That's just it!" he shouted. "You've let us be too independent! Barging ahead, not knowing what to do, needing someone to tell us, but oh no, we shouldn't come to you, we'd be leaning, we'd be dependent, we wouldn't be having the guts to make our own decisions. You've demanded too damned much independence! And you're a hypocrite. You believe in good, but you told me to go out and commit every sin." I looked at him in astonishment.

I refused to talk with him further. "This is *crazy*," I thought. "He's not

173

making any sense." I sat down in the Lincoln rocker and picked up the *Tribune*.

"So you won't talk any more," he chided. "You're always that way, you just won't discuss things." He went out and slammed the door.

Yes, this was crazy! I was the one in the family that talked. I was the one that liked to get to the bottom of things. But I wasn't going to go on in a nonsense talk that was getting nowhere.

I spent the day going to a conservation seminar, making some chili and a big tossed salad for dinner; then went out to the board meeting of the The Thursday Evening Club. By the time I got home it was almost ten o'clock, and I was not happy to see Chris sitting on the same bar stool waiting for me.

"Where's Dad?" I asked, hoping he was around and that his presence would prevent another of our "intimate conversations." And then I noticed that Chris's eyes were soft.

"Dad turned in early. His back was bothering him. No wonder after watching those fool Bears tonight on TV." Then, "Mom, I've been feeling depressed all day. There was hardly the tiniest grain of truth in anything I said this morning." He paused, looking the other way. "I'm sorry I talked to you the way I did."

I did not ask him why he had said the things. I was only glad for his friendly move. Though the day had been busy, he had been very much on my mind.

"Could I talk to you for awhile?" he asked. He didn't usually ask! I wished I could say no—I *was* tired—and I was afraid that if we did talk we might get back into some craziness. But I said, "O.k." And he wasted no time in getting in deep.

"A lot of things I've done I'm unhappy about."

"Chris, we all have done things we're not happy with. How could we always do everything right? We're all just struggling human beings. How in the world could we fail to make mistakes?"

He wanted to talk about some of his. "One of the things that bothered me most was when Tim was thirteen and he came to me all elated and confided, 'Hey, Chris, I can make sperm now!' I smirked, 'I've been able to do that for two years.' Instead of thinking of him and feeling joy with him, I tried to humiliate him, belittle him—by telling him his younger brother had matured long before he did. Matured! In body *only*—what a childish ass I was, what a lousy brother."

"Chris, that was so long ago. It doesn't do any good to dig around like that—we could all find plenty of things. One of the things I remember I did when I was in college. A girl, Amy Slocum, and I were trying out for the drama club. I forgot my lines, and tried to shove the blame on her as if it were *her* fault. I rationalized that she was no actress anyway, and I was a good one—which was true—so it was o.k. Of course what happened was that she passed the tryout and I didn't. The drama coach knew very well what I had done. It took me a long time to stop hating myself for that one. The coach didn't let me in the club for a year."

Chris's face brightened a little. Then he said, "Another time, I did an awful thing to Rick. We were just getting started on our butterfly collections, and we were both anxious to get a yellow swallow tail. Somehow we weren't seeing any. One day when we were over in the field, he had his net with him and I didn't have mine. Along came a yellow beauty, and instead of calling it to Rick's attention, I chased it away."

We smiled together, a little sadly, and he seemed more relaxed. "How about a piece of that carrot cake with some whipped cream?" I suggested.

As we sat at the dining room table eating our cake, he told me "I found some great new rocks in Indiana. Wait, I'll get them." He brought them to the table, and we studied them together. I showed him my new agate and carnelian necklace.

Our love for each other was shining and it was just the same old wonderful. We talked for an hour or so in the easy way we had talked so often. Chris had always been the most communicative of the three boys. I remembered how, when he would come home from high school, he would take fifteen minutes or so before he flew out to shoot baskets or play softball with the neighborhood gang (our home was often the center of activities) to tell me all about the day's happenings, which might be anything from how he had swiped a little snake from the zoology lab and set it free; to his progress with a new girl; to how he got demerits for giving a fake message on the loud speaker system.

When we finally decided to quit for the day, I turned toward my bedroom door on the first floor, and Chris started for the upstairs where his and Jeff's room was. His dog was looking expectant. "O.k., come on, boy," Chris laughed. "You can sleep on my bed."

"Be careful not to wake Jeff. He's had a big day. 'Night, Chris."

"'Night, Mom."

Our eyes met, and Chris said, "Oh, Mom," in a voice that was almost a sob.

Oh, how I loved him.

Notes by Chris when he got back to the University of Texas. Fall, 1967

So it was, then, that I had looked through the 'scope and seen the tiny creatures swimming there; I longed to know their world, longed to know

175

something of their preference; for, here before me, were mysteries I knew not existed. This longing to know them, is it not the same longing, the enrapturing mystery that I feel in the presence of a stranger, of a new person among my affairs, whose face I like? Are these not the same longings which grip me when standing amongst the ancient books in an old and well-used library I come across a certain yellowed and tattered volume entitled *The Science of Alchemy?* Is this not the same longing which grips my heart when I—all unknowing—stand looking into a laboratory of scientific achievement and there, before me, stands apparatus of great consequence, coiled glass tubes, retorts, things boiling in beakers, strange colored liquors in flasks, unfamiliar odors?

Is this not the same longing that I feel as I stand before a tree, a mountain, a cathedral, a butterfly, a blade of grass? This longing that I have, is it not a certain respect, is it not a certain love, a concern and a care; do I not want to see these mysterious creatures fulfill their destinies, do I not want to protect them from harm that may befall them?

Has not this longing certain other names such as the "call of the wild"; "spring fever"; "humbleness"?

And yet, what did I do? I took the tiny creatures that I saw under my 'scope—I grew them under a number of conditions. I found out how much they weighed, what they ate, how they swam, I stressed them and strained them with too much heat, too much cold, too much dissolved matter. I killed them with toxins, I discarded them when the cultures grew old and unuseful—in short I did everything opposite to my respect and my love for them.

And is this not how I often treat the mystery stranger whose face I like—do I not proceed to weigh him to find out various insignificant facts about him, how many brothers he has, what is his job, how wealthy is he, do his beliefs coincide with mine?

And is this not how I often treat the ancient books on Alchemy—do I not begin to read them and finding certain scientific improbabilities, do I not pick them apart? Do I not weigh them and subject them to various stresses and strains that are contrary to my respect and love for them?

Is this not how I have often treated the tree, the mountain, the cathedral, the butterfly, the blade of grass?

And what I ask—what was the consequence of these mistreatments? The consequence of these mistreatments turns out to be the most insidious kind. It was not obviously horrible at all—it is a certain lulling of one's appetite—it is a certain peaceful slumber—it is the acceptance of contentment and security in place of beauty.

I told myself that I now knew the protozoans I had studied. I could recite a good deal of their statistics. I could tell you which could withstand

176

hot conditions and which cold; and so, slowly the mystery I felt at first seeing these tiny creatures transformed into a feeling that I understood them—a secure feeling, a feeling of prediction, a feeling that there was hardly a situation under which one could place these creatures, the outcome of which I would not be able to predict. And so mystery and beauty transformed into security and predictability.

And is this not how it often went with the mystery stranger? Did not, after finding out how many brothers he had, after finding out his financial situation and his beliefs, did not my original feeling of his mystery and beauty transform into a more secure, more relaxed feeling? That I could now smoke and drink comfortably with him, that we could share certain pettinesses, joke and laugh together? Was it not instead, rather than the gaining of a friend, was this not instead the loss of one? Was not the camaraderie we shared over dirty jokes and beer, was this not in truth the secure communion between men gained at the expense of beauty and mystery? Had I not gained a comforting comrade at the expense of beautiful love?

And the book of Alchemy—when I saw that even the mysteries upon which it dwelt seemed to contain certain contradictions concerning the transmutation of baser metals into purer ones which I could not fit into my framework of thought—did I not begin to feel easy with the book? Did I not begin to feel that I now knew the book, that it was "merely" the product of certain delightful men but—alas—dreamers? And was this not a secure and comfortable feeling gained at the expense of the mystery and beauty of their secrets?

And so also with the mountain, the cathedral, the butterfly, the blade of grass—and so with all that we call matter and think we know so well. When we accept matter as something that we know, aren't we really accepting a security in place of a beauty? When we say we know and understand matter, aren't we really saying only that we can predict certain things about it? Isn't our feeling of comfort with matter really just a feeling of familiarity and predictability? Have we not sacrificed the beauty and mystery of matter for this security? And is this not then what one has to do in order to regain mystery and beauty and truth into his life; does one not have to slay his secure feelings towards matter and in so doing re-enter the mysterious world in which matter is but one tiny unknown aspect?

Do not two people, in order to become more than just congenial comrades, have to slay within themselves the wish for the other to fit into certain patterns and categories, certain predictable modes of action? Is not it a common desire towards Truth which creates true friends who respect (though not necessarily agree with) each other's thoughts, and a common

177

desire toward security which creates two congenial comrades who fear to argue and do their best to cover up unpleasantness?

Do not I have to slay within myself that comfortable framework of thought called "scientific" in order to get at the Truths, the Mystery, the Beauty, the Meaning within the rare alchemical text?

And do I not have to likewise slay certain comfortable notions within myself in order to fully see the tree, mountain, cathedral, butterfly and blade of grass? Do we not have to slay all of our wish for security and false camaraderie in order to try to be ourselves, our unique and truthful selves, our universal selves?

To anyone whose answer to these questions is no, I say they hold science to be a god and they mistake their comfortable feelings with matter as knowledge of a truth.

I make the following accusation: I accuse members of our society today of acting like small frightened children running to Mother Science for comfort. She has comfort, but she knows not Truth. Each person knows Truth, knows when he has done something wrong. He is told by certain fears, anxieties and other bad feelings when something is not right. Yet because our society is one of small children, we pretend that these fears are nothing much at all, must be overcome rather than encouraged, intensified. Fears combined with a feeling of emptiness are ourselves telling us that we are embarked on a wrong course. That is why we are given those fears. One can only overcome his fears and feelings of emptiness by doing what he knows to be right.

Early November, 1967

The call came at noon, just as Mother and I were having lunch. Mother was there for one of her two day visits.

"Hi, Mom."

"Hi, Chris!" I wasn't surprised to hear his voice. He called every month or so, just to have a chat—often a long chat of a couple of hours or so.

"Mom, I just want to tell you. I'm quitting grad school."

I guess it wasn't too much of a shock to hear this—he had threatened many times that he might. I think the first thing that jumped into my mind was the war and how he'd lose his deferment.

"I'm just not getting anything out of it at all. Everything they teach here is the inverse of anything I really want. I've found out that the true Reality is the inverse of everything I've been trying to do." There was a pause. "Mom, I've been reborn."

I didn't know whether to be happy or frightened. After all, wasn't I the one who believed that the spiritual life was all that really mattered?

He went on quickly. "You remember I told you I had been feeling a little disoriented a couple of times? I see that this was because I was drawing away from the world. I think the thing that really pushed me over the hill to Reality was when I had lunch the other day with three professors and a couple of grad students. The talk was laughable and really sad. All they talked about had to do with power and prestige, that's all they think about. Getting papers published, being impressive, that's all that matters. Mom, that's not what I want. It's the opposite of what I want. I've got to get out of here. Do you understand?"

It was hard for me to say anything, knowing Mother was listening. I felt empathetic with what he was saying, yet I was afraid for him. "Chris, I think I do, yes."

"You know, Mom, I don't think it's necessary to work. I think the Lord will provide." I felt uneasy. I thought of all the people I knew in my volunteer work at the state hospital who didn't work—*couldn't* work.

"Chris, Grandma is here. We were just having lunch." That would let him know that she was right in the same room with me and that I wouldn't want to talk.

"I'll call you tomorrow," he said.

Art and I worriedly discussed the call that night.

The next day I took Mother to the train. Soon after I got home, Chris called. I said, "Chris, I hope you will wait awhile before going into action. Why not finish up the semester? There is no need . . ."

He interrupted me. "I signed out today. I'm all through. I'd like to come home and talk to you as soon as I finish a paper I'm writing." Then, "I'll need some money."

"We'll send you the 'plane fare." I felt as if I were someone else talking. "When exactly will you come?" He thought it would be the following Tuesday, five days from then.

"Please send some extra for my dog. I'll need to get a new case for him." Then, "Mom?"

"Yes?"

"You do understand that I've been reborn?"*

"I think I do," I said tentatively.

"I'm so lucky. I've been so lucky all my life. I'll see you, Mom. 'Bye."

We hung up. I went immediately to the post-office and mailed him a check for the fare, the dog, and fifty dollars extra.

And then we waited to hear from him. The days passed. I kept busy with my own affairs, and tried to believe that something wonderful *had* happened to Chris. After all, hadn't I had a spiritual awakening myself?

*What had *really* happened was that he had made a decision to *seek* a rebirth. He had not yet actually been "reborn".

Not so suddenly, of course, rather slowly, over a period of several years. It did happen to some people this way. But—well, I didn't know.

Tuesday came and went. There was no word from him. This was not like Chris. He was almost always very good about not making us worry.

We called his number. No answer. But it was not disconnected. He had a private 'phone in the room of the building where he lived with several other graduate or would-be graduate students, some of whom were quite deep into drugs. Every day I called many times.

Finally on Friday someone answered the 'phone. It was Chris's good friend, Larry. His voice was so faint and hesitant, I could hardly hear him. I strained to catch what he was saying. God, how I strained. I was desperate for his words. "Larry, I can barely hear you. Can you speak more directly into the 'phone?" For a minute he would, then he faded off again. It was maddening. But I caught most of what he had to say.

"Chris decided he couldn't take a 'plane. He and his dog are walking home." Walking! From Austin, Texas to our house was a distance of a thousand miles!

"Why?" It was unbelievable.

"He can't ride in 'planes now. Not in automobiles either." His voice fuzzed off again, then came back. "He believes that there are evil messages in all the noise the 'plane makes. He can't use the telephone either. That's why he didn't call you. But he did give me permission to answer his 'phone and talk with you if you called."

My heart was quickening. Oh God—strange messages—I'd heard all about those from my state hospital patient friends.

"Larry—do you think—well, is Chris ill?"

This time his voice was firm, directly into the 'phone. "There is no question of insanity," he assured me. "What has happened is that Chris has become a real man." I grabbed at his words, tried to believe he was right. "He has also discovered the reality of evil."

My hope dwindled again.

"Thank you, Larry. If you hear anything of him, please let us know immediately." He assured me, faintly, that he would.

"Good-bye, Larry." I hated to hang up, to break this little connection, this little life-line to Chris.

I told Art about my conversation. We were both immeasurably relieved to have found out *something*, but extremely concerned about what I had been told. We spent three more anxious days. I hardly dared to go out for fear I would miss some kind of message. We made up our minds if we didn't hear by the *next* Tuesday, we'd have to report him missing.

On Monday I did go out since my cleaning men were there and could answer the 'phone. Sure enough, Chris called when I was out. The men said Chris would call again in an hour. I was scared he would not. Then the 'phone rang and I raced to it. It was Chris. Dear God, it was Chris!

"I supposed you've been worried about me."

"Oh, Chris," was all I could say. I tried not to cry. Then, "Larry told us quite a bit. I think I'd have died if I hadn't talked with him."

"I walked from Austin almost to Dallas," he explained. "It was cold and raining most of the time. My sleeping bag is not waterproof. The thing became too much when Ben developed a sore pad. I made the decision to sin, and hitched a ride with someone who offered.* Being reborn, I was sinless up to then." His voice sounded like the same old Chris, even if his words did not.

"Where are you now?" I asked quickly. I couldn't lose track of him again.

"I'm at Love Field in Dallas, at the airport. They won't accept the check you sent. I do look pretty bad. Could you wire me some money?"

"I'll have to go to the bank first. I'll get it off as soon as possible." Thank God, thank God.

"While I'm waiting, I'll buy a decent shirt. Mom, you understand, don't you? Because I've been reborn, everything is different to me, everything Real is the inverse of what appears to be real." I couldn't argue with him on that. "I've been lucky all my life—I've had good looks, a wonderful mother, a great childhood, plenty of money and care and intelligence. Now I'm lucky again. I have died in order to be reborn. I can see things as they Really are."

I worried that he would never get on the 'plane. But he arrived on schedule, dog and all, in a beautiful new white shirt.

Though he had referred to his wonderful mother, we hadn't even gotten home before he was bawling me out!

---

*Later he told me that he had considered just lying down and dying and giving himself up to God, but that he thought of us and decided not to do so. He didn't want to deal us that blow.

PART 6
1967-1970

Late Fall, Winter, 1967

Excerpts from paper written by Chris in November, 1967, just after quitting grad school. (It describes what Chris felt to be his own condition before his "rebirth.")

With no particular malice nor derision in my heart, but with a great deal of relief and a small degree of apprehension, I must now proceed to pry away at that particular framework which constitutes a good deal of Western thought and culture. I have only recently become aware of the poison of this structure, the weakness of the metaphysical assumptions upon which it rests, the way it obscures Reality and its beauty, makes it nearly unrecognizable. For the need of a name, I'll call this framework "bourgeois," though I might better call it unenlightenment, unawareness, lack of inner guidance, etc. It may even be one aspect of the Devil himself. For those such as I who have experienced its horror, who have felt torn into two, then torn into many parts, felt as if they were being squeezed and weighed upon to an intolerable degree, it is a devil. This order of thought, which until recently constituted my own framework of thought,* is that into which each Western babe is born and must struggle against for a lifetime, more often to die than to be reborn. It exists as certain principles, values, etc., which pervade Western thought.

The bourgeois knows above all else that everybody is right. He knows that all philosophies, all religions are right. He knows that at the root of all troubles lies a certain inability between the two arguing parties to compromise. He knows that all problems are soluble by compromise. And it is this that builds the bourgeois into what has often been called "other-directed"! The bourgeois is constantly seeking approval from without, the

---

*As Chris says in the same paragraph, he felt torn in two; so we know that this was not his only framework of thought. We who knew him best experienced a very different side of him much of the time.

bourgeois will be spiritual in front of spiritual men, cynical in the presence of cynics, stoic with stoic. The bourgeois is all things at once, a bit of a coward, a bit brave, loving, hateful, Godly-devilish, spiritual-selfish; and so on. But he is only a little bit of each of these, for the farther he goes toward one pole, the other pole calls to him and, due to his need to compromise, he always comes back and apologizes to the neglected pole, for he seeks all approvals. . . .

Into the bourgeois world steps a man who claims that one must do what he believes in, not compromise with other beliefs, and this troubles the bourgeois no end. He must somehow compromise with this idea that all compromise is bad. So the bourgeois latches onto certain "causes" with which he will not compromise, possibly a belief that a certain war is wrong, possibly the belief that compromise itself is good. He holds dearly to his "cause"—he must not give this up because this would be giving up his compromise with the non-compromiser who entered his world.

The bourgeois only feels happy when he has everyone's approval (except those opposed to his cause). He only feels he has succeeded when everyone "loves" him, when he has perfectly compromised everything (except his cause). And often he becomes a scholar, trying to learn all points of view perfectly so that he may become an even better compromiser. Indeed it is the bourgeois goal to know all points of view perfectly; to be, in fact, infallible, for to be shot down (disapproved of) is his wretched fear. Disapproval is the one thing he can't tolerate. And so he goes about collecting knowledge, collecting facts, he dabbles in science, in politics, in history, in religion and philosophy, ad infinitum, in order to be able to say clever things in the presence of scientists, politicians, historians, priests and philosophers and win their approval. . . .

But I have saved the most bourgeois phenomenon 'til last—the most complex, the hardest one of all to get ahold of and to murder within oneself. The bourgeois classifies everything. Herein lies the treachery of the bourgeois system. He has a mass of drawers into which he must put everything, everything must fit into his classifications scheme. People are of one type or another. Everything fits.

This whole paper is bourgeois. I feel a need to get all sides of the story in to be infallible. The reason is because if I said things in an unclear way, not given adequate examples, the bourgeois mind would seize upon this unclarity, this mistake, this minor error, and use it as an excuse to disregard all the truths therein. If there is the slightest personality quirk in a man, if there is the slightest weakness in a certain theory, if there is a small crack in a beautiful old piece of china, the man, the theory, the piece of china, become worthless, he can see nothing of their value or truth.

Most bourgeois would like to reject their system of thought but there are none perfect enough for them to accept. They will seize on the tiny flaw, dwell on it, harp on it, and in the end they will reject it in its entirety.

Efficiency of time is also a bourgeois trait. . . .

Naturally, money is important. Money is the measure of greatness, of value, of truth, to the bourgeois. . . .

Few of us, if any, are wholly bourgeois. The true bourgeois is nothing more than a little old lady sitting in her rocking chair nodding her head at everyone, constantly reiterating, "How nice! Isn't that sweet!" The true bourgeois seeks a certain paradise where everything is sweet, in order, complete, everyone approves, everyone accepts me, the Devil is sweet, God is sweet, there are no problems in this fantasy paradise. But probably there are none of us who are true bourgeois; we know of pain, ruthlessness, sorrow and hatreds and evils; and so in our minds we seek after this unreal paradise.

There are many of us who feel we've taken a long and hard stand against this bourgeois picture, there are many of us who feel that we have rejected it wholeheartedly, have stood in protest to it for our whole lives. But every time we are affected by someone "shooting us down"; every time we realize that we have missed the beauty in a piece of cracked china; every time our inner voices come to us in the form of fear and tell us that we are doing things against our nature; then we vaguely realize the truth—that though we thought we had staunchly stood up against the bourgeois for our whole lives,* even so has it made inroads into us, has it slowly eaten away towards our hearts, mashing decency and beauty, Respect and Love, transforming them into ridiculous aberrations. . . .

The bourgeois world is no more than a series of inverted truths; instead of looking within for guidance, we look without. Instead of culturing our own gardens, following our own affinities, and recognizing our own linkage, our own uniqueness and beauty, we look to others for Truth, we let them tell us what is beautiful, what is right, what is good, what we should do and where we should go.

---

*This bears out what I said in the last footnote. (See page 185)

The bourgeois group lives in a peculiar space-time world containing nothing supernatural, forgetting that our space-time world is hardly an accurate picture of Reality, forgetting that there is only a supernatural world.

Each of us must leave the bourgeois completely behind in order to become fully human, be aware of Reality. . . .

The greatest problem today is that we pass ugliness by to such an extent that we actually repress it. Everything we do is in search of a "beautiful" paradise. Everywhere one looks there is a dwelling upon beauty—we hang onto this paradise. Then the Devil can do his work unnoticed, he has hidden himself from us and at this time, he has an upper hand. It is this treacherous and universally sought-after paradise that must be overthrown.

Two most important virtues—to seek only the Truth and to accept one's fate. One must arm oneself against Evil, the Devil. So long as one is well equipped against Evil, no harm can befall him, though he may be thrown into prison or an insane asylum, though he may be murdered.

One must sacrifice his present body if it becomes necessary. One must sacrifice his present body if it becomes appropriate to do so. Only a voice from within can tell one.

Part of a letter from Ralph, apartment-mate at Cornell, to Chris.
November, 1967

Hi old room-mate,

I was going to call you tonight, but decided not to because you don't deserve it. After not writing since last Xmas you certainly did not deserve a 'phone call. But if you don't answer me before Thanksgiving I am going to call you and give you all holy hell.

You'll never guess what made me nostalgic for our old days together. My new roommate here, Keb, you probably remember him from Cornell, he was a big frat man who always tugged at his collar, informed me that he's probably going to be engaged and asked me tentatively if I wanted to be best man. Well I couldn't help but remember the last time I was offered that post,* and I figured that one of us would have to break the ice, or else we would never hear from one another again. I thought I'd call because I didn't have your address, but the operator gave me your address.

---

*When Chris thought he was going to marry Margie.

A lot has happened since last year. I can't believe I'm in my second year of Harvard law school. I didn't do too well last year but I was at least promoted so I'm happy. Actually last year was a reaction against the whole Ithaca environment and my more or less monastic first 2½ years at Cornell. I went out a lot last year, soaked in the really invigorating atmosphere of Cambridge and Boston and said "yes" everytime somebody asked me whether I wanted to go out for a beer. Meanwhile, I really . . .

I decided to include this fragment of a letter I never finished.*

More notes by Chris, probably late 1967.

Correlations:

Unaware: looking without for approval. Painting to keep blues away.

Aware: Looking within for Truth—God. Creating tools by which to drive Devil away.

The devil's formula—by concentrating on the good and beauty we become unaware of the evil, we lose sight of it. By this a paradise is formed which is immensely hard to relinquish but must be in order to discover and remain aware of the devil and his work. Fear to look evil straight on. Fear that we may become a part of it as well we may. Fear to acknowledge its possible all-pervasiveness.

Note to Chris from Ken, old Cornell friend.   Late 1967

Chris Jens, what's happening?

The Little Prince—I finally read it—thanks.

I'm at Stanford U. Passed my qualifying exam last week (for Ph.D., not PFC). You're always welcome to stay with me in Palo Alto.

Brain protein is now my thing—that and Spanish Harlem—united by magic. What else could?

Love and magic invite all sorts of things—win all sorts of battles—and girls—girls must be listed separately now. No longer come under "battles"!

Growing up without growing old—neat trick—sure you're managing it, too. You were well on your way when I knew you—that's why I'm writing you. Renew our friendship?

                                   Ken

---

*No other letter found.

189

December, 1967

After he came home, he talked to me almost constantly. He said he *had* to talk.

When he wasn't talking, he was reading or writing or drawing pictures.

He had brought home a book that his friend, Larry, had lent him. It was by René Guénon, a writer on Hinduism, entitled *The Reign of Quantity and Signs of the Times.** It is concerned with the idea that these are very evil times in which materialism has taken over. All that Guénon said backed up Chris in his belief that the world today is a very evil place.

At first Chris said he felt very happy. But evil began to take over. Chris saw evil everywhere. He told me about his experience in Texas when he had found the bone that was very beautiful and smooth on top. When he picked it up and looked on the other side, he was horrified by its ugliness and decay. It was right then that he became fully aware of evil in the world, the bone's other side being a symbol of evil.

What disturbed me most was that he was dwelling not on the goodness of God but on the evil of the "devil." I was amazed by his belief in the devil. I had always told him that *I* thought that the devil is none other than our selves as opposed to our Selves—that is, our earthly parts which have desires and needs.

He would get a strange look in his eye when he spoke of "the adversary." He also had experiences of "God." I reread William Jame's *The Varieties of Religious Experience*** and decided Chris was having such experiences.

One day he went into the city and bought a book, *The Philosophy of Nietzsche,**** by Nietzsche. "I have always been afraid to read Nietzsche," he confided. He spent the next few days absorbed in this author.

Chris was lured by the idea of becoming a superman, à la Nietzsche. And he spoke often of becoming a monk. After reading Nietzsche, he said one night at dinner, "I can't decide whether I want to be a monk or a superman." He wrote and illustrated a little book, a poem, called *The Jewelled Flower*. The main character was in appearance a grown up version of St. Exupéry's "little prince." The poem goes like this:

> Long I looked
> for the jewelled flower;
> searched.in taverns
> and the church's spire.
> Sought I it from

---

*Published by Luzac and Company, Ltd., Great Britain
**Published by The Modern Library, Random House, New York
***Published by The Modern Library, Random House, New York

strangers, friends and foes.
Sought I it in gardens
and in groves;
orchards both of apples
and of books.
Sought I it in
wise and kindly looks.
Sought I it from
that which seemed profound.
Sought I it where
only naught is found.
Then one day
I did a magic trick:
Closed my books and
stopped my wandering feet,
Sat me down before
a merry fire,
Closed my eyes and
felt my fearful heat.
Found I then a mystery stranger there,
And he made a secret
sign to me.
So I followed softly
by his side,
Trembling, neither
caused by fear nor pride:
Led me to a
strange and marvellous sea.
And its edge, I saw,
reflected me.
Found I floating there
a wondrous sight—
T'was the jewelled flower
of my delight.
Seek I now the plant
whose flower this is,
While the many think a
shame it is.

The poem contains a number of clues to the way he was thinking in
those days. He very much believed in magic (including black magic) and
archetypal persons such as the mystery stranger who appears in the illus-

tration as a Wizard. He enjoyed archaic ways of speaking. All of which indicated that he was being invaded by the collective unconscious about which Jung writes, which we all share and which contains all the myths by which man has lived, and archetypal characters which can become very real, and awesome because they are numinous.

One snowy night before Christmas, he got into an argument with his father and demanded that his father kick him out of the house. "I'll never leave if you don't," he hollered.

He suddenly decided he would go back to school, but was informed he would never be able to get back his draft deferment.

Symbols and hidden meanings continued to be important to him. He was constantly seeing meanings that others did not see. Then after Christmas, he seemed to be gaining what seemed to me a true spiritual belief (all is good, all happens for the best, even evil serves God, we are all part of God, which, though he did not seem to realize it, was the spiritual idea he had heard mostly expressed when he was growing up). On Dec. 30 he talked with a group of friends with great zest about his ideas and felt great. But the next morning, he came to me and said he was very depressed. He put his arms around me and clung to me and said, "I get so far up and so far down." He told me he had suddenly seen that God was lonely and that was why he had created man—God was pathetic, God was no better than he was. Later his brother Jeff told me he had heard Chris crying in the night. Chris recovered from his low and laughed it off later in the day. That afternoon he had a date with a new girl in his life who had pursued him, and whom he liked a lot. She also had psychological problems and had been a patient in the state hospital. He picked one of the poinsettias off our plant and made her a corsage.

Winter, 1968

Early January, 1968

The date extended into the night, and finally into the morning in our living room and in the kitchen. When I got up I could hear him going back and forth from the living room to the kitchen. Not knowing the girl was in the living room as I came into the kitchen, I asked, "What's going on?" He looked flushed and excited and answered, "Great things have been going on. I'm free of you at last. Lucky I didn't have to kill you to get free. Lucky I didn't have to kill myself."*

---

*Hadn't Chris now projected to *me* that part of *his* psyche which was symbolized by the archtype of the "terrible mother" known as the "dragon" which the hero should slay if he is to attain the "treasure" which in turn symbolizes the attainment

192

The Jewelled Flower

(Reproduction of original booklet.)

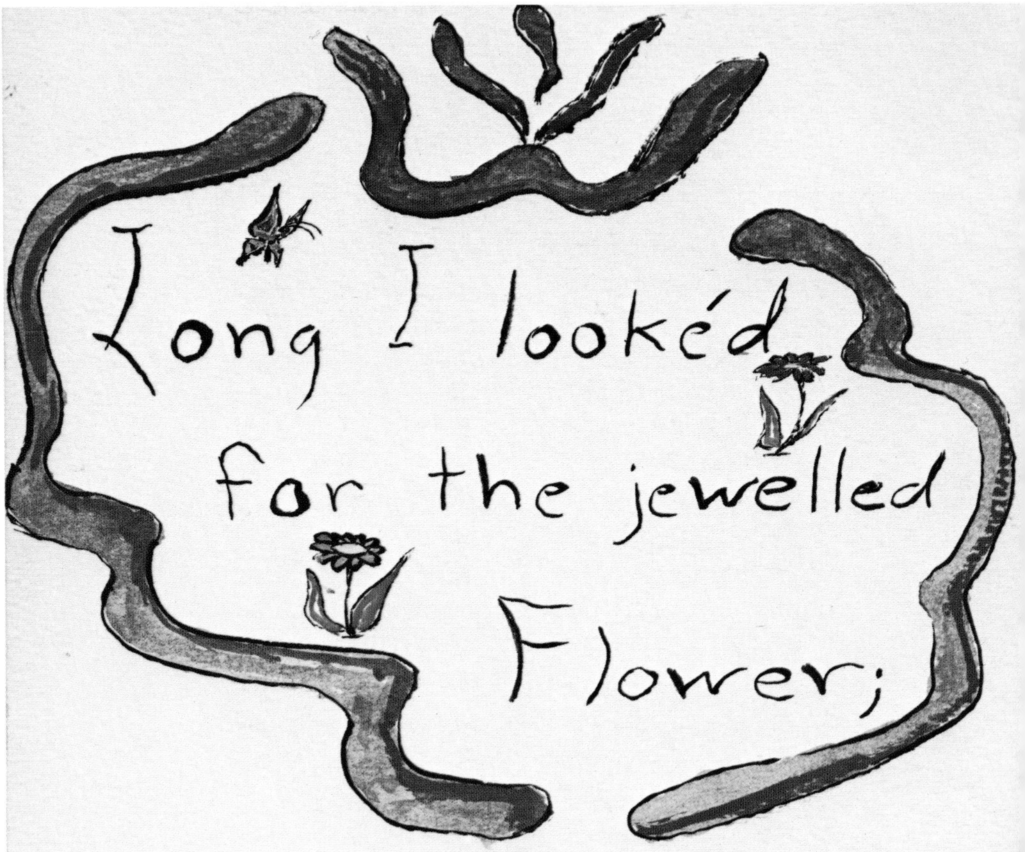
Long I lookéd
for the jewelled
Flower;

Searched in taverns

and the Church's Spire.

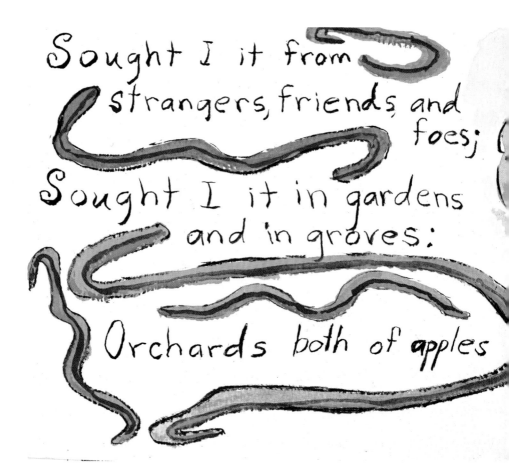

Sought I it from
 strangers, friends, and
  foes;
Sought I it in gardens
  and in groves:
Orchards both of apples

and
of books;

Sought I it in
wise and kindly
looks.

Sought I it from
that which seemed
profound;

Sought I it where
only naught
is found.

Then one day
   I did a magic trick:

Closed my books and
   stopped my
       wandering feet,

Sat me down before
   a merry fire,

Closed my eyes and
   felt my fearful
       heat.

Found I then a
    mystery stranger
            there,

And he made a secret
    sign to me.

So I followed softly
by his side,

Trembling, neither
caused by fear
nor pride;

Led me to a
strange
and
marvellous
sea,

And its edge, I saw,
    reflected me.

Found I floating there
    a wondrous sight—

T'was the jewelled flower
    of my delight.

Seek I now the plant
whose flower
this is,

While the many
think a shame
it is.

End

After he took the girl home, he was back in a very excited state. During the morning, he talked as if he had been intimate with the girl of the night. Since we knew he was in a precarious state, we were alarmed over the possibility of another pregnancy. Hard words passed between him and his father. There was an emotional scene, with me shedding some tears, and saying I wished indeed that I had always managed to do my job well, but at least I had tried to give them the best I had to offer. Whereupon Chris rushed up and threw his arms around me. At noon when we were starting to eat our New Year's Day dinner, his sister-in-law suggested a toast to Chris's new girl. A strange look came over Chris's face and he said, "Oh, no you don't. I know her. She's like all women. They're mean, conniving tricksters." We were all taken aback, as Chris had always liked girls. Now he was including even the girls he liked the best. He used some anti-social words, and was reprimanded by his father, whereupon he shouted them out louder. (He had a queer look; actually he looked like the devil himself; his eyes were narrow, he almost had horns and steamy breath. We all thought so.)

"They're all out to shoot you down!" he shouted. "I'm not going to be tricked by their evil!" We all looked from face to face at the table, silently agreeing that *he* was the one who seemed evil at that holiday table.

Tim joined the hollering match, and the afternoon was a shambles, with only the men involved. Chris told Dad to wear the pants in the family, he shouted that men are essence and women substance. (According to what he was reading in Guénon, essence is quality, substance quantity—or we might say, essence is spirit and substance earthiness.)

This kind of thinking, prevalent in myths and religions, which makes the masculine represent spirit and feminine represent earth also brings us to the idea that man is good, light; and women, evil and dark. His excitement was so high that I called our psychologist so that he would be standing by. At one point Chris said to me, "What's the matter, Mom? Don't you see our family is healed today?" His sister-in-law was up in a bedroom

---

of wholeness? One must wonder how Chris managed to think he did *not* have to slay the dragon ("Lucky I didn't have to kill you.") which symbolized that in his psyche which must be overcome (i.e. fear of the unconscious) if he were to become whole, fully himself. What had happened that night with the girl? Whatever it was, he evidently felt as if he had overcome his fear (killed the dragon) without having to kill me (to whom he had projected the dragon archtype). How complex these psychic activities can become!

"Lucky I didn't have to kill myself." Here do we not see a portent of things to come, when he will find that he has not slain the dragon, i.e. has not overcome his fear of the unconscious, that indeed he cannot slay the dragon (and cannot, perhaps, bear to kill *me* to whom he has projected the dragon!); and that the only chance he has for wholeness is to kill his body and hope for another chance, a rebirth?

crying. In the evening he called up the girl and said, "You know you are going to marry me." She evidently spoke of another boy, and he talked of the girl in New York (Karen). He continued very excited. He raced up the stairs shouting, "I am not named Christopher for nothing. I am the one who will have to be crucified!" At another time he made an aggressive sexual remark to me.

The next morning, after he had cried a large part of the night, he went out with his dog, and I was afraid he had left. When he came back he told me, "Mom, I can never be happy until you and Dad get together." I realized now that his father and I were symbols of his opposing thrusts (one might say, competition versus non-competition) which would have to be combined if he were to become whole, fully himself. In this case he was projecting one side of his basic conflict to me and the other side to his father. (For that time, he preferred this projection to me rather than the projection of the dragon archetype!)

His father came out of his bedroom with a letter Chris had shoved under his door. It said, "Mom never wanted anything from you except that you be gentle with her. Dad, be gentle with her. Beg her forgiveness." Later, he told his father to "wear the pants." He spent the day in a very depressed state. His father went to work; the rest of the family were home. At one point Chris said, "I have no will." At another, "I am God and so lonely. You are all just illusions. I created you." I took him to the psychologist that night—Jeff went with me, as I was afraid to be alone with Chris.

The next day Chris continued to be very depressed. He would not let his father go out of the room. "I'm afraid of Mom," he said. "She'll trick me." Art remonstrated, "You know she's never tricked you!" Once Chris shouted, "Man is the high and mighty. Woman is the low, cunning trickster. That is what woman is." This was not easy for me to bear.*

Art said that it was important that he get to the office—he had an appointment with someone from out of town. I could not believe he meant it. "You can't leave. You're needed here." "I'm needed there, too," he replied. Soon Chris suddenly said, "I feel a terrible pain. I can't stand this terrible pain!" He walked across the room, carefully picked up a large wooden candle holder and hurled it through the window.

I called my psychologist friend. We hoped to get Chris into a hospital immediately. We were both extremely frightened of him, and afraid of what he might do to himself. We both felt grateful that he had only broken a window and not someone's head, probably mine.

In the afternoon, as we waited for the call from the psychologist, Chris said to me, "I can never live with my mother and father. I might do

*In this episode with Chris, he had evidently projected to me one of the negative archetypal women.

194

something bad. Like make love." Was this seemingly incestuous thought perhaps a symbolic way of expressing a fear of regressing to the primal source, to the "maternal abyss" of the collective unconscious, and possibly being swallowed up? Or, to put it another way, fear of being devoured by the dragon, "the terrible mother"?

I held Chris's hand all the way to the hospital. I, who had majored in abnormal psychology; who had recovered from an exceptionally distressing neurosis; who had worked so many years as a volunteer with the mentally ill; who deeply loved this son; who had wanted so much for him to be independent—"himself"—could not help him. All I could do was love him, love him, love him; but he was in another world.

More notes by Chris—probably January, 1968.

Experience of role—choose your own role, allow each his own—choice of your own universe. Inability to choose the universe I want, wish not to be separate is the governing force, wish to be whole. Wish to be sure there are others, not lonely. Lonely God will create any universe—for the reassurance that something else cares about him. Each are different aspects.

Final choice—all lie down and weep together or all kill each other.

Another note:

Even thinking about the Devil fills me so with fear and horrible thoughts that my growth is treacherously impeded and I become nasty and more like him.

Late January, February, 1968

Chris made many diagrams. "Cues" and "innuendoes" were very much part of his thinking. He read things into what others did and said, saw meanings that were not there. E.g., his father brought him an electric razor at the hospital and said something about listening to it, perhaps, to see if it was working right. Chris read into this some strange message. E.g., before he left home for the hospital, his father gave him a green and black capsule, a very mild tranquilizer which he had on hand for himself. Chris did not take it, probably because of suspicions of it, but hid it behind a desk. He escaped from the hospital one cold winter night and ran home 15 miles, with no coat, to get the capsule which had somehow become symbolic to him of something very important.

In this first hospital (which we did not like, nor did he), he made two attempts at suicide, once by trying to push the sharp end of a broken

195

billiard cue into his temple and once by diving head first onto a drain in the bathtub (on my birthday).

This latter attempt resulted in his being put into maximum security.

He was very peculiar and hostile during his month in the hospital, and believed the hospital to be full of evil forces.

Soon after he was hospitalized at the first hospital, he received a letter from his draft board that he had been put in the 1-A classification, having lost his student deferment. There was nothing to do but write them the truth, which was hard to do. His psychiatrist also had to write. He was reclassified to 4-F. Chris, who had formerly seemed so desirable to the draft board, was now a reject.

Chris continued seeing "cues" and "innuendoes" in everything. Every simple happening was complex for him. At first he suspected all the other patients and the staff of communism (he knew of people abnormally suspicious about communism with whom I had worked and he latched onto that). But soon he felt the "cues" and "innuendoes" came directly from the devil.

There were a number of things we did not like about this hospital, so we had him transferred to another one.

The second hospital was homey and warm, in contrast to the first which was bleak and chrome-decorated. Chris was often quite hostile, yet he always seemed glad to see us. Compared to the other patients, he appeared amazingly well except for his spells of catatonia when his head would be pulled over to one side, and when he had delusions of being Christ (I was the Virgin Mary, Dad was—I never knew—Joseph, or God).

One night his dog had a cerebral vascular accident and died in about five minutes. It was devastating to me to have to tell Chris that Ben was dead.

He had developed the idea that he would die on his birthday in February and was closely watched. (He had, remember, failed in his suicide attempt on *my* birthday.)

Because Chris had been away from home for so long, we were able to keep his situation quite a secret. I did not tell anyone except our immediate family that he was hospitalized. I knew, oh I knew, how hard having been "mentally ill" would make it for him. My years of volunteering with the mentally ill had taught me how they suffered from stigma, even when they were quite well again.

Letter from Ralph to Chris. (Chris was in the psychiatric hospital, unknown to Ralph.)

Dear Chris,

Well one of us has to break the ice, and I guess that it's going to be me. I can't think of a letter that I sent you in the 1½ years since we've seen each other that's really said what I've wanted to say. Anyway I've really had a compulsion to talk to you these last few days and in fact I've wanted to call, but that would cost too much, more than I can afford right now. Last night I fell asleep with my light on and sleeping with my girl friend of the last year and I suppose the mood or the memory of seeing you and Margie sleep like that all the time caused me to have a vivid dream of you and our times at East Buffalo Street (I can't even remember the address). Anyway it's horribly depressing to think that I've lost almost complete contact with you, Margie, Brad, Marion and even little Mary, all the people I was close with. My friends here are very good friends and in many ways I'm just as happy. I have a really fine girl friend (altho I still get restless); but it's still sad that I have no contact with the people I really loved at Cornell. If you don't write now, after this emotional appeal, I'll never forgive you; I will, of course, but please write anyway.

Anyway, I'll move on to slightly more prosaic topics, my life up here. It's much better now than it was this last year. I'm much more involved with the law now and doing interesting things. I'm working for a Community Legal Assistance Organization and am even on the board of the Harvard Civil Rights—Civil Lib Research Council, which doesn't do much. But at least I feel as if I am moving in the right direction, and I'm working hard for the first time in two years. I have some of the restlessness out of my bones. But not completely for good. I'm certain that when I graduate from here I'll want to travel, and for a long time. I'm thinking very seriously of enlisting in the Peace Corps. Sometimes I still feel that I erred in going to law school. When I look around and see the predominant type here, well-shaven, dressed in suit and tie, diligent, hard-working, and I realize that I'm probably the only guy there who doodles in his note-book, well I think, you blew it again, how did you get yourself in here? But I know that if I had to do it over again I'd still come here: it's a really nice place, dozens of quaint shops, interesting, and has many very kind people, very pretty girls, very willing to become friends, and sometimes willing to sleep with you if you convince them that you are indeed a very, very confused law student. This is a very rare, rare occurrence. My point is that I don't feel the masculinity hang-up that I sometimes felt at Cornell. Maybe it's because I'm older; maybe because the dominant social ethos here is being cool. It's probably because I have a girl friend.

Meanwhile, I'm also doing things at least a little, for the first time, that you always tried to get me to do, like painting and writing poetry. Your influence, Chris, is still existing even over the span of time and distance.

I'm going to have to end this letter soon, because I'll have to stay up very late to get all I have to do done tonight, but first I want to give a little pitch for the New England countryside. It's really charming, more rustic and fairylandish than New York State. The New England autumn is phenomenal. I never saw anything like it. It makes up for the harsh and miserable winters. But there's a lot to do, tobogganing and horseback riding. I can't believe that I never tray-slid at Cornell. I went tobogganing for the first time two weeks ago. Anyway what I'm trying to say that you can share in this anytime by visiting for as long as you want, with or without companion, is it still Margie? Of course, alas, Texas is far from Massachusetts.

Now please Chris, stop everything right now, and write to me, even a page that couldn't take more than five minutes. It will make me feel so fine: and try to visit me before I finish law school, either in New York or Mass.

See you, your buddy,
Ralph

Chris did not—could not—answer this letter.

Poem by Chris—written during hospitalization,   Winter, 1968.

There is a rock-like quality about me now—
I have no will, no interests,
I write only by chance—
I have no inner flame, nor fears.
There are no rivers flowing within me.
I am a soggy log—my heart beats
but only from inertia—it will not stop
because there is nothing that wants it to.
My mind is aware of Truth, but rejoices not at all.
It cares not nor does it work Truth over—it
knows Truth only because Truth happened to be
present within it when it stopped—I could be
whipped yet would not feel, I could be presented
with beauty, and worship not, I am neither
happy nor unhappy, neither empty nor full.
I would not see naked women, should they dance
about me. I feel no peace, no gaity, no sorrow,
no pity, no contempt, no loneliness, no love,
There are just a thousand streams about me all of

which are filled with water, yet have ceased to
flow: I am capable of doing things, but there would
be no reason to. Were someone to enter I could
talk enthusiastically or intelligently about anything,
perhaps even creatively, they would think I was in a
gay mood. This must be the state of most people
around me from which they know no departure. I may
eat, I may not. I might show contempt but feel it not,
I could not show love.

Part of notes written for hospital by Lee, winter 1968*

What was the patient's personality before illness?

All in all, Chris has always been a non-comformist. Wanted to do things
his way.

Always very energetic. Lots of projects going, even as a small boy.
Sometimes had ideas bigger than he was able to carry out. Popular always
with his peers, male and female, and loved by adults (except by teachers
when he was too audacious!). Was elected Vice President of senior class
in high school as a write-in candidate. Voted most humorous in high school
class. Impulsive, and somewhat of a "sore-head" because quick to anger,
but also quick to apologize.

Having been brought up in a household which emphasized turning a
search-light on psychological hang-ups and which was deeply imbued by
the pursuit of spiritual values on the one hand; and on the other hand
deeply involved in the power and prestige principles encouraged by a free
economic and political society, Chris found himself caught between the
two thrusts. He has great innate abilities and affinities in both directions.

When he was a sophomore in college, he began to reject the spiritual
beliefs of his mother and became a materialist. He denounced her ways
of thinking with vehemence (those ways being basic in most religions).
Became for awhile an advocate of Freud's theories as opposed to Horney,
the neo-Freudian, in whom mother had great faith. It was also at this time,
after having utterly failed in a big love affair while using mother's spiritual
and psychological ideas, that he became hostile with mother. (Before that,
while there had been hostility, the major feeling was warmth and admiration, as evidenced by much communication.) He began to build up father,
with whom he had never been close and to whom he had always felt
hostile. He was living with a room-mate who was in Freudian analysis,
and under the tutelage of this room-mate Chris had decided he perhaps
had an Oedipus complex.

---

*Notes approved by his father.

199

During junior year in college began to express the fact that he often felt uneasy with people. But people continued to love him.

Spring, Summer, Fall, Winter, 1968

Letter from Lee to Chris (never delivered)

Spring, 1968

Dear Chris:

For how many years now—three, four, or more—there has been this grave complication between us. At first, it was startling, hard to bear. It was not that you were getting ideas that were different from mine—that would never have bothered me, I knew you had to work out your own philosophy; and if it was different from mine, but worked for you, fine. Fine, within limits, of course. I'll admit I'd have a hard time having you around if you had become say, a devotee of the Klan or the Mafia.

No, it was not that you were thinking new thoughts—loving, as I do, to see people thinking for themselves, that even delighted me—it was the way in which you attacked me and my beliefs, or rather, my way of life (using the word beliefs makes it sound as if I am positive, close-minded, which I am not), the hostility which you displayed. Yes, I was hostile, too—in answer to you. Not in reaction to your new ideas, but to your *hostility*. There was almost no length to which you would not go in trying to hurt me, belittle me, crush me.* It almost broke my heart, because I knew that we were good friends. It had seemed to me that you and I had always had a lot of enjoyment together.

It got so I didn't want to be with you, for I knew whatever I said, about *anything*—you would be against it. Everything about me was bad, you seemed to think, even my cooking (which you had always enjoyed before).

I was baffled. I was sure you loved me, underneath. *What* was wrong?** I knew it was not simply that you had a new and different philosophy. You were intent on destroying mine, so it seemed. You seized upon my every weakness, you tried to cut me down, to prove that my philosophy was not good, did not work. It seemed to be a *passion* with you.

Of course, there was ambivalence. Often you sought my help, talked things

---

*It seemed to go beyond adolescent rebellion. And he was now in his twenties.
**What I did not see was that much of our problem came from the fact that he was projecting to me various aspects of *his* inner conflicts, a device which enabled him to get them outside himself, experience them as not his own, and not have to suffer the pain of haranguing himself, but rather experience the less painful haran-

over with me, even expressed a dismay over the way you had been treating me.

But it went on.

Now, a lot has happened. You had some experiences in Austin. I guess when you came home, you felt as if you had found some answers, and that this time, you could win me over to your new beliefs. I'm not sure. And before long—after how many hours of talk, when I thought we were at last settling our differences, even though I was concerned about some of the bizarre ideas you had when you first came home—you went to the hospital.

Now it is nearing the time for you to come home. And I see that things are pretty much the way they have been for these several years—you are still very hostile to me, still trying to "shoot me down" (an expression of which *you* are fond).

Now it is more important than ever that I understand what is going on between you and me. For above all, I don't want you to have to go back to the hospital, I want you to be able to live your life. It is also important that *you* understand what is going on between us. We must both understand, so that we can meet the problem and dissolve it. For obviously, it must be dissolved.

Our differences—as I see them now—all seem to center around people. I choose to dwell on their good side (be it ever so small)—I may not always seem to be doing this, because I am against neurotic activities. I will do nothing to help along a neurosis (except in an emergency), and so I may appear to be not dwelling on good in my actions. But to me, I *am*: because to me, it is sinful to make people comfortable in their neuroses, to "handle them"—sinful, because, to me, it is unloving.

So, our differences center around people. I choose to trust them, in spite of their obvious unlovable, selfish characteristics. You choose not. You

guing of me. (He was, of course, *entirely unconscious* of the fact that he was projecting.) I wonder why I was so often the one to whom he projected the above, various archetypes from his collective unconscious, etc. Was it that, since we were so close, he felt he was part of me, and that therefore he was hardly projecting at all? It certainly was not because I was so quick to receive projections—rather, I fought them when they seemed completely foreign to me. (However, in the case of the projection of some part of his conflict, what he was projecting from himself was often the same as some part of me, which made it hard to recognize that he was projecting.) Did he project so often to me perhaps because he knew I would fight or defend, whichever was needed, with great ability, and he actually wanted those parts of himself that he was projecting fought or defended? What a confusion! And all interlaced with our very real love for each other! Not a selfish, warped love on either of our parts, but a *real* love. Not just of mother and son, but of two human beings who really related. He was trying so hard to find himself, and our very love added to the perplexity (e.g. by arousing suspician of Oedipus!).

feel that I am fool-hardy. I think your kind is too suspicious. And on and on.

All of your philosophical undertakings seem to me an attempt to reconcile how *I* feel about people with how *you* feel about people. You had to keep including what *I* feel because you really believe in me, and have seemed afraid *not* to stick to what I believe. And yet, you have not been able to do so. You have been caught in a conflict indeed—on the one side was what *you* are, and on the other side what *I* am.

What we must see now is that we must both be ourselves. You must give up trying to change my beliefs so that you will have no conflict. You must also give up trying to make yourself believe what I do *if you do not*. No matter how dependent you have felt on me, how tied—it is now imperative that you relinquish this tie, to feel that it is not fearful to be what *you* are. The only way to get over your dilemma is to take out of the philosophy which I presented to you as mine *only* those parts which suit you, and add to those what you believe differently from me.

You must give up trying to change me.

And you must believe that even as I must be myself, you must be yourself. This must be true, even if we have to give each other up. I don't think this will be necessary—that our views will be so far apart. But if they are, that is the way it will have to be.

Whatever happens—I'll always love you. No matter what your goals, I'll know they are what they must be. I'll know that *if* you get yourself in hand. If you do *not*, and spend your life going in and out of hospitals, I'll know you cannot solve your dilemma. But even then, of course, I'll love you. No matter what.

Letter from Jer, old childhood friend, to Chris. From Viet Nam.

May 15, 1968

Dear Chris,

I just came back yesterday from a 5-day leave to Singapore. Damn it, it was great to get away from Vietnam.

Singapore is a very beautiful city, and it's as clean and nice as any city in the states. Unfortunately, though, my trip was a let-down.

It sure has been great getting the two letters from you. I get a bit sad and start feeling old when I think that we grew up together and were best friends for ten years, and yet now I haven't seen you more than a few times in the past six or seven years. Your parents moved out to the country and I guess we both blew the Glen Ellyn scene. I haven't called Glen Ellyn my home since I graduated from high schoool in '63. It was a good stable place to grow up, but you can shove it now. It ain't my place anymore. I've tasted freedom and happiness too much since I've left Glen

202

Ellyn and I've had too super a dose of reality tossed in my face since I got drafted to be able to hack middle class suburbia anymore.

After reading your two letters, I can see you are definitely fouled up as far as seeing what you want out of this great big world that we were born into. As for oriental philosophy and the Orient, in general, I've had it. I don't want to come to this section of the world or have a thing to do with it when I get out of here. The Orient stinks.

Aside from this prejudicial raving (I admit the army is mainly to blame and the Orient is a fascinating place) I'd guess you've fallen the victim of one or two things, based on my own experiences in this "great" world. First you've been the victim of an unhappy love affair, and second, for better or worse, you've made the drug scene. Am I right?

If I've gained anything from the army, but mainly from being in Vietnam, it's been a deepest sense of appreciation for the things I had back on the block (army expression for when I was a civilian). Nothing in my life could ever approach the misery we go thru over here. Now I value the things I took for granted—like getting up in the morning, getting on a good suit and going to a respectable job. Or coming home and making my own meal and sitting down and watching TV with a can of beer in hand. Or going out with a girl who's going out with you because she likes you, not because you have money. God almighty damn, Chris, things are all right back in the world. Happiness is everywhere. I didn't know it then, but I do now.

By the way, I really liked living in the city. You ought to give it a whirl. It's a fantastic place with a lot of great people our age. Ever consider teaching there? I knew a couple of guys who really liked it. A job always has its bad points, but no job is as wretched as this stinking army. I hate the army real bad.

So much for my cogitations. It is very late and I have to get up early (6 a.m.). I now have 158 days left in the army and I'm staying low. Write again. Great to hear from you.

Friend still,
Jerry

Summer 1968

He had stayed in the two hospitals a total of four months. At first we were encouraged—the chances were this episode was one in a lifetime, and he would be able to take up his life again. When he came home, he was very remote, not at all the Chris we had known all his life. He was also hostile. He spent his time taking very long walks, and in his room. (Chris always refused to take drugs when not in a hospital). He said he couldn't concentrate on reading.

Instead of improving, he deteriorated. One night he cut his abdomen with a pen-knife. After about two and one half months at home, we were quite worried. Late one night we got a call from the police department of a neighboring town. They had found Chris sitting on an island in the middle of a busy highway. (We had thought he was in an upstairs bedroom.) On questioning, they decided he was probably under the influence of drugs because of his odd behavior. They took him to the station and put him in a cell. He hollered, "Somebody kill me!" We picked him up, and took him back to the hospital the next day.

Letter from professor under whom he worked at University of Texas to Chris.*

August 28, 1968

Mr. Christopher Jens
Glen Ellyn, Illinois

Dear Chris:

I am writing to tell you that the man and environment course that we talked about briefly has been approved for the spring and will be given then. I hope that you will be able to get back to Austin soon this fall to continue your work and that you would find it of interest to help us with this course in the spring. I think you would find both most invigorating.

I am off to Iceland and then to Kentucky but will be back on September 16, the day registration begins.

Sincerely yours,
Avery Megan

October, 1968

For three months he stayed in the hospital. He seemed glad to see us when we came, but he was not himself. He developed a relationship with a girl who was suicidal. When we visited him, we all talked a lot in our usual fashion, Chris included. We stood out, for most of the visiting families had hardly any communication with their relative patients. The best they could do was have a game of cards.

As soon as he got-out of the hospital he announced he was leaving for Texas, where he felt he had friends. He wanted his father to buy him a

*Chris wrote the professor that his interests had changed.

bicycle, but was refused. Dad gave him $100, and said he could spend it as he wished. Chris ended up taking the bus. If we had not had the psychologist's o.k. on his going, we couldn't have managed. It was a trying experience to see him go off by himself through the trees, not knowing what he would really do. He got to Texas where he found a room for himself near where he had lived before, and got a job in the kitchen of the hospital.

Letter from Chris to family while he was in Austin, which came with Christmas gifts.

December, 1968

Dear Folks,

I give to you an author, Herman Hesse, whose points of view are very dear to me. Debbie's gift I have chosen for the profundity of some of the pictures.*

I am, for the present, leading a solitary life of reading, praying, wandering and cleaning dishes, none of which should really be separated.

I will think of you all on Christmas as indeed I do at many other times.

Merry Christmas!

Love,
Chris

Winter, Spring, 1969

Letter from Chris to Lee on birthday card.

January 21, 1969

Hello,

Happy Birthday!

I now have a new address—608 N. 25th St., Austin, Texas, 78705

It's a small room, very cozy with an adjoining bathroom for $40 per mo., with kitchen privileges. Just what I wanted! Like a little "monk's cell." I was promoted to head of the dishroom at the hospital, with a $30 per month raise, which I surely need, as I am always broke.**

I am at present acquiring all the books that I want to read, including those of René Guénon's (in French) that are available. I am teaching myself

---

*Not a Hesse book. The rest of the family each got a Hesse book. Mine was *Narcissus and Goldmund* (Published by Farrar, Straus and Giroux).

**Because he was always buying books on mystical and occult subjects, and traditional religion. We sent him $150 a month to augment salary.

French and can translate one page per hour and a half on the average (after only a week!).

I am presently reading Guénon's *Les Principes du Calcul Infinitesintal* (the Principles of Calculus) which the library here has a copy of and which is a remarkable work. Out-of-print books cost a fortune to acquire. For instance, this month I'm having to pay $29 for one of Watts's books that is out of print.

It's obviously a racket, but if you want the books (at least they find them for you) you have to pay.

I am also in the process of acquiring a remarkable crucifix from the 18th century (Mexican)—has certain alchemical symbols on it which are highly interesting. Cost is $60 which I am paying little by little.

No more news. Hope your day is good.

Love,
Chris

February, March, 1969

He managed for four months, from October almost through February. His 'phone calls to us were quite frequent, for which we were thankful.

Some of the people with whom he was working in the kitchen had been in state hospitals; one of them, a young woman, fell in love with him. We heard later that Chris had suddenly begun acting oddly. (He was nearing his 25th birthday.) He had strange looks on his face. Once he threw his arms around one of the sisters and cried, "I've lost my God!" His actions got increasingly bizarre, so that his fellow workers were extremely worried about him.

One of these, a young man, was going to have to go away for a couple of days, and felt he could not leave him. He went to Chris's room, but Chris was gone. So was his bicycle (which he had inherited from one of the roomers). His friend notified the police to pick Chris up if they could find him. They did, at the edge of town. He told them he was going to Chicago to his parents' home. The police took him to the Christian Social Center where his co-worker was waiting, along with a minister. They did what they could for Chris to help him relax, and called us in the night.

We left for Texas as soon as possible, but we were too late to keep Chris out of the state hospital.

We found Chris in what seemed like a large cage, housing many utterly dejected looking men. One man was vomiting on the floor. I had been a volunteer for years in a state hospital but this was the most depressing ward I had ever seen. We asked for Chris. The aide called him. As Chris approached the aide he made a flying tackle and threw the aide to the floor.

We were allowed to talk with him in an office. He had refused to talk with anyone, but he did talk with us. His answers to our questions were very slow in coming, but they did come.

It was heart-breaking to leave him in that hospital, but it was impossible to get him into the private hospital. We arranged for a private psychiatrist who would work with him at the private hospital later.

A further complication was the fact that Chris had been bitten by a sick raccoon, which had then died, and which we found decaying in his room—too far decayed to be tested for rabies, so the officials said. There seemed nothing to do but put Chris, already so burdened, through the series of painful rabies shots. Perhaps if our lives had not always been so full of psychological and physical complications, which had conditioned me, I could never have stood the utter sadness of it all as we boarded a 'plane for home.*

After he had been in the state hospital only a little over a week Chris was given permission to go back to his job during the daytime. (We had spoken with the sister who was the administrator of the hospital; she said how much they all liked Chris, and that he was a very good worker. She told of how, just a week before his breakdown, he had received a raise, and a very good report; and he had told her how thankful he was for the job.) He only lasted a couple of days. One afternoon he grabbed a knife, handed it to the girl who was in love with him, and shouted, "If you love me, you'll kill me!" The job ended, needless to say.

Two weeks later, he called me from the state hospital grounds—he already had another grounds pass. He told me he was quite depressed, but that at least the food was good, especially the desserts. Then he said, "I just called to say I love you, Mom. I wish it were Christmas and we were decorating the tree."

There was an opening at the private hospital, and Chris was taken there by two guards. Just as he was entering the ward door he managed to escape. He ran across the field. Later he told his father, "I just felt I had to buy something." A book, no doubt—theological, mystical. He lost his place at the hospital. His father visited him at the state hospital when on a business trip. Chris said, "If I could only *be* somebody."

He was accepted at the private hospital about three weeks later. We went to Texas, and he spent the weekend with us, in a motel. The doctor had told Chris, "Now try to communicate with your parents." Little did the doctor know how we had always communicated. And there was no

---

*We could stay no longer. Art had to go back to work; I was in the middle of a course in nursing.

difference. Somehow, some professionals didn't quite believe that Chris was always the most open and communicative of our three sons.

We went downtown to get him some new clothes. He was dressed in state hospital clothes, which were far too big for him.* It was tragic the way a handsome young man like Chris could look so definitely a state hospital patient because of his clothes. My husband went into a store to get something for himself. Chris and I sat in the car, he in front, I in back. Suddenly he turned, and I thought he was lunging at me. I visibly jumped. Chris said, "Mom, are you afraid of me? Afraid of your own son?" Yes, I was. (All that weekend I saw to it that I was not alone with him.) Perhaps I had imagined something, but I was afraid. I said, "Let's go find Dad." We walked down the street, a strange looking pair, Chris in his hospital clothes and I in a trim suit and hat, with our arms about each other (he had insisted).

He was quite content in the new hospital after he was given shock treatments because he wouldn't eat and was uncooperative. Our permission had been given.

We hated the idea of shock treatments. We talked it over with the psychologist here. He said that if it had not been for his intervention with Chris's psychiatrist at the second hospital Chris would have had them before. But he said, "As long as they will refuse to keep Chris if he doesn't have them, perhaps he'd better have them, they might do some good." As the shock treatments proceeded, Chris came out of his depression for sure, and went into a manic state, which didn't sound any better to us. Eventually he settled back into his "religiosity" as he called it, spent a great deal of time with the Catholic chaplain, went back to reading Guénon and dwelling on the evil of the world; gave some consideration to going to a Catholic college where he could study more about religion; considered also becoming a pharmacist; taking up wood-working; and ended up doing none of these.

Letter from Chris (in hospital) to family.

April 15, 1969

Dear Folks,

I got your Easter card and was pleased to have it. I thought I'd write a little note to tell you that I like St. Joseph Hospital and things seem to be going well here. I've had several good talks since I got here and I'm beginning to feel I can trust the people here. Physically, I could feel better, but the good health that I have been blessed with seems to be holding out well, thank God. In fact, thank God for all the things I've been given,

---

*As they say, state hospital clothes come in three sizes—big, bigger and biggest.

208

including two remarkable parents. The basic changes which appear to be occurring in me are from fear to thankfulness.

I decided to smoke, but to try to keep it at a fairly low level which takes a fair amount of perserverance

I've used some of my free time to design a chair somewhat similar to the one which I made before, but with several basic changes. There is a dream beginning to bud in me of myself becoming expert at this kind of chair, and turning them out quickly enough to sell for a living; perhaps even owning a shop some time and making these chairs full time. One thing I feel, I'm ready to settle down and get to work on a life career, if God is willing; and I would like a career in which many of my dreams, desires, and "unquenchable longings" can find fulfillment. Chair-making seems to satisfy my creative, mechanical and practical side, and is specialized enough so that I could become expert enough to make it work.

These are all the things that I'm thinking at present. 'Bye for now.

Love,
Chris

Letter from Chris to Lee.

April 22, 1969

Dear Mom,

I am writing today after having had a treatment (electroshock). Although it affected my memory for awhile, I seem to have gained most of it back, just a few hours later. I will be having them every other day, I believe, and I hope they do some good.

Mrs. D.* brought the whole collection of books by Guénon to me last night, which came in the mail a few days ago. She took them back as I didn't think it was wise to read them in the hospital. They cost about $84 altogether, and Mrs. D. is sending the bill to Dad. I don't know whether they are a curse or a blessing. Whichever they are, however, I now own them.

How is nursing school going these days? Are you still getting A's on all your tests?

Each day at the hospital is unique, and though it's a small area to move around in, it is surely not boring.

I'll quit for now.

Love,
Chris

---

*Chris's landlady.

Letter from Chris to Lee. (Letter addressed to "Ma Jens")

April 24, 1969

Dear Mom,

I am sitting at my desk right now reading your letter of April 17 and feeling very happy to have such a wonderful mother.

I haven't been able to make many friends here that are really close because I've been too tied up with my own thinking. I'm hoping that I can start being a better friend to the people around me but the problem is fear—I keep fearing rather than loving and this puts me in a bind.

I have another problem also—I move around like somebody with no firm foundation, and no solid beliefs. This is probably the result of my searching for the truth and therefore not ever tying myself down to any specific point of view. It is also a result of my inability to give myself wholly to someone else, an inability to feel love for someone else more or less constantly. This is what I would like to be able to do.

I am very sorry I have been such a disappointing son. It is my prayer that I can rectify this. Perhaps I can do so to begin with by acting more consistently on the basis of love and understanding which I know to be Good.

I love you very much, Mother.

Love,
Chris

Letter from Chris to family.

April 27, 1969

Dear Folks,

Just a note to let you know how I'm doing. I can't say I'm glad to have shock treatments; they do seem to be helpful in some ways. But I don't like the bulldozer method of doing things.

Trudy Bingham, my girl friend from work, stops over to see me twice a week.

This afternoon, weather permitting, we are going to have an ice cream "social" with home-made ice cream, etc. It should be a little fun. Goodbye for now,

Love,
Chris

Letter from Ralph to Chris (who was in the private hospital).

April, 1969

Dear Chris,

I'm sorry that I haven't gotten back to you sooner—I lost your letter originally; I was very upset because I intended to look for the book right away.

When I came home for vacation last week, I looked for your letter again and fortunately found it in my old letter pile.

Today I searched for Guénon's book and found it in the Far East collection located in the Fogg Art Museum—unfortunately it cannot circulate. The only thing I can do is photocopy it. It's 330 pages, photocopies at a nickle per page it is $16.50. I didn't want to invest that until I was sure that you wanted me to. Let me know if you want me to do it, I gladly will.

In the meantime I'll rummage around old Cambridge book stores. They might very well have it and I'll pick it up if I find it.

I was delighted to hear that you're happy, Chris*—and I admire your spunk, chucking the whole system and doing what you want to do. I can't right now. I look at what you're doing and appreciate its cosmic implications because right now I am so involved with everyday headaches of living in this system that all I can think of now is that. I'm frustrated: 1. have to knock off five papers in the next 1½ months; 2. suffering from spring fever; 3. practically broke. But I'll be graduating soon and that will make me feel really fine.

Next year I'll probably be in Hawaii or Micronesia. I applied to the Peace Corps and they invited me to be a Peace Corps lawyer in Micronesia. I probably will accept it unless I get a position with the Legal Aid Office of Honolulu. As you can see, I want to get away; far away from my environment of the last three years.

I'll let you know where I will be and if you decide to visit the far east, which I think you should visit, you can stop off.

What's happening with your girl, Margie? Are you still in touch and is she in Texas?

I've been going with the same girl now for three years—but I've been gripped with wanderlust, once again. We'll probably end the relationship when I leave Cambridge, but who knows?

I'm sorry, Chris, that I haven't commented more on your ruminations. I've thought about it, but anything I said now would be phoney because I am frankly too much occupied with my own hang-ups to think much

---

*Chris had probably written Ralph before this last hospitalization. Chances are that he had never told Ralph about his previous hospitalizations.

about the broader meaning of our sojourn on earth; also I am working my balls off to get out of here. But I think about you and I hope that we can get together some day and have a long spilling out of our thoughts in many areas. In the meantime write me and tell me what you want me to do with the Guénon book.

Ralph

Letter from Chris to family.

June 8, 1969

Dear Folks,

This past year or two has certainly been an extraordinary one for me. I have seen a great many things nothing short of miracles and super-rational, super-normal occurrences. At present I am discussing seriously the Catholic faith with Father Kipka, the Chaplain of this hospital, and reading several books he has given me concerning the Sacred Heart and other mysteries. Also, I am reading Guénon and Schuon whose books in French I have obtained. No more room on this card—let me tell you quickly that I have a great deal of thankfulness for the way I have been brought up and I love you, both of you, very much.

Love,
Chris

Letter from Chris to Blackwell's.

June 8, 1969

Blackwell's
Broad Street
Oxford, England

Dear Sirs:

Please excuse the tardiness of payment. I was in the hospital for several months.

I would like to obtain copies of the following works, if you can locate them:

Gnosis: Divine Wisdom, by Frithjof Schuon
The Transcendent Unity of Religions, by Frithjof Schuon (Faber 1953)
Spiritual Perspective and Human Facts, by Frithjof Schuon
Language of the Self, by Frithjof Schuon (Ganesh 1959)
The Reign of Quantity and Signs of the Times, by René Guénon (Luzac)
The Crisis of the Modern World, by René Guénon (Luzac) 2 copies

212

The Symbolism of the Cross, by René Guénon—3 copies
East and West, by René Guénon—2 copies
Thank you.

> Sincerely,
> Christopher E. Jens

Letter of Chris.

> June 9, 1969

Dear Folks,

Enclosed is a bill for three books that I ordered from England which Mrs. D brought out to me tonight. They are books that I am delighted to have and I am hoping you will not mind paying for them for me. I surely appreciate the financial assistance that I can count on you for, and consider it a real blessing.

Doctor T. says I only have a couple of weeks to go. He has given me ground privileges which I am using fairly frequently. Right on the edge of the grounds is a little stream with a couple of trees and bushes growing by it. In the trees is a non-stopping chorus of some sort of swallows with long two-pointed tails, and hovering over the stream are a number of remarkably beautiful dragon flies with scarlet bodies and luminous wings. It is a great pleasure to sit there and commune.

I do not as yet have plans for when I get out of here, so I can't give much hint—I have been considering everything from going home (coming home) to being an apprentice woodworker at Goodwill Industries, to going back to General Hospital to work, to going back to school to learn pharmacy, joining the Catholic Church and possibly eventually becoming a contemplative (monk) and many other things. At any rate I am praying to God that He lead me in the path that will most please Him, and that will allow me to become a decent person, which is one of my goals.

I have many friends in this hospital, and I bet I'll sort of miss them when I get out! There has been a great deal of rapport shared in many directions.

Goodbye for now. Thanks for everything.

> Love,
> Chris

213

Letter from Mrs. D., Chris's very kind and concerned landlady, to Lee and Art.

June 11, 1969

Mr. & Mrs. Jens,

Thank you for the rent check. I was out to see Chris several nights ago and he looks and feels marvellous. He expressed to me his appreciation of the wonderful help and understanding you have given him during his hospitalization.

We are looking forward to once again having him on our block.

C.D.

Letter to Lee and Art from Dr. Tomasek, Chris's psychiatrist in Texas.

June 13, 1969

Dear Mr. and Mrs. Jens,

I received your card and note this morning and would like to comment to you about the fact that your son Chris has again taken up religion as a major topic.

He was thinking of woodworking and pharmacy up until this past week. After he has spent considerable time with Father K., Chaplain at Holy Cross Hospital, he has become more interested in religious interests than anything else.

As you know I plan to keep him in St. Joseph's next week and dismiss him on Friday, June 20. I have asked him to plan to see me on a twice-a-week basis so I may be able to follow him and work with him in therapy. He is agreeable to this.

There are those people at the hospital working with Chris who feel that he is getting more religion than they feel he needs. I have encouraged Chris to think of other subjects as well as religion and to put off any major decisions for at least a few weeks.

I will be writing you next week after he has been discharged.

Sincerely yours,
W. M. Tomasek, M.D.

Letter from Chris to family.

Dear Folks,

This will be a fairly hard letter to write for I am going to try to express some somewhat complex matters.

I received your letter of Wednesday which expressed some concern over my reading Guénon, and interest in how my plans are shaping up, both short term and long term.

First, you spoke of the correlation between my avidly reading Guénon and going into the hospital. The truth of the matter is that my going into the hospital correlated to the following:

1. My realization that manipulating little creatures and their environments was in direct contradiction to my love and natural feeling for them, and hence my dropping out of Graduate School.

2. My avid reading of the Bible, other religious and traditional scriptures, and Guénon, who says nothing different than the scriptures but simply goes into greater details of some of the principles mentioned in the scriptures.

3. My faith that there is a remarkable something going on in this most extraordinary world, and an avid desire to know more about it.

4. My avid desire to become as decent a person as possible.

5. A prayer which became tears, then more and more intense tears, then tears by which I was drawn upward and at the very height of it all—a union and a flowing into an "immense internal expanse" which left no doubt that it was God.

6. The beginning to hear "hidden" and deeper than "everyday" meanings, sometimes profound, sometimes disappointing, sometimes downright scary in the things people, radio songs, magazines and newspapers, etc., said. Thus you can see that my going into the hospital correlated to a good deal more than Guénon only. In my explanation it correlated to my conversion, followed by a confrontation with the adversary (Satan) who took me by surprise, in my weakness. I am praying with all my might that I will gain the strength to "withstand future attacks" from the adversary.

This is where I am right now. As to my future plans, I have done a great deal of thinking . . . first of all I have been doing a good deal of talking with a fine man—Father K., the Chaplain of the hospital—and I am, at present, studying carefully some of the Catholic literature to see if I could honestly and with good conscience become a Catholic. I am pretty sure that I can. At any rate, I have discovered that what I really want to do, with all my heart, is nothing other than to learn and study religious doctrine (as well as "traditional" doctrine) and try to improve my relations with God, and people. Father K. and I talked about this for a while, and he suggested some six or so universities which are strong on religion and religious doctrine. I have sent away to them for information, catalogs, and applications forms. I believe that after the summer I would surely like to attend one of them. And as for the summer itself, I would simply like to take it free and easy, talk to friends, priests, etc., make a beginning on the gigantic number of books I have obtained, do a lot of praying, communing, maybe become a Catholic (if I am not one already!). I feel that I am running towards almost completely, and only slightly am I running away.

At any rate, to do these things I would need your support financially and would like your support mentally and spiritually. Please let me know how you feel.

With much love (and thankfulness for all the aspects of my upbringing).

Chris

P.S. Doc T. says I will go home* Friday. Also, would like to spend some time in Glen Ellyn, if possible, this summer if it works out. See you soon.

Letter from Chris to Art.

June 15, 1969

Dear Dad,

I learned that today was Father's Day so I thought I'd drop you a little note wishing you a happy one—a little late!

I haven't had a cigarette now for three days, so it looks like I may be quitting again!

I've told you about most of the news previously, so I'll simply renew to you my thankfulness to both you and Mother for my being alive, loved and supported in many ways. May God continue to bless us and have mercy!

Love,
Chris

Summer, 1969

June, 1969

While he was hospitalized, the girl who had fallen in love with him at his job visited him regularly and brought him gifts. He seemed quite fond of her. She told us, "You have a wonderful son."

---

*To his room in Austin.

216

In June, after a month in the state hospital and three months in the private hospital, he was released. We went to Texas to help him get reorganized. He had been having some difficulty with the girl. Evidently she felt very possessive by now. She had to be hospitalized for one of her emotional upsets. He wanted to be relieved of the problem. We had felt uncomfortable about her, for fear of a possible pregnancy since she apparently adored him, though we had no special reason to believe there had been intercourse.

She had been an extremely deprived girl, having been in foster homes that were allegedly full of wickedness. She was far from stable, and with Chris as unstable as he was, it did not seem to be a desirable situation. Now, as he was leaving the hospital, he wanted to escape her. We didn't know exactly why. He suggested that he come home with us in order to get away from her. We felt that was not a good reason to leave, simply to escape, and that if he wanted to end the relationship it was only fair to tell her so. As a result, he stayed in Texas. How he managed the severing of relations I don't know, except that she finally told him she never wanted to see him again.

He moved back into his room which was beautifully clean due to his wonderful landlady. He expressed some fear of going into it because of the antique wooden cross he had bought with the alchemical symbols on it which evidently held great meaning for him. The weekend with him was pleasant. We took a long ride into the country and he showed us some favorite spots. When we finally took him back to his room because we had to leave, we stood for a few moments on the sidewalk with him. I noticed a young man and woman standing on the corner leaning toward each other, their arms around each other, seemingly holding each other up. The man turned out to be Chris's great friend, Larry, who took drugs and was obviously stoned; the woman was someone Larry had met when *he* was a patient at the state hospital. Chris and Larry embraced. As a result of our meeting, we were asked if we could take the woman home, and Larry to the home of another of their friends who was deeply absorbed in "traditional" religious study. We did both. The last we saw of Chris that weekend was he and Larry walking with their arms around each other up the path to the home of the friend. We did not feel very comfortable about the relationship. While Larry was extremely intelligent, he was not only deep into drugs, but he was a promoter of Chris's extremist ideas, encouraging his study of Guénon, whom we had come to fear (because Guénon put the stamp of approval on Chris's hatred of the world as it is; and because he encouraged Chris's belief in the power of evil). It was not that we believed there was no evil in the world, but we did not worship "Satan" by believing so much in his power that God was almost rendered

217

helpless before him, which is how Chris seemed to feel. (We also believed evil had its place in the Plan.)

He tried to get the job back in the hospital kitchen and was refused. He was told he was overqualified, but of course they were afraid of him.

Letter from Ralph to Chris.

July, 1969

Dear Chris,

I should have returned your letter right away, now I'm not sure where you are, whether or not you have the same home. It was a good letter, your last one. I'm not going to say that it sounded like you had both feet on the ground but I felt that you were really in the mood for communicating which made me feel good. I don't believe that you wasted a lot of time during your "wanderings"; you needed the time to coalesce your philosophy and sense of direction.

What hurts *me*, I think, is just the feeling of loneliness which I've found is impossible for me to avoid unless I'm in the protective womb of (figuratively speaking) a girl-friend. But that's a hassle of its own.

Are you going to return to school? Do you have any desire left to make a career of ecology or conservation? I still feel that you have a contribution to make there.

I'm thru with law school and happy about it. My last year I worked hard and got a lot out of it, but I couldn't have gone any longer at it. Now I'm working for O.G.O. in N.Y. as a legal counsel. It's interesting work, we're managing the bureaucracy arbitrating disputes in community action projects, etc., but I hate the G-S routine. It's only a summer job which I'm happy about. Micronesia and Hawaii fell through—Nixon fucked me up—but now I might go to Samoa (West) with the Peace Corps. I hope this doesn't fall through because I'm restless and I want to get away from pollutedly hung-up Americana. Samoa is probably just as bad in other ways, but maybe I'll enjoy myself for a while.

I'm leaving my girl for the Peace Corps and I'll probably lose her as a result; but God, I just couldn't settle down right now, although maybe in the future.

Let me know what you're going to do. It would be great to talk some time. I feel I haven't had a really good conversation in ages. By the way, I took the Massachusetts bar exam. I might settle down there some day.

Write soon, be happy.

Ralph

Letter from Art to Chris.

Dear Chris—

I was pretty disappointed not to have heard from you Sunday nite "after dark."* It is possible you called and we were not there as we didn't get home until a little after nine o'clock. But I sure wish you would persist as I feel we should be in touch at least once a week and I, of course, can't call you.

Have there been any changes in your routine? Are you considering any? Special student? Job? Etc., etc. Have you reached any decision about staying there or coming back to our vicinity as I suggested? Please let me hear from you not later than next Sunday nite "after dark."

Love,
Dad

Letter from Chris to family.

July 8, 1969

Dear Folks,

I thought I'd take some time out and write!

Each day is much like the other, extraordinarily hot, but sometimes really quite beautifully cool; somewhat windy, and usually clear nights.

As for my own activities, they have not been very numerous, a fact for which I am thankful. Most of the days are spent translating works out of French—Larry and I have spent a good deal of the last two weeks together translating a biography of René Guénon: *The Simple Life of René Guénon* by Paul Chacornac. Mostly Larry reads while I write in English the translation; we can only do about 10 or 12 pages a day that way. Lately, I haven't seen so much of Larry so I have been doing the translating myself. I can do about a page an hour, getting most of the meaning, which I am pleased with. Today I will finish the book. (Guénon's life was extraordinarily interesting, at least to me!)

I have been going downtown to a Catholic Cathedral (very fine!) for mass and have also attended the services of the Eastern Orthodox Church not far away. I find them both to be meaningful. The Orthodox service is wholly sung and chanted with responses from a small choir, with a good deal of incense burned. The Catholics do the same only at "high" mass evidently. The Catholics have changed so much in the past few years, having ceased to read and recite the mass in Latin.

---

*When he was supposed to call every Sunday.

This change I find "upsetting" because not only do I feel that the Latin increased the dignity and holiness of the service (as well as serving as a "link" to the middle-ages) but there are also some strictly "theoretical" reasons, and very important, for the use of Latin in the mass. These changes from the point of view of "progress" are disappointing; from the point of view of "adaptation" they are less so. I hope the second is the only one for which the church made her changes.

I saw Dr. Tomasek again today. I would be very interested to get to know him better.

Very little else is happening. I am doing a fair amount of walking and riding my bicycle, visiting the libraries, parks, etc., when not translating. I will probably go out and get a job in a week or so. I have been immensely enjoying the free time, given over to "scholarly pursuits"; at this time I would like to center my life around "scholarly pursuits."

I have decided that the best thing to do is to simply get a job and continue the studies that I have started already, for these at present are the ones that interest me most; and as far as I know the "traditional" point of view is taught very incompletely at universities and colleges. Thus I am going to continue my French studies of Guénon, about twenty works, as well as thirty or forty other works by various authors. At the same time, I plan to intensively study Christianity, its doctrines and history, and perhaps become a Catholic. Lastly, I may investigate some other languages, particularly Hebrew and Arabic. At any rate that seems to be enough to fill a year, at least, especially if I am working. Thus I may not actually enter school for half a year or more. I will see how things work out. That will also give me time to make the proper arrangements with a school.

There is a fig tree outside my door on which are numerous maturing figs. The first of the harvest are already ripened and are delicious.

I don't seem to have lost any weight yet, as none of my pants fit yet. I am quite over-weight compared to my usual and normal.

Goodbye for now,

Love,
Chris

Letter from Art to Chris.

July 16, 1969

Dear Chris—

After thinking about it a great deal (more or less constantly) and talking to Dr. Tom. Monday, we (Mom and I) have decided to ask if you would not consider coming back to this vicinity where perhaps we could be of greater help to you in your quest for independence. Our greatest wish for you is just that—*true independence*. And we feel, at this time, that your progress toward this goal is not as rapid as it should be.

Moreover, we feel that the environment you are in, and the persons you are spending most of your time with, as kind and nice as they may be, are not really able to be of constructive help to you—and you may not be a particularly good influence on them.

If you came back to this vicinity, you could have your own place, as you now have, perhaps in one of the nearby towns, if you preferred; where you could come and go as you wish, eat and sleep as you wish; and come over to see us when you felt the need to talk to us or to get some guidance or assistance with your problems; or some help toward a more ordered and disciplined life, in which you would resume responsibilities to and closer relationship with other people—all other people—on a regular basis.

I would be happy to come down for a couple of days. We could get all your things together and arrange for them to be sent back. We could, if you wish, start looking now for a suitable place around here, so it would be available for you immediately when you came back or as soon as you wanted to go to it.

In view of the fact that you must leave your apartment by Sept. 1,* won't you think about this and call us up soon so we can discuss it?

I know you will understand we are wishing to do only what is best for you.

Love,
Dad

August 1969

Chris did not wish to return home at this time.** We were now fully supporting him (albeit meagerly in the hope that he would be encouraged to try to get a job). Though he had spoken of getting a job, we knew of no effort to do so. He continued in his very expensive taste in books—all dealing with traditional teachings, alchemy, magic, occultism, mysticism.

We hoped Chris would go back to school and take at least one or two courses, so that he would not be so isolated, limited only to Larry and the few other "traditionals."

Guénon continued to be his favorite author.

---

*The house was to be leveled.
**He moved into a room in a building with grad students.

221

From Dr. Tomasek to Art.

August 8, 1969

Dear Mr. Jens:

Just a note to let you know that Chris is staying unchanged in his thinking. He has made no real progress, neither has he digressed any. His daily routine consists of translating French, sometimes visiting in the park; and a young lady named Jane* comes to visit three evenings a week. She is considerably older than Chris.

Chris's decision to attend the University is seemingly based on a soft touch—i.e., with him in school you will pay the bills and he won't have to go out and get a job. This allows for less involvement with people and a comfortable life.

I am planning to continue seeing him on a weekly basis and he seems interested in coming in on a weekly basis.

Sincerely yours,
W. H. Tomasek, M.D.

Letter from Art to Dr. Tomasek.

August 10, 1969

Dear Dr. Tomasek—

Thank you very much for your brief report of August 8.

We have been in reasonably close touch with Chris, speaking to him by telephone approximately once a week and in occasional exchange of letters and we agree with you that he isn't showing much change at this time, if any.

I am recently encouraged, however, by his decision to go to the university and resume the disciplines of some formal education; his last word to me was that he expected to take a couple of courses. We feel that the resumption of regular contact with more people might help him to develop other relationships and encourage him back to greater responsibility for himself.

I realize that the time may come when a complete cut-off of support may be the best therapy and assistance we can give him.

I guess I don't need to say that we have been completely unsuccessful in our efforts to bring him back to the Chicago vicinity or area, so we will just have to see how it goes.

Mrs. Jens joins me in expressing our thanks and good wishes.

Sincerely,
Arthur M. Jens, Jr.

---

*We never knew who she was.

Letter from Chris to Jeff.

Dear Jeff,

I thought I'd write you a little birthday note since I haven't seen you for so long.

I don't know exactly where to begin—maybe just tell you a little about what I'm doing.

I'm engaged in remarkably interesting studies at present. They have been basically the same for the past two years, interrupted, of course, (or should I say "besieged") by my sojourns in the hospitals (the exact nature of which I shall not go into for reasons of prudence). Basically, what I'm doing is trying to find out what's going on, and what my role in it is, God willing. As it turns out, the more one truly loses his biases and his "ignore-ance," the more one sees that the only place to seek the answers to such questions is from traditional teachings; and the more one studies the trad-itional teachings that are available (in our times and in our place, coming upon undistorted traditional teaching is truly rare and in many cases "pro-vidential"), the more one sees how they are all different forms of the same essential Truth (for the Truth is One and One only), and that Truth is really and truly "true," the more one sees that there are unbelievably remarkable things going on!

At any rate I have found only four or five trustworthy authors who expound traditional doctrines (René Guénon, Frithjof Schuon, Marco Pallis, Ananda K. Coomaraswamy, and perhaps Martin Lings and Titus Burckhardt) in western languages; and as yet I have found no trustworthy translations of the Hindu Doctrines, or any other Eastern doctrines for that matter (although there is some value in some of these translations that exist). Even the best of translations would still be lacking many things such as the numerical values of words, the sounds, and even some ideas which are untranslatable. Hence to truly study the doctrine one ought to learn the language. But the above authors and the translations that exist are surely enough to get one started!

That all is a quick summary of what I'm doing—reading, organizing, hoping and praying.

And if you get the chance, you might write and tell me what's going on in your world.

Love,
Chris

Letter from Jeff to Chris.

Dear Chris,

I've never been a writer of letters, but I realize how self-centered I've been in the matter of communication with you. I imagine you feel by now that I hardly recognize your presence in Austin. I'm sorry for the impression I've given, but it isn't the correct one. I think of you quite often, but, of course, how are you to know that? I'm sorry, ashamed, for my absence in your life; my actions have not been brotherly to you, at a time when possibly you need them most. I have been overly absorbed in myself as of late, too "busy" to take in the accounts of others, which is the main business of life. This will change, hopefully, as time passes. Thank you for the note on my birthday; it is always good to hear what your feelings on our lives are.

Love,

Jeff

Fall, Winter 1969

Fall, 1969

The one course he signed up for was history of the papacy. He went to one class, decided he did not like it at all, that it would disturb his "well ordered life of study" and dropped out with my permission.

Every day Chris went to mass at the Catholic church. Later he decided that the Greek Orthodox church was more traditional, and that the Catholic church was making too many changes. He continued to study a great deal. Larry had left and evidently his main contact with humanity was riding his bicycle to the park and watching the people; and conversations with his landlady who took a beautiful interest in him which we greatly appreciated. Her teenage daughter was enamored of him.

Letter from Chris to family.

Nov. 11, 1969

Hello,

I thought I would send along some notes on some important Christian words that have been so abused as to have been almost totally inverted, and have come to mean nearly the opposite of what they truly mean.

First is forgiveness. The Lord tells us that if a person sins against us, and then repents, we should forgive him immediately. And if he sins against us seven times, and repents seven times, we should forgive him each time. Thus true forgiveness means to hold fast against another's error until such time as he shall repent, at which time you thank the Lord and bless the repented sinner who has found his way back to the Path.

That is a far cry from modern "forgiveness" which is no more than a sort of nebulous "disposition" that one assumes whereby one does not even bother to call another unto repentance. And if a person does not have this "laziness," and does bother to call others unto repentance, he is told to be more "forgiving."

Similar remarks hold for the word "understanding." A person who does understand and know will call those who are in error unto repentance, and he is qualified to do so by the very fact that he does understand. And yet such a person is commonly accused of not having any "understanding," and told to be more "understanding"!

As for the word "peace," it has come through various deviations to be a correlative of war. In truth, "peace" has no opposite, being one of the attributes of God, who is without opposition or contradiction. However, "peace on earth," which is a reflection of God's peace, has for an opposite disharmony and disequilibrium—in short, disorder. When disorder arises among the peaceful, it must be eliminated in order to restore the balance which is "peace." One of the traditional means to do this is by a holy war. War is only legitimate when it is a reflection of the Greater Holy War, the war against the enemies that a man bears within himself. When war is thus a "lesser holy war," then, and only then, is it legitimate; and it is thus a "tool" of peace whereby disorder is restored to order and peace. True warfare, it might be added, with its discipline and hierarchy, is one of the most obvious manifestations of order (which is nearly synonomous with peace) that there is. Modern war, however, is surely a far cry from traditional war, and is only another manifestation of the disorder that has spread into every domain of human activity.

There are many other words and notions that have similarly become "twisted" among which are love, religion, knowledge, etc., but I'm getting tired.

Things have never been better for me, for I am filled with hope and have been given a privilege and a freedom rarely given to men of our age—that privilege and freedom is that I can confess with all my heart, and all my mind, and all my strength that I love and worship the Lord, our God Jesus Christ the Redeemer and Savior, incarnate of the Holy Spirit and Virgin, and that I await the terrible Day of our Lord with prayers and trembling. And I might add, that this Faith is not the "blind faith" of the moderns, but on the contrary due to the numerous and glorious lights which I have been and am receiving, which are rectifying my faulty vision. And this "blind faith" with which the religious are accused by the profanes, is really an irony, for it is precisely the faithless who are blind.

Love,
Chris

"He that doeth sin is of the Devil." 1 John 3:8

Letter from Chris to family.

November 29, 1969

Dear Folks,

I believe it is high time to clear up certain confusions in what regards our family, and particularly, my relations with you. It should have been done long ago really, but there are, perhaps, many good reasons why it hasn't been done yet.

First of all, I recall that some while back you expressed the opinion that somehow I "blamed" you or somehow held you responsible for my problems. This is not and never was the truth, and in fact is the opposite, in some sort, of the truth. The truth is that I feel and always have felt a deep and profound thankfulness both for the fact that you brought me into the world and that you gave me all the things that you did give me. The reason is that I deeply like myself, I love being, I love all that this being entails. Hence you can see how ridiculous it would be for me to "blame" the very agents through whom my being was accomplished in this world for anything fundamental at all. "Blame" at most is but very relative and applies only to special limited circumstances, never to anything basic or fundamental for which "blame" is no longer applicable. "Blame" also entails a certain moralistic overtone, completely foreign and strange to my nature, for I think in terms of truth or error, correctness or incorrectness, right actions or mistakes without, at least in principle, allowing any element of the sentimental (or moralistic) to join in, save joy over truth, and sometimes, anger over error. Thus at most, I took it upon myself sometimes to point out what I considered to be errors on your part, both in regard to your own relationship and in your relationship with your children, and myself in particular. But I in no way wished to "blame" you for them; I brought them up solely in order to get rid of them, to bring the errors and their effects to naught, as happens when an error is uncovered, shown up for what it is, and reflected upon for a time. And that was all my intentions ever were. Hostilities arose only because you considered that I was "blaming" you (or because you didn't think they were errors) and also because

226

of my insubordination, no doubt. The former was a mistake but the latter has some grounds in reality. Rather than becoming angry you should simply have pointed out my "insubordination." All this is to say that I don't and never did "blame" you for anything whatsover—at most I have recognized, as I said, what I consider to be errors and have broached them to you only hoping that they would vanish into the nothingness that they truly are, and that all error truly is, when it is discovered. The fact is that, quite the contrary to blaming you for anything, I have only thankfulness for all the positive things you have done, and as far as the errors and negative things go, they are, at least for me, as if they were not; for I have discovered their airiness. There are still, however, some things that as yet I do not understand, and, although they appear as errors, I have yet to discover them as such; but we don't need to go into that right now.

At any rate, I love you both very much, both because of the beauties which you each are the expression of, and because you are the vehicles through whom I am in this world and through whom I have received many valuable teachings and inheritance. By means of these marvelous gifts I hope to get back to my Lord, who commands all of my love, even that for my parents.

Love,
Chris

P.S. Dad—The checks came. Also, if you would prefer, you can combine the checks into one from now on, sending $50 checks twice a month or $100 checks once a month, whatever you will prefer (along with $48 checks for rent). I might take this opportunity to express again my gratitude for these checks. The results of the freedom that they provide me with are truly prodigious and profound. I know you have some qualms, but let me assure you that I am working long and hard, and with definite plans and goals, and that I know what I am doing. Aside from these benefits, perhaps some day I will be able to serve as a channel, God willing, for benefits and blessings of many different orders. This, while being only secondary to the interior work and the battle against error and limitations, is still not to be neglected and shows that there is a "practical" side also, aside from the beauty and glory, and blessedness.

By the way, I thought you might be interested—I have obtained a key to the Orthodox Church here and I have permission to use their organ. I'm putting my piano lessons to some use now. I will be the substitute organist when there are none others. (The regular organist went away somewhere.) I have been working at it for 2 weeks and am getting better. The hymns are simply beautiful and one can allow himself to yield to them completely in the perfect faith that they are a direct expression, in musical mode, of the highest Truths, since they have come down to us from the ancient

Byzantine Empire, a time when men had not yet immersed themselves so deeply in matter; and hence were still in possession of those Truths that are concealed to all those who "think they can only know what their senses bring to them," in spite of the obvious falsity of such an assertion.

Mom—I got your note and enjoyed it very much, although I was sorry that you felt mine to be impersonal since the ideas expressed in it came from my heart.

I know you enjoy buying things for people, and I appreciate the thoughtfulness that I might enjoy making my room "Christmasy" as indeed I used to. You were correct, however, in sensing that my interests do not run quite along those lines at present. I know that it must be somewhat frustrating for you, since I know you like to find things that are meaningful to other people. Therefore, let me jot down a few things that you might keep your eyes open for, since they would be meaningful to me, and alas!—nothing is left of my entire savings, I have spent it all on necessary books. Here is my list for possible gifts.

1. All books on Art, Chinese, Indian, Moslem, Japanese, Egypt, mediaeval, North and South American Indian, etc., etc. All traditional art. The only art I am not interested in is artwork of the Renaissance or in the West, which no longer remain true to traditional principles. Also, the fewer words and the more pictures there are the better, since I have almost no interest at all in what the modern commentators have to say; at most it is often pure trivia, if indeed it is not actually subversive.

2. All doctrines and writings of the saints, particularly those from the 1st through the 14th centuries. Even more particularly of value to me are volumes which contain the original Latin or Greek along with the translation, but this is not essential to me.

3. All books concerning Masonry, particularly the Masonic doctrines and writings themselves, but also descriptive.

4. All Sacred Scriptures from all countries, and you don't have to worry about "repeats" because a number of different translations are valuable, each having its own merits and demerits.

5. All mediaeval or early Christian works (1st—15th centuries) with translations alone or with the original Latin and Greek.

6. All works concerning Alchemy.

7. Anything that, in its origin is "traditional"—that is, originates from, and is a manifestation of, the Traditional spirit, no matter where.

That is a pretty good list to start with! I also have a rather large number of specific books which I will buy some time, but at present cannot afford because of their rather exorbitant cost. If you would like to know what these are let me know.

Love,
Chris

Paper written by Chris for Art.

November, 1969

Some reflections concerning the quotation from St. Ignatius of Loyola:
". . . every good Christian ought to be more willing to give a good interpretation to the statement of another, than to condemn it as false . . ."*

Because we do not know the context of the statement we do not know to what degree it is true. It is surely not an absolutely true statement, but is at most a relative truth. The reasons for this are obvious:

A true Christian, by very definition, must acknowledge that Christ is a "divine messenger" and an "incarnation of God," that God *is* and that the teachings of the Scriptures are written under the inspiration and guidance of God.

It is therefore obvious that anyone who states either outright or by implication that any of the teachings of the scriptures are false, or that Christ is not a "divine messenger" or that God *is not*, has directly opposed himself to Christianity. Thus, (and I am sure St. Ignatius would agree) every good Christian has no alternative but to condemn as false such statements. If, in fact, he did not condemn such statements as false, he would not even himself be a Christian for he would not be denying the negation of Christianity and, hence, to some degree at least he would be accepting this negation.

I might add by way of note that these are the fundamental *principles* of Christianity; thus when a person claims to "believe in a Christian principle" and yet still denies any of the above mentioned fundamental principles, this is none other than a flat contradiction and an indication of the confusion of him who has stated this. This so called "Christian principle" that one hears about so frequently these days is none other than a nebulous morality no longer attached to any superior and transcendant principle and constitutes a "residue" of Christianity in truth, sort of like a body which the being has abandoned.

To get back to the main topic, the denial of these fundamental Christian principles can be either outright or else implicit in a statement. The outright denials are of course easy to spot and it is the implicit denials that provide

---

*Art thinks he probably had sent this quotation to Chris.

a great deal of confusion because they are more "hidden." However, whenever one reflects long enough on a certain statement and discovers in it the implicit denial of a traditional truth, he should, being a true Christian, denounce that statement as false, just as he should do for an outright denial of that principle. And, I might add, almost every modern conception and tendency can be shown to be such an implicit denial of traditionally taught principle Truths, if one cares to go to the bottom of the matter, rather than to keep himself to outward appearances.

Thus, as has been shown, St. Ignatius' statement surely does not hold good and probably was not intended to in regard to anti-Christian statements, which include a good many of the statements made in modern times. It remains, however, to consider the occasions on which St. Ignatius' statement does hold good. It is obvious from what has been said that only if a statement is not anti-Christian, then should a Christian be willing to "give a good interpretation" to it, and will affirm all of the essential Christian principles and is in no sense anti-Christian. The "so-called Christians" are often anti-Muslim, however, and it is to these that St. Ignatuis' statement is most fitting since it is these very "Christians" themselves who make a statement that is truly anti-Christian, namely, that the Muslim Doctrine is false, whereas in truth it is non-Christian.

To summarize: falsehood, as well as errors when they can be shown to be so, must be denounced and condemned. Surely no one would disagree with that. This includes all orthodox traditional doctrines and statements.

Letter from Chris to Lee.

December 1, 1969

Dear Mom,

I got your box of Christmas things today and was deeply touched. I hung the hanging things out near the steps leading up to our apartments and everybody will be reminded that "The Season is at hand!" The candles I will be able to use all year long, at the sides of my wooden cross, somewhat like on an altar, and am glad to have them. The nativity scene music box is charming but for various reasons I think it might find better use somewhere else. I have in mind two little girls, daughters of Addie C., who would be absolutely delighted by it, I'm certain, just as I used to be by our music boxes at Christmas. But the best gift was none of those things—the best gift came while I was opening them and pondering them— and I saw my dear mother bustling about in the stores and in the bitter cold—I saw her searching for gifts for everybody, things that would be just right for each—and I saw how happy she was, happiness blemished only by her one stray son who, for some reason, won't be home for Christmas! Oh, my dear Mother, how I love our Christmases, the snow, the crystal clear stars, the tree, the ornaments, Good King Wenceslas, and the family. Surely you must know that I love Christmas more than anyone in the family, yourself, perhaps, excepted. It is that very love kindled in my heart by our home and family that has led me to the very spot where I am now. It is that very love which is growing each day in richness, fullness, yes, in plenitude so that more and more and closer and closer do I come to a perpetual Christmas, a continual birth of the Lord, our Lord, by the action of the grace of the Holy Spirit working in the pure and chaste womb of the Blessed Virgin, our most Beautiful Lady. Would that I could bring all of them with me, all the beings, all the Christmas shoppers, and all my family, but—praises be to God—they each have their own life to lead, and their own "law" to fulfill. And I must fulfill mine.

Thank you for all those wonderful gifts.

Love,
Chris

Letter from Ralph to Chris (written on a Christmas card from Samoa).
December 22,1969

Dear Chris,

I went and joined the Peace Corps. I am a Peace Corps lawyer here. I remember your skepticism when I first told you I wanted to travel out here. You were right. I wandered out here chasing fond dreams of paradise—I found a friendly place far from home that looks disturbingly like the visions of paradise I had in my imagination; but it is something quite different from what I bargained for. I'm not happy—but I'm learning, and hopefully growing a lot. I've been almost thrown out of the Peace Corps three times so far because of rebellious activity. Viva la revolution!

Take care and let me know where you are.

Your friend,
Ralph

Winter, Spring, 1970

Chris had had many years of piano lessons. We were pleased that he had now taught himself to play the organ at the Greek Orthodox Church in Austin well enough to replace the organist. He enjoyed it so much and we were so glad he was being productive. He spoke often of being baptized.

231

Somehow, he held off. He did not say in which church, the Greek or the Catholic, which he also continued to attend.

For Christmas, he had not sent us separate gifts, but wrote a paper for us all on the true meaning of various Christmas traditions.

We continued to try to stay as optimistic as possible about him, and to believe that he was at last "finding himself" after so many changing views through the years.

We were in good touch with him by 'phone and letters throughout the winter.

Letter from Chris to Ralph.

Winter, 1970

Dear Ralph:

I got your Christmas card and was enchanted—a message from the isle of palm trees.

What a pity that you are not happy. It is strange that someone unhappy and not at peace should be a representative of something called the Peace Corps. But then I have the slight suspician that the Peace Corps itself is not all that "peaceful." Far from it, as proves its presence in Samoa. Here is a people of pure strain and pure tradition on islands of beauty, with grass homes and flowers and birds and mountains. A people truly at peace, without any needs, at perfect equilibrium with the cosmos. But modern profane Western man, dressed in the sheep's skins of "Progress!"; "Civilization!"; "Peace!"; etc., comes in like a ravening wolf, gobbles up and destroys all the traditional institutions; that is to say, all the means by which true peace and equilibrium can be "gotten and holden"; substituting for it a lot of artificial and illusory needs, bulldozing over God's wild gardens, and imposing in their place either trim lawns all tidy and neat and without a grass blade out of place; or else garbage pits and junk yards full of scrap iron and vile smelling poisons. Would that they had left God's wild gardens! Finally, they beat into the heads of their victims a whole standardized series of falsehood and half-truths; that is to say, modern education, that formidable weapon by which children of God are transforming living mouths which once burst forth with spontaneous praise and thanksgiving and love into dead mouths which recite certain pat phrases and standardized conventions in no wise reflecting the true nature of things; and, rather than giving life and understanding, on the contrary, take them ever further away. Truly "modern profane education" is just another form of the bulldozer.

Ralph, repent and turn from these "people," these beasts, and make a

232

pilgrimage to the true Isle of God, that Garden of Eden wherein grows the Tree of Life with twelve fruits (said to be a palm tree, by some!). Take no more part in their works of darkness. Become again one of the elect people of Israel. "I will be their God and they will be my people." For modernism in all its forms is death.

Love,
Chris

Letter from Ralph to Chris.

Winter, 1970

Chris,

Thank you so much for your words. If you knew how much they meant to me I believe you would feel truly gratified. I know that you sent them with the intention of giving me much more than just a "good feeling" that my dearest friend from college still thinks of me. You are trying to win my heart to a truer way—to convert me, if you wish, from the path of darkness. I know you appreciate the confusion I feel but also a potential I have not yet realized. I am truly gratified that you feel I have the potential to be of the elect people.

I was being truthful when I told you I was not happy here. But Chris, I do not want you to think that I have just been a sheep led around by the halter by these corrupt venal swine that call themselves Peace Corps staff. I have made their lives difficult and unsettled whenever I could. If it means anything we have already brought most of the staff to ruin. Right now I am on "probation" and will probably be kicked out of this country soon. I am, of course, ready to go at anytime—but first I do hope to continue my education here.

Chris, we each have our way—that is a truism, almost trite. You have found your way, but you were always so much closer to what was basic to your self. Of course that is one reason why I and so many others are so profoundly attracted to you.

I have much further to go to find myself. This has been my "wandering" in a sense. I have met many very wonderful people who took an interest in me and who have tried to teach me. I have seen a wonderful traditional culture and watched it being destroyed. Your sneaking suspician is so perceptive. The "Peace Corps" is a travesty of the word peace and of the valuable in people. The Peace Corps staff and the "star" volunteers hold the real Samoans in the most complete and total contempt. But they can get away with it because by this time the Western imperialists have built a client caste that will do their dirty work. What can I do to destroy this!

233

There is only one way, I feel, be true to myself. There will soon be much death and destruction in the world, of this we have to be certain. And although I am afraid, I suppose we must welcome it. We cannot expect to fight God without being hurt ourselves. I am only glad that I was born late enough and had the good fortune to call modernity, especially its education, crap. Although I at times hate to admit it, I have to agree with you, modernity in its present form is the most unbelievable, excruciating death—but I don't completely despair for the future. Haven't there been valid cultures built before? What about the ancient Minoan culture and the true cultures of love that once flourished in the Marquesas Islands, in Yap, the Eskimoes? Maybe we can return to their form of love.

Chris—thank you so much for your rejuvenating letter. Please send me further guidance. Don't despair for me. I'll be leaving soon. I'm not one of these unhappy people that must constantly wander. And God help me, I don't believe I'm an imperialist. I came here to fulfill a wanderlust. That wanderlust thrust me into a situation that illuminated the excrement that we call Westernism. Your words really hit home. I felt that they illuminated thoughts that I had only half articulated. But where do we go from here? Is there a communal solution or must we each follow our own way until enough of us come together and move the world. Must we be Jeremiahs and welcome the impending doom or can we avert it?

Peace and love,
Ralph

P.S. At the risk of sounding redundant I want to thank you again for loving me enough to condemn me for sticking with a situation that I am really not happy with. Other people who love me, Lennie and Patty (my girl), have gently suggested that I leave, but have not had the courage and audacity to condemn me outright. Chris, your letter just might push me into doing something very important.

Letter from Chris to family.

January 19, 1970

Dear Folks,

Here are some notes I would like you to send on to Tim and Debbie, Grandma, and Tänte. I have misplaced the addresses of the last two, and I thought you would be interested in the ideas expressed in the letter to Tim and Debbie, as well as Grandma.* (Tänte's is the same.)

I have played the last three services of the Church. I am almost mistakeless and the hymns have been of the greatest spiritual benefit to me in a

---

*This one is missing.

234

number of ways, doctrinally, as well as "technically." I will probably be baptized and confirmed soon. I have talked with the priest and I as yet have a few uncertainties. I am proceeding with caution and prudence, for receiving Christ and the Holy Spirit is no small affair. One must be sure to be properly prepared lest "the partaking of Thy Body, O Lord Jesus Christ, which I, though unworthy, presume to receive, turn against me in a judgment and condemnation." (From the Catholic Liturgy.)

I am very well and at present reading the Epistles of Paul again as profoundly as I can. They are completely full of the most remarkable revelations, if one takes the time and concern to study them carefully.

Love,
Chris

Letter from Chris to Tim and Debbie.

January, 1970

Dear Tim and Debbie:

I received your gift and was glad to hear from you. The scripture you have cited is a fine one,* and one of which the majority of our contemporaries, having turned from God and His sacred tradition, haven't the least comprehension. Indeed the "bourgeois," if he has any concept of joy at all, finds it in having everything "neat and tidy." How the bourgeois loves his "trim lawn." The "flower children," on the other hand, try to find their joy in utter chaos, complete with self-induced illusions and a certain music which literally drives every thoughtful pondering from their mind and renders impossible any true contemplation. Truly the "hippy" idea of joy is an unbearable noise coupled with a chaos of flashing lights and pictures, while undergoing drug induced delusions!

The truth is that true joy can only be found in Reality. Neither the happy chaos, nor the bourgeois tidiness has much at all to do with Reality. Reality is neither a trim lawn, as the bourgeois suppose; nor an incoherent junk yard, as the hippies suppose; but it is a most marvelous wild garden, full of butterflies, flowers, bees, and habitations for all creatures, as well as grasses, thorns, and stones. Reality is a most complex, but always coherent unity with multiple aspects and dimensions, most of which, though conceivable, are perfectly unimaginable and can only be gotten with the intellect through the grace of God and spiritual "exercise." One such exercise is making a joyful noise unto God. This can be done by prayer, by hymn,

---

*They had made him a banner saying "Make a joyful noise unto the Lord." Psalms 100:1.

by sacred music, sacred poetry, by continual recitation of the divine name, etc., and is intimately bound up with the traditional science of rhythm, totally unknown to the moderns who think that praying and singing hymns are just sentimental games of naive people. This is not without irony since to think such takes an incredible naivety.

But the scripture itself tells us what a joyful noise ought to be: "Make a joyful noise unto God . . ." Say to Him, "How terrible are thy deeds" Ps. 66:1 & 3.

Love,
Chris

P.S. I hope you can find your way to the R.C. Church, or to the Eastern Orthodox Church, for it is only through God's traditions that reality can best be "gotten and holden"; and these are the only two authoritative traditions in the West, all the others being deviations or modernist inventions. I might also add that traditional affiliation offers salvation after death, if one has not attained it during his life. These and similar matters are of no small import.

Letter from Chris to Lee.   January, 1970

Dear Mom,

Remembering it is soon to be your birthday I decided to write you a short note . . .

I am very well, thanks be to God. Love conquers all; that is to say God, the merciful and just, who is Love, conquers all those who oppose themselves to him and hence lead many of his sheep astray, by punishing them and destroying them; and He conquers all those who ally themselves to Him by winning them with His beautitudes until they *are* no longer, but rather Christ in them, in the plentitude of the Love of Jesus Christ, "the length, the breadth, the heighth and the depth of the Love of Jesus Christ." "Perfection, which surpasses all understanding" and fills all things. Praise be to you, O Christ.*

Love,
Chris

----

*These quotations must be from traditional doctrines.

Letter from Art to Chris.

Dear Chris—

Am more or less on the go all the time (only peace when I get home with Mom), and this will last for at least the rest of the year. We (F.S.J.) are committed to this program and I guess I can't (and really don't want to) quit at this stage. It's the same old thing—don't build commitments to other people unless you are ready to carry them out. Many people expect me to do just what I'm doing and would feel terribly let down if I stopped doing it.

We were thinking of your birthday and thought a little bonus check might help for something you especially want or need just now. So enclosed is $100. Happy Birthday! and love,

Dad

P.S. Jeff and 6 other members quit (were fired) from Phi Gamma Delta (naturally a controversy over principle) and he now lives at 120 Bartland St.; if you would like to write him, I think he could use a little friendly support at this time.

D.

Notes jotted down on a card by Chris, Winter, 1970.

A job providing food for peace and contemplation and food for the belly must:

1. Not be complicated.
2. I must feel pleased with it and not ashamed of it.
3. Not involve a lot of interrelationships with people.
4. Not involve any binding agreements that I cannot break if necessity should arise. No oath of allegiance binding forever unless I could find something to which I would want to bind myself. Reason: I fear I will lose much and gain little.
5. All this so I wouldn't have to be distracted any more.

Ideally, wrapt in eternal and everlasting bliss.

Ideally in this aim—a room, food as long as I need it, my books, no distractions.

Ideally—a guru, sitting at his feet.

I feel sorrow, guilt and fear around the people that I know. Fear because of possible irremediable ills. Are these irremediable ills? Can I get past them?

Do I want to get away from Austin? I would like to find a place of

237

peace where I can study—contemplate without continually being besieged by a lot of peculiar impulses.

I have never yet tried wholeheartedly to realize any specific possibility in all its developments and prolongations.

To become or not become.

I came to dislike, then to fear people, because they were doing things which were not in accord with my nature.

Letter from Chris to Karen.

February 20, 1970

Dear Karen,

I have thought about it for awhile and have decided to send you this gift for your birthday. It is a square, but certainly no ordinary one. It is the "simplest" of those that are commonly called "magic squares"; although the profundity of this application goes far beyond simple magic. The property of these squares is that all the horizontal, all the verticals, and the two diagonals add up to the same amount. In this case it is 15.

4	9	2
3	5	7
8	1	6

Love,
Prince Christopher Q Robin

Soon to become "His Majesty," if the Lord would will it. "Come, with thy crown and thy anointing oil, O Lord, Yea, Come Lord."

April, 1970

He was apparently happy in his studies and his music, when suddenly a message came through Dad's secretary. Chris was on his way home and would arrive the next day, Saturday. I asked her why he was coming; she said she did not know. He was to arrive, we thought, on the bus at 11 a.m. He was not on it. More worry. His father met the evening bus at 11 p.m. He *was* on it, but hard to find because he was in a 'phone booth, in an isolated corner of the station. Later (after his death) we found out that he had been making a 'phone call to the girl Karen. He asked if he could come to her in New York, because, "You are my last hope." She recognized that he was not himself but, bless her, she told him to come ahead (though she was engaged to another man). Even now I would die a little if I had to think about how she had refused him, and I am grateful that he died feeling wanted by her. However, he made no effort to get to her.

As soon as he and Dad walked in the house, I could feel Chris's hostility. Yet, he had written these notes: "1. Abandon books and 2. Be near to my family. Share with them and get their advice and help and be with them. 3. Do lathe work for a living, but live elsewhere if they desire."

He needed us—yet he was hostile, especially to me. We talked a long time, until about 2 a.m. He was very talkative.

It was obvious from our conversation that Chris was once more in a precarious condition. Also, he was extremely thin from weeks of fasting in the wilds. Dad said to me, "Lock your door tonight." (Dad and I had adjoining rooms.) The next morning we were relieved to find Chris still in the house. Once more it was necessary to talk about hospitalization. Chris remonstrated a bit, but soon gave in. It was sad that he was someone who was a possible danger to himself and others. We took Chris to the hospital that afternoon. He made no effort to get away. It was the same friendly, homey hospital where he had been before. Even his old suicidal girl friend was there, having once more made an attempt.

May 8, 9, 10, 1970

I was busy fixing an elaborate casserole—one of Chris's favorites—to have ready for the next day when he was to come home from the hospital. I felt quite happy and hopeful. During this stay in the hospital, which had lasted about two months, he had seemed very much like his old self. "Chris is the best I've ever seen him," Charlie, one of the aides, had commented. Other members of the staff agreed. We all felt that maybe Chris had finally made it through his chamber of horrors, had fought his way through to that integrated personality on which we had been pinning our hopes.

I thought about how just last Sunday, when he had been home for the final trial visit, he and I had had such a wonderful talk. That was the day (oh, God, what a horrible and great day) that one of our beloved cats was found dead by me in the morning—I can hardly bear to think of it now—in the clothes washer-dryer. (We had all heard the thumping when the machine was going through its cycle the night before, but assumed it was just Chris's tennis shoes which I had thrown in.)

Sometimes I think that Henry, the cat, had to be sacrificed so that Chris and I could have the wonderful talk in the nearby Arboretum, where we had gone, weeping, while Dad had prepared Henry for burial and dug the grave. Henry's death centered our thoughts on what was really important, what we really felt about people—and love—and death—and meaning—and how we all have our roles to play.

We parked the car and headed for the bench in back of the Thornhill Building where we could look out over the trees—how Chris had always loved trees!—and talked for about an hour. For *then,* there were only the two of us in the whole world. And it was good.

"Will you go to Mass this morning?" I asked. "There will be plenty of time." It was only about nine o'clock.

"I think so. I hope that young priest is there. I really like the things he says." I noticed how much his hair was thinning at his forehead—it really showed, here in the sunlight. His beautiful near-sighted eyes seemed to be trying to scan the distance.

Then he looked at me. "Oh, Mom," he exclaimed. "I love you!"

I smiled and touched his outstretched hand. "You'll be hating me in five minutes."* We both laughed.

He put his other hand over mine. "I always loved you, Mom." There were tears in his eyes.

Then, "Dad would be relieved, wouldn't he, if I chose suicide as my answer?"

Now I looked into the distance. It was not new to me, the idea of suicide; he had made those minor attempts, odd attempts which did not seem serious at all—breaking off the billiard cue and trying to push the jagged end into his temple; diving onto the bathtub drain; pushing the pen-knife into his abdomen. Then there had been what he had said when he had first quit school, "I thought of just lying down and giving myself back to God. But I thought of you and Dad and how it would make you feel." Oh, I knew he had it in his mind, that he had that possibility if his dilemma could not be solved any other way.

And I remembered that sad remark to me one recent Sunday after he had walked the four miles home from church. "God didn't give me the tools to be the person I want to be."

No, it was not new to me, this idea of suicide. I had learned to live with it. Now I answered, "Oh Chris, no, no, Dad wouldn't be relieved.

---

*When he projected to me, for instance, the role of the devouring dragon.

Just the other day, after he heard about the instant death of Bill Avery's son in that awful accident, he said, thankfully, 'We've still got Chris. We've had troubles, but we've still got him!'"

Suicide. Why didn't I right there and then fall on my knees before him and beg him, "Chris, Chris, you must not even think of such a thing!" Why did I not beseech him, "Don't do such a thing to *me*! I love you, I can't bear to think of life without you!" Why didn't I? Because deep down I had decided that he had a right to make his own choices without interference. He was sane now. He had never seemed more sane. Supposing I did beseech—and win? Supposing he gave in to me, loving me, not wanting to hurt me so, even though he really wanted to make that choice? How he would have hated me for forcing him! No, I *would* not interfere.

We walked back to the car hand in hand.

When we got home, Art was sitting in the back yard. I felt so sorry for him. Henry had been his favorite cat; there had been a special bond between them. I leaned over him and put my arms around him. "Poor Daddy," I whispered.

Chris put his arms around both of us. "Oh, my parents," he said, his voice breaking. I thought of that time he had said, "I can never be happy until you and Dad get together."

By folding us both in his arms, did he feel for a moment as if he were whole?

But now he was about to come home. As I simmered the diced green peppers and onions in butter for the casserole, I was not thinking of possible suicide, I was dwelling on how well he had seemed, how much he had been enjoying his woodworking in his basement "shop" here at home, of how now perhaps he could really get into woodworking as he had always dreamed of doing. At least the army would not be breathing down his neck—his "mental illness" freed him from that forever! I thought about how if it hadn't been for the draft, he probably never would have gone to graduate school, about which he had so many qualms, feeling that it would tempt that competitive, manipulative side of him that he hated so much, but could not resist. And how he could have been, perhaps, a happy woodworker in his shop, and never have broken down. And yet—and yet—it was something he *had* to face in himself, that dog-eat-dog side—better to face than repress. To take the gamble, even if he might lose.

The 'phone rang. It was Chris. "Hi, Chris! I'm just making your favorite pork casserole for tomorrow!"

"I'm coming home today!"

"But, Chris, I thought it was tomorrow morning."

"The doctor said I could come home today—this afternoon."

"But Dad won't be home till dinner-time. He'll want to be with me when we come to get you. This is a big occasion!" And somehow, I felt strangely uneasy about getting him by myself.

"I'm all signed out. I've got to come home *now*. They—," he hesitated for a second, "They've given my room to someone else," he pronounced convincingly.

I had to give in.

I picked him up about three. The aides and the nurses gathered round to wish him well, and it was evident that they were all immensely fond of him. "We'll miss you, Chris," said one pretty little nurse, and kissed him on the cheek, with tears in her eyes.

One aide called after him, as we went out the door, "Bet you feel great, Chris!"

"Well, pretty good," he answered. Pretty good? Only that? I worried a little.

On the elevator going down were two older people, a man and a woman. They were obviously feeling happy, and confided to us, 'We just found out that our brother doesn't have cancer after all!"

"How old is your brother?" Chris asked.

"Sixty seven."

"Sixty seven! I'm only twenty six, and I feel like an old man." I worried again.

We walked through the basement of the hospital, and then Chris said, "It's faster to the parking lot through the underground tunnel. I'll show you." There was no one in the tunnel, no one but us. I quickened my steps. I was afraid somehow. He seemed so well. And yet—I was afraid.

I took the forest preserve route home, the one that he loved. The apple trees had just come into their delicate pink buds. It was a perfect May afternoon, the kind that used to make Chris dance inside, but he did not seem very happy. "Don't you ever feel nervous just generally, Mom?"

"No, not often. Not any more."

"I can't imagine being like that."

"I guess I couldn't have either at your age, Chris. As you know, I had some really bad problems to get over, what with all my phobias. You can get over your fears, too. You have so much going for you. You're so intelligent, you've got so much charisma, wonderful health, and you're such a great looking guy." I smiled and reached for his hand.

His answer was, "I'm all positives on the outside, and all negatives on the inside."

Now I was really worried. I asked him if he felt he had been mentally ill. He answered, "I think I have been what people call mentally ill." It was a good answer.

As we drove up our long driveway lined with choruses of daffodils, through the trees all lacey with blossoms, Chris did not seem to notice the beauty. A pheasant dashed across in front of us, and the brown thrasher was singing his entire repertoire as we entered the house. A day for utter gladness, but I was growing more fearful by the minute. Chris seemed very nervous.

As soon as we got in the house, he paced around. I grew very frightened, being alone with him. I had never seen him quite like this. I said, "Chris, why did you leave the hospital? You don't seem ready to be home." He only paced harder. Then I said, "I'll take you back to the hospital." And he said, "Make it the state hospital. You can't pay out all that money any more." And I cried, "I don't *want* you to be in the state hospital!" I knew it too well, I had been a volunteer there for fifteen years. I could not bear to think of my son being there.

He left the room and ran up the stairs, ran down, went outdoors, came back. I was getting increasingly alarmed. The 'phone rang. It was my husband calling from the airport, saying he would soon be home. I quickly told him about Chris's agitation, and that I didn't know what would happen. "Come as quickly as possible. Chris is acting wildly," I whispered.

"It will take at least half an hour to get there." (It was an hour before he could make it through heavy traffic. I hate to think of what he went through, of the thoughts he must have had.)

Chris continued to race about the house. I debated over whether to lock myself in my room. Then I heard him rush out the front door again, and this time I knew somehow that I had to rush after him.

I followed him. "Chris!" I screamed. "Chris!" (We live far back from the road, no one else could hear me.) He paid no attention as he scaled the wall next to the driveway, a red gasoline can in his hand. I too scaled the wall (which I could never do normally) and chased him into the field near our house. I kept screaming "Chris! Stop! Stop!"

I saw him lift the can over his head, light a match and in a split second the flames started. He shouted, "Goodbye, Mom!" He fell to the ground in flames, and I reached him yelling, "Roll, roll, roll!" and for a minute he did, and then stopped. My dress was of nylon and I was afraid it would make more trouble, so I could not use it to smother the flames. I pulled up large weeds and beat at the flames. Finally the fire was out, but I knew it was too late.

Yes, I had felt he had a right to make his own choice. But when he chose to die, I tried to stop him.

I asked him to get up and walk to the house, which he did. He lay down on the floor in the kitchen. I called the hospital and asked them to get me an ambulance. "My son is terribly burned." I was told to wrap Chris in wet cloths. I soaked two tablecloths and wrapped them around him. "Are you in pain?" I asked. "No, it isn't bad," he answered. The nerve endings were gone. "I thought of the Buddhists," he said, referring to those monks who had sacrified their bodies in fire.

"I don't know how much longer we have," I said, "so I must talk now. Why did you do it?"

He replied, "I was afraid of what God would make me do." I did not dare ask him more. I was afraid he would say something that I could not bear to hear, something I might misunderstand, or misinterpret; and I might never be able to ask him more about it.

I ran up to the field, and it was still burning. I knew grass fires can be dangerous. I called the fire department. "There is a grass fire." The ambulance arrived. The driver and his helper looked at Chris. The driver exclaimed, "My God!" I told them I wanted to take him into the city—to the Northwestern Memorial Hospital. "Lady," the driver said. "I would advise a closer one."

I left notes for my husband. I sat in front with the driver and directed him to Central DuPage Hospital nearby. I was a zombie, I did not cry, I did not feel.

Chris was rushed to the emergency room. I waited in the other room. Art arrived. "What happened?" he asked, his voice hoarse. He went in to see Chris, and Chris said, "I'm sorry I didn't do it completely."

Finally the doctor came to us in the little chapel where we now were. He told us it looked very bad. He indicated there was no hope, but told us of a burn center which specialized. I said, "No, no heroic measures." Art agreed. I believe we *both* faced the fact that Chris had a right to die if he wanted to. And we feared what he would have to go through if he had managed to live. In my nursing course and my volunteer hospital experience I had learned the extreme care that burn patients need.

I had a nurse call the Catholic church and ask for the young priest Chris liked so much. I had her explain what had happened and of Chris's interest in Catholicism, and that perhaps he would want to be baptized. The priest came to the emergency room. Chris asked how it happened that he had come and told the priest yes, he wanted to be baptized. The priest came and talked to us and told me that Chris had said, when asked what he was thankful for, "I have always been thankful for my mother," and that he was thankful that I had called the priest.

The head nurse came from the emergency room. She was crying. She said to us, "He loves you very much." I asked, "Can it be kept quiet, that it was a suicide?" Art said, "That isn't possible." The nurse said, "I will not tell myself, but it would be very hard to keep it quiet." I realized that that was true. My feeling was that so many people had believed in Chris's greatness, I hated to think of their reactions, their disappointment. "I don't care what people think about *us*," I told Art and I meant it.* (Certainly after he died it was not kept quiet. It was heard over the radio and on one TV news broadcast, complete with a picture of him. The ambulance men must have given out the news. However, only the simple report of his death in the hospital, which I sent in, was printed in the local papers, and nothing was in the city papers.)

If it had not been for a little book, *The Purpose of Tragedy***, by Hugh Shearman, which I had bought from the Theosophical Society and saved, feeling some day I would need it, I don't think I could have made it through the night. I slept slightly, off and on, but read most of the night. I felt an amazing amount of strength as I kept my mind on what are to me the eternal values.

The next morning we went to the hospital. I remember hanging on Art's arm, crying, as we made our way up the walk to the hospital. A man stopped and asked, "Can I help?" I knew I had to gain control before we entered Chris's room. As we looked in the door, I could see his feet and part of his legs. It was comforting to see that he was still alive, though we knew he would soon be gone. His feet and legs had escaped the fire for the most part.

No one who has never seen a severely burned patient could know how Chris looked.

The nurse said, right in Chris's presence, "It must be terrible to see your son like this." All the burned parts, which must have been at least seventy to eighty percent of his body, were blackened peeling flakes, and red flesh underneath. His eyes were swollen shut; I don't think he could see us but maybe he could. Water leaked from them; part of the loss of fluid—or tears?

The nurse said he had been talkative. He had tubes everywhere, and it was very difficult for him to talk, but he managed.

He said, "I'm sorry to cause so much trouble."

"Chris, it's all right," Art said. "You did what you had to do."

I said, "It was the way of the kind of person you are. We understand."

"The priest came again this morning," Chris told us.

"Do you feel less anxious now?" I asked.

"I'm more at peace than I've ever been before," he whispered.

I smoothed his legs, the only part of his body that was normal, with my hands. We stayed about half an hour. We were afraid we were tiring him, it was so difficult for him to talk. His mind seemed perfectly clear.

---

* In the years since Chris's death we have never felt shame over his suicide. Rather, we are proud of him for the valiant struggle he made to become what he wanted to be, and for his refusal to compromise.

** Published by the Theosophical Publishing House, Adyar, Madras, India.

When we left, I said, "We'll be thinking about you every second." "Every second?" he asked. "That's an awful lot." It was hardly an exaggeration.

We did not call any of the family, but decided to await developments. Our youngest son has always resented not being called, not having a chance to have some last words with Chris. But we just never even considered it. We couldn't bear to have his brothers see him like that, to have that memory of him. Perhaps we were wrong.

We went back to see him in the afternoon. I just couldn't seem to keep the weakness out of my voice. I don't remember what we said exactly, but it was mostly reassurance that he should not worry about what he had done, that we understood that he had to do it, that he had no other choice in the end.

Perhaps it seems strange that we did not stay there at the hospital all the time. But we felt it was wearing for him to have us there, that all he needed was the reassurance of our love and understanding. We told him we would be back the next day. We never saw him again. He slipped into death early Sunday morning, May 10th, 1970. It was Mother's Day.

PART 7
1970-1976

Spring, 1970 – Spring, 1972

May, 1970

Letters arrived after friends learned of Chris's death.

Margie did not write because she had expressed her great sadness over the 'phone.

Betty wrote of her sorrow over the death of someone who was so aware, so sensitive and so vulnerable. She told of Chris's great effect on her and said that he had influenced her as much as anyone ever had.

Letter from Glenda to Lee.

May, 1970

Dear Mrs. Jens,

I find it somewhat difficult to know how and where to start this note to you.

My feelings for Chris run so deep that it is difficult to express them.

I feel a great loss. I feel as though a part of me has died with Chris. I am basically happily married, but Chris was with me spiritually at all times. He did a great, great deal to shape my thoughts; my awareness of things around me; my whole feeling for life.

As best as I can tell, very few people ever feel the type of wonderful, trusting, thrilling and peaceful love I felt for Chris. I am selfish enough to believe that no one else could have loved him so completely.

I felt secure in knowing he was near enough for me to find if need be.

My life is fuller and better for having known and loved him. My only regret is that I wasn't able to tell him how near and very dear he has been to me all these years.

Sincerely,
Glenda

From Valerie (old neighbor) to Art and Lee.

May 20, 1970

Dear Art and Lee:

We thank you for the gift of Chris—all that he was. He brought so much happiness to our family when we were neighbors and he was a small child. We loved him dearly. Now he has entered into a new life, Life Eternal.

Kitty* gave birth to a daughter the day after Christmas. Her name is Chris.

In deepest sympathy,
Valerie

Note from Valerie to priest.

May 21, 1970

Dear Pastor:

Enclosed is a small gift for the Christopher Edward Jens Memorial fund. Our family and the Jens family were next door neighbors when Chris was a small boy. He was a boy full of happiness, a gentle, loving lad and we loved him dearly.

Chris brought his gift of joy and sensitivity to all who knew him. We'll never forget him.

Sincerely,
Valerie A.

From Mrs. C. D., Chris's Austin landlady.

May 22, 1970

Dear Mr. and Mrs. Jens, Jeffrey and Timothy,

Thank you for your letter. A sense of relief swept over me as now Chris is totally involved in the Truth which he so feverishly sought; he is at peace, and in this I find comfort. His last months of meditation, prayer and study surely prepared him for the end.

Words fail me, yet I must find some way to express to you the special place Chris took in my life. His search for Truth and the meaning of life always made me vow to try to be a better person; his gentle approach to any living thing (even the cockroaches) made me appreciate more my surroundings; and his passion for hiking and camping showed me that I should walk more with my children and enjoy the simple things. I would

---

* Val's daughter who was Chris's close friend early in life.

not be truthful if I said I did not have moments of extreme anxiety because of his fasting. And there were times I had the 'phone in hand ready to call you, but shortly things would look up and I'd think "Am I meddling?" because obviously Chris wished to try to handle the problem himself. The last time I about called I got your office number but I couldn't recall Glen Ellyn. The following day Chris told me he had made the decision to go home. He truly is now "at home."

I wish to share with you one last experience that to me was typical Chris. He dropped me a little note from St. Louis saying he wanted certain books. He closed the note by the following: "Thank you. I doubt that I can come back to visit for awhile. I will miss Austin. Thank you very much! Love (a little, anyway!)—Chris."

Mauricio, Barbara, Teri, Janie Rodriguez and all the residents of 2505 Rio Grande, particularly Isidro who also lived with them at 608, join me in extending to you our deepest sympathy.

C.D.

Letter from Larry to Lee and Art.

May 30, 1970

Thank you for informing me of Chris's death. It is of importance to me to know the exact manner of his death.

As far as I know Chris never took drugs, except for the medications given to him in mental hospitals, and was always against their use.* His protestations were one reason I quit taking drugs. One time I talked him into trying marijuana, in November 1968. He said it had no effect except for increasing the buzzing in his head which bothered him continually and which resulted from a medicine given to him in one of the hospitals.

Since Chris was Catholic he has entered an extracorporeal modality of the human individuality. I hope that he is in Paradise. In any case it should be possible to communicate with him. I am thinking of something far different from spiritualism which at best only communicates with the psychic residue of the individual concerned and which is dangerous to everyone concerned. Do be careful.

I wish you a long and joyful life.

With love,
Larry

---

*I had asked Larry about this.

251

Letter from Karen to Lee.

June 1, 1970

My Dear Mrs. Jens,

It must only be that this world of ours simply is incapable of dealing with beings such as Chris—beings who have far more than one share of intensity coupled with sensitivity and warmth and giving. It is difficult for me to describe Chris; save to say that, he was so rare and such a special person and I am glad to have known him. In my own way, I carry him still within myself for I learned from him how to believe in magic and, even more, how to share this belief. And you know, I'm not sure that you can ever meet another Chris in the same lifetime—but rather must simply be glad to have been close to one and, in your own way, continue to share the gifts you received from him and pass them on.

I am so sad to know of his death. My sadness is so deep that it took hold not suddenly, but with a gradual pervasion. I am sad because he played a very special and lasting part in my life, but even sadder with the realization that in our world of war and violence and inhumanity a being so fragile and honest and beautiful such as Chris could not survive for the world would not allow his dreams to come true and it would not even allow him to dream.

As for me, I have just finished medical school and begin internship July 1st. I am going to specialize in pediatrics. In my own way I will try to teach the children what Chris was able to teach me.

Thank you for your letter.

Karen

Letter from Ralph to Lee.

Sunday, June 7, 1970

Dear Mrs. Jens,

The very sad news found me in Western Samoa where I have been serving with the Peace Corps since October. Chris meant very much to me. Without him my years at Cornell would have been very empty. Since leaving him I have not found a more loving friend. He gave much to me. He had been very much with me during the last 4 years and his rich spirit will always be with me. We had been corresponding during the last year and he had helped me through a difficult period. In his letters to me he recounted the deep spiritual conflict that he underwent—in a sense I felt that he was undergoing something for me, also.

252

I know Chris was always satisfied with himself and with his life. I am sure that he had to do what he did.

I feel very fortunate that I was blessed with Chris's friendship. I am heartbroken that I will be unable to reunite with him in this world in a physical sense; but his creative, vital spirit will continue to offer me guidance.

Later this month I will be leaving Western Samoa and begin working in Honolulu. This is a decision Chris helped me make.

In August or September I will probably be returning east and if I am able to, and if it isn't trouble for you, I would like to visit and talk with you.

Thank you very much for writing me. More than feeling sad I feel grateful that God sent to stay with us—even for a short period—such a wonderful human as Chris.

Sincerely,
Ralph

Letter from Lee to Larry.

June 13, 1970

Dear Larry,

Thank you for your letter which we appreciated getting.

You asked how Chris died. It was by burning. He lived for thirty-six hours afterward. It was during this time that he became a Catholic. I called a young priest from the church here where he had attended mass and Chris asked to be baptized. He of course received last rites. The priest twice was able to see him again before he died. When Chris (whose mind was perfectly clear at all times) was told that the priest was visiting him again, the priest told me that he tried to get up and had to be restrained—this in spite of his very bad condition. A memorial fund was established under his name and many donations have been made to the church. As a result, Chris's name has been put on a plate which is attached to the small crucifix carried by an altar boy at every mass. The priest thought this especially appropriate since his name is *Christopher*.

One time Chris said "My name is not Christopher for nothing. I am the one that will have to be crucified." Do you know any of his feelings on this?

Thank you for telling us about Chris not taking drugs, which was all the same as he had told us. Now I would like to ask if you and Chris ever involved yourselves in any other experiments, such as magical ceremonies. I know that many young people have been trying all sorts of things. Chris did not tell of any such things, but he spoke of unusual experiences, such as becoming aware of the terrible loneliness of God. He expressed an interest in occultism. Once he said to me after I said that we must go through much suffering before we can become truly loving, and finally rejoin the One, "I don't want to suffer. I want happiness *now*." I'm afraid that is what a lot of kids want—instant Eden—and I do not believe you can get by without a certain amount of suffering. Chris, in spite of his distaste for suffering, suffered drastically himself. I am wondering how much was due to his trying to force his spiritual evolution to take place faster than he should have expected. There are those, I understand, who believe it is possible indeed to get powers that one has no business having at that particular stage of his development since they are to be handled with greatest wisdom and are very dangerous otherwise. Those who so believe say that such a person might be overwhelmed by fear of powers that he has stirred up which he can't understand or control.

So, Larry, I'd appreciate anything you can tell me about Chris's possible attempts along this line. I'd also be interested to know what you meant in your letter about possibly trying to contact Chris.

We who are Chris's immediate family are deeply grateful to have had him as part of us. We all loved him so much. He had a radiant beauty about him that was felt not only by us, but by many others on whose lives he had a great impact.

Please tell me all you can, Larry.* Call me up collect if it's easier. Thanks.

Sincerely,

Lee

P.S. When I first talked with you on the 'phone just after Chris quit school and was trying to call him, you said, "He has become a man." I am wondering if you continue to think that, in view of the great fear that Chris had, which interfered so with his joy.

Letter from Lee to Larry.

November 4, 1970

Dear Larry,

We think of you often. We hope everything is going well for you.

I don't have a copy of my last letter to you—that is, I have one, but where is it?—and I'm not sure exactly what I asked you. I do know I was not specific about asking you about the following, in letter or 'phone conversation.

Did you and Chris (or did Chris alone, to your knowledge) attempt in any way to "open" up "chakras," those centers in the astral and mental

---

*I could not find Larry's answer to this letter but I know he assured me that Chris did not try to get greater powers.

bodies which, according to occult writing, are centers that can receive impressions and correspond to sense organs in our physical bodies? That is, did you two try in any way to "link up" your chakras to your physical brain? It is my understanding that Laya yoga deals with this type of activity. It is also my understanding that this can be extremely dangerous without the careful eye of a highly advanced guru.

Did you and/or Chris use any particular method to try to enhance your psychic abilities; that is, did you try to heighten your awareness of sights and sounds on the astral and mental planes?

If so, did you feel that you were successful in these pursuits to any extent?

Chris gave me the impression of someone who has received more of something—whether from his own unconscious or the Collective Unconscious or from the astral or mental levels—I don't know. From observing him and hearing what he said, I would think it was some of all.

Did you and Chris ever use any technique to attempt to get in touch with your spiritual Selves, so that you might link up their experiences to your physical brain and make better use of spiritual gains made?

Any light you can shed on this will be greatly appreciated.

I wish that we lived closer so that I could talk with you sometimes.

Hope to hear from you soon.

With love and every good wish,
Lee

P.S. Did you and Chris do anything that brought those more or less repressed fears out into the open? We all have fears and the main way we manage in this life (until we become more Godly and less selfish) is to keep them more or less repressed. Was Chris, through some procedures, I don't know what, from then on forced to keep his fears unrepressed?

Larry, please tell me all you can. After he became a Catholic he said he felt more peaceful (though not perfectly) than he ever did. He seemed to.

L. J.

Letter from Larry to Lee.

December 3, 1970

Dear Mrs. Jens,

To my knowledge Chris never experimented with any type of Yoga or drugs. (I have done both, with and without expert guidance, with so far disastrous results, particularly with drugs, which I have quit completely. Now I am practicing a type of Yoga in which the chakras are bathed in different colored light under the guidance of Dr. Frytz whose metaphysical knowledge is extensive.)

Chris's unusual (and I believe, profound) knowledge and experiences seemed to come to him spontaneously. Initially occasioned by certain books that I recommended to him. It began with Jung; he broke through to a new world with *Demian** by Herman Hesse; and Guénon plunged him further into it.

The last few times I saw him (last winter) he considered himself an initiate. This means he was probably in psychic communication with an organization that he considered initiatic. But whatever his connections he seemed to undergo a type of increasing disequilibrium.

If you want to understand his world view read the works of Guénon. If you do not read French, Guénon's French is very easy and you could learn to read his books in a couple of months. It was Guénon's writings that Chris read primarily. And he claimed to agree with them in every detail.

There is a group of people in Austin who knew and loved Chris who wish to found a Chris Jens Memorial Library for the use of students of tradition. These people asked me to inquire about the possibility of obtaining Chris's library to serve as a nucleus on which to build.**

Love and Peace,
Larry

Letter from Mary Rutledge, piano teacher.

January 19, 1971

Dear Friends,

Since receiving your greeting at the holiday season, I have given so much thought to the added note concerning Chris's passing.

Anyone as expressive of the qualities of willingness to learn, of the outgoing attitude toward his fellowman, of sincerity towad the music he might be performing at the moment and who had such a fine dignity (with which all of your sons impressed me)—anyone who expressed all this can never pass out of our spiritual consciousness.

I loved to see each of your fine boys enter the studio and always looked forward to their "half hours."

Do keep in touch.

My dear, love to all of you.

Mary Rutledge

---

*Bantam, Inc., New York

**We decided not to give the books (about 500) to this group, for fear it would disband and the valuable books might scatter.

Letter from Anne to Lee.

March 14, 1971

My Dear Mrs. Jens,

I have no idea where to begin. I received your letter last night and I was torn between going straight to Glen Ellyn today or writing you. I thought that for now I should first write to you. Thank God, Chris has a wonderful and dear mother. And thank you so very much for writing to me. I am so sorry about Chris.

Last night I sat up for hours asking "My God, what has happened—how did this happen to Chris??!!" I searched for anything I might still have from Chris and I'm sorry that all I could find was a Christmas card I received from Chris in 1964 and the note he wrote to me in my 1961 year book.

I think your writing a book is an excellent idea. You may, of course, use anything I might have written to Chris. You may use my real name without any hesitation. I loved Chris and our friendship was something many people never have. I have only been back to Glen Ellyn twice in the last six years, and I do wish now I had been able to see Chris.

I would like to know where Chris is buried as I would very much like to go visit.

I am living here on my parents' 52 acres. My husband and I are renting from them as we, too, are very addicted to woodlands, open meadows and the country. It has been this private, country living that has helped me to find myself.

I have been teaching for the past three years. I am now working with the special education program in our district. I have a new program this year working with children from 9 to 13 years old. They are all very confused little children. Each of them has difficulty adjusting to school, life and their own self-concepts.

Last year my husband and I became foster parents and have a girl 12 years old. In October of this year we adopted a ten year old boy. Both of these children have had their special difficulties.

Thank you so much for writing to me, Mrs. Jens.

Please do let me know how you are doing and if you do the book—I do hope that you will. I have this feeling that the book has to be done and that Chris would want you to do this.

Forever yours and Chris's friend,
Anne

Letter from Father T., who baptized Chris 36 hours before death, to Lee.

May 26, 1971

Dear Mrs. Jens,

I received your letter but did not need it to remember Chris's first anniversary, as he had been on my mind throughout the year; for as you said in your letter, in many ways he was an unusual person.

When I first saw Chris he was very calm and very clear thinking. He didn't seem to be in much pain although he had difficulty talking. I told him that you called me since I was the priest who had said that Mass he attended the Sunday before. I went on to say that you mentioned that he was considering becoming a Catholic and asked him if he wished to be baptized. He said he had been thinking about it for a long time and that that would make him happy. We spoke for a few moments about the goodness and mercy of God and then I asked the nurse for a little water to baptize him. The doctor said it was all right to pour the water on his forehead. He became even calmer after being baptized and I thought he might be in shock but as he still spoke very rationally I think rather he was just in peace. He spoke of you and Mr. Jens with a real sincere love and gratitude. He said several times he was sorry for causing you all this trouble. He didn't say why he did what he did. He spoke of his happy home-life but said he had become troubled. He asked me to thank you for everything and especially for calling a priest to baptize him. I left him then as the doctor and nurses were working on him.

I saw him twice the next day. I had the early mass at 6:15 so I went to the hospital around 7 a.m. The nurse was with him and he was more restless. He was turning from side to side in the bed and wanted to get up. I don't think he could see me but I told him who I was and he remembered me and that I had been the priest who baptized him. He still didn't complain of any pain and still was able to talk about things clearly but with great difficulty. I told him I had just finished saying Mass and that I had offered the Mass that he might find peace. He said he had already found it and that he was no longer fearful. I saw him again later that day after you were there. I feel he was truly in a state of peace from the time I first talked to him until his death. He again spoke of the happy childhood and home-life he had had and didn't know what had made him so disturbed. He said he had been troubled for a long time but was now happy.

In our church the day of a person's death was often called the "dies natale" in Latin—birthday—as it is the person's birthday in eternity. I think this was especially true in Chris's case. He really began to live on the day he began to die.

I hope these thoughts of mine have been of some help to you. If I can

258

do anything else let me know. If you want to call or stop by, please feel free to do so.

You and yours are still in my prayers that God will grant you peace.

Sincerely,
Father T.

Letter from Larry to Lee.

June 26, 1971

Greetings:

Chris experienced and was obsessed by God. He felt that no one who did not love and seek God was his friend. He believed everything that Guénon said and that not from a blind belief but rather after strenuous searching and suffering. He considered me a very close friend; he was always loving everybody, like we* all do. He was in communication with us and that's how the business of his life came to express himself. I find Guénon rather frightening, though not as highly as Coomarasway, not repulsive like Schuon.

The two people I loved most, Chris and Laura, have been taken away from me. Sometimes I think Guénon killed Chris. Chris's experiences tallied exactly with Guénon teachings and not exactly with any other. My own tally exactly with none though some of the statements of Alan Watts and Aldous Huxley are evocative. In any case you should read all of Guénon's work in French if you really want to understand the world Chris lived in. I have studied all of Guénon's work, and Chris and I had many discussions concerning points of doctrine. I wrote you that Chris considered himself an initiate and his death may have been an initiatory test.

I wonder if he had some extraordinary experience since I saw him last. I'm sure he had or he would not have gone back to see you. He at one time considered all of you in the power of the devil; he felt someone in such a family has to be Christ to redeem that family and that it should be he in this case.**

Unfortunately I convinced Chris of the reality of evil in late summer 1967. (I know now I should have waited.) After that he was almost always haunted. He found centers of evil influence everywhere. At one place, in a grove of trees where he found a bone which was smooth on top and shaped like a flute; he turned the bone over and the underside was hideous.

---

*Traditionalists—i.e., "tradition freaks"
**At other times he felt *himself* to be in the devil's power, as we knew from what he wrote.

He took it to the university but all they could tell him was that it was some kind of fish.

I could show you a rock in the park by a stream where Chris loved to sit and read the Psalms and the Gospel and the Catholic Devotions. This he regarded as a sacred place.

To Chris, one of the most stimulating quotations was, "I am a hidden treasure, I wanted to reveal myself so I created the World."

Not only was he obsessed with God, he was obsessed by evil; all the "tradition freaks" are. According to Hindu traditional doctrines we are nearing the end of a huge human cycle called a Manvantara, the last Yuga of which is filled with evil. (We are nearing the reign of the anti-Christ.) Chris found this to be true before reading Guénon, but he found everything Guénon wrote affirmed his belief.

At the point of the Manvantara where we are now, in the darkest part of the darkness, the worst things are possible, all the possibilities rejected by men in previous ages must find their realization. This can drive a normal person insane, or at least fill him with horror and brings a diminishment of interest in all contemporary movements.

Chris was the gentlest, kindest, most devout, and, I believe, most intelligent of all the people I've ever known. I'll never forget him.

Once, Chris believed he had found the world axis and at first he went up but he fell to the bottom. I believe that this was just before he was placed in the mental hospital for the first time. Chris believed that the mental hospitals were a sort of axis or hub of the modern world.

His trips to the mental hospitals were really bad. He received (as I do) innuendos from other people whom he felt were leading him astray. He considered most of them to be doing it unconsciously since they were possessed by the inferior cosmic psychism. Also he was given drugs which produced a buzzing in his head which after a year or so finally went away.

Chris always called Guènon "Blessed Guénon" as he believed that the material in Guénon was the most accurate, and valuable material in any modern language and best suited for his needs for learning the traditional symbolism and methaphysic. Chris thought my turning him on to Guénon was perhaps the best deed I have ever done. I wonder if it was not my worst. Guénon confirmed what he had experienced and frequently gave him insights. He said he would always be grateful to me for introducing him to Guénon.

The last time I saw Chris he said that he thought Guénon's works on Hinduism were more important and he intended to study them in unbelievable detail: They are, *Introduction Generale des L'Etude des Doctrines Hindoues, L'Homme et son Devenit, Selon le Vedanta* and *Etudes sur L'Hindouism.*

Sometimes I suspect that Chris was too dangerous for the evil powers which rule the world now and that he was in a way murdered by them.

Chris assisted mass in the Catholic Church every day and liturgy in the orthodox church as often as possible.

He considered Christ's life to be the pattern of the life of an initiate. He felt himself undergoing many of the same trials and tests. Chris read the King James version of the Bible primarily. Last time I saw him he was studying Latin in preparation for studying the Vulgate.

Chris took no drugs (not even coffee). He had no sex life whatever. All he wanted was God. He refused to see anyone except me and a few other traditional students.

Love,
Larry

Letter from Father L. to Lee and Art.

February 24, 1972

Dear Mr. and Mrs. Jens:

Thank you for your generous gift to St. Petronille's in memory of Christopher. Indeed we cannot forget him. Daily at our services the beautiful processional cross is carried to and from the altar bearing the plaque "Christopher Edward Jens—Peace with God—May 10, 1970."

Definitely we will see and be with him again.

The enclosed card pictures the greatest and holiest shrine in the Holy Land—the Holy Sepulchre of our Lord Jesus Christ (D.N.J.C.).

It was my joy to celebrate Mass on the Empty Tomb, shown on the card in the center of the Church of the Holy Sepulchre, empty—yes, because He arose. As His faithful followers, we too, as the Master, will arise and have our own glorious Easter Day.

At that Tomb I did pray for you, for all my friends, acquaintances and parishioners. I did also beg there Christopher Edward, to pray for us that God's blessing may be on us while we are here on earth and that we be united again with him and our Blessed Saviour in eternity.

The Empty Holy Sepulchre gives us all that confidence and hope—we shall see and be with him again.

Sincerely yours,
Father L.

Part of a letter from Larry to Lee.   March 29, 1972

. . . Concerning tradition: I have had a long series of remarkably horrible experiences while reading traditional authors. It is my opinion that Guénon was possessed by infernal aspects of certain archetypes. I believe that his disease is contagious and that it spread to other people thus starting the Traditional Movement. I believe Chris was infected with this disease and that I am still infected, to a certain (possibly fatal) degree. I believe that tradition opposes the mainstream of human development which is the conscious relationship with the eternal and immutable archetypes. Thus does universal nature come to know itself.

Love,
Larry

Letter from Ned to Lee.

March, 1972

Dear Mrs. Jens:

I am writing to you this evening on the same day that I received your letter. Chris always told me that you were warm and understanding and I see it's true.

I am also one of those very sensitive people. Words aren't adequate to express what I want to now. However, if you bear with me I am sure that you can gather the sum total of what I write from some rather disjointed parts. Anything which I write about myself is for a purpose. It is to give a fuller meaning to my words and the relationship I had with Chris and what I know and still know of him. I, of course, extend a late but sincere sympathy.* I said I write, but most of what I write pours forth from my heart, which is perhaps only ½% expressed in my words.

I am so grateful to you for taking the time to write such a letter to me. Chris was very special to me. I still and always will talk of him to people I am close to. He will always be in my life. To say he was special isn't adequate.

I've never written a letter of this nature but I will try.

Chris and I shared a very important time in our lives. It was very real. We lived together for 1½ years and became very close. I thought highly of him. There were few barriers he would not try to break. I realize you knew him in your own way; but I knew him also, and all of what we shared I want to tell you openly. I know you will understand.

_____

*I could not find Ned for awhile after Chris died.

262

I loved Chris. I am deeply affected to hear he is gone. It is more than tragic. The world, I am convinced, is headed in a bad direction. If survival of the fittest means Chris is lost, then we are in a sad way.

Chris loved animals and growing things.

One term he decided that sleep was a waste of time. He wanted to sleep 2 hours a day (2-4 a.m). So he decided he could walk through the woods with his dog** before dawn. I felt for that.

I, too, encountered trouble because I am over-sensitive. I conquered some of this because I was removed enough from people to see the awful truth about our nature—our growing animal nature. There is one distinct pattern with no morals except our own image of them. One species, to survive, developed areas of the brain, and we, that species, have been over-developed and a certain extinction is rearing. Of course, we are the last to know. The species going extinct is always the last to realize that something can be done. And thus we are subject to great dilemmas and questions posed to us with no answers! The problem is more in the nature of a disease, in man's nurturing the questions! We peer out and perceive darkness and light and are affected. Often I go to the shore in the middle of the night and run from civilization and hear the waves crash and I am primitive—rushing feelings shoot through me. What am I? Should I ever return to the materialism? Is my destiny here? Well, I'm presently adjusting to all of this.

I am no success. I loved a girl deeply for four years; but the relationship failed, though she loved me. I graduated from college, couldn't hold a job (I) was almost shattered by reality), and now I drive a taxi. I am getting stronger, but I've been in the hopeless dilemma; logic and a very good psychologist pulled me through. I saw that we are animals, as I've described. It's unreal but true. From another world a person or being would see the changing growth on this planet, us included. If only Chris had seen that he could change and still feel as deeply as he did. I still love him so. It wasn't hopeless. I know nothing can bring him back. He is part of you and I'm writing to you—he would have wanted me to.

Later: This is all disjointed but try and follow—

When I received your letter I took my dog and went to the woods and felt so deeply, tears were unnoticeable. I still feel deeply. Chris was the closest person to me that is gone. This is a first and at times I don't know where to turn.

My thoughts are somewhat erratic now but I want you to know who I am, that I am real, and I shared the deepest moments of the young Chris— which were just as real or perhaps more real than later on. He added so

_____

**A "campus" dog.

263

much to my life. I'll always go on for him. He told me he loved me, too. Love is a word, but he felt much more than what it commonly represents. My life is changed somewhat now, I realize it as I write.

Perhaps I get over-anxious, as I write, for you to know and understand me. I feel great frustration over miscommunication. We were originally a directive-command type of communicators, but words led to partial deeper and segmented thought; and communication now is difficult, but I try.

I'll always love Chris.

He told me lots about you and your husband. I was always there to see how he handled the new situations which developed in your relationship.

Sincerely,

Ned

P.S. I hope I can develop what I have inside. Trial and error is the prevailing attitude I have.

Chris is real to me. He will always be. I've never met anyone like him. We shared the world in our own way for awhile.

After thoughts—

I have kept Chris's letters to me. I often re-read them because I want to feel close to him.

I smoked his brand of cigarettes (L&M). I can picture him lying in bed before going to sleep having his good-night cigarette. He loved to have a sweet, good-feeling conversation before retiring. I wish I had been in his life more before the tragedy. He is part of me. Some of my feelings originated with him. He gave so much and I absorbed much, being who I was. He seemed so secure. I copied the little things and sayings he used, to try to feel as he did. Chris made the world much more beautiful.

I'll close for now—Brian, Chris and I spent 1½ years as a threesome. Has Brian been in touch?* He and perhaps you are the only ones I can express myself to. I feel that I will be sad for awhile. A part of me has died and my instinctive reaction, my illogical feeling is that of disbelief. I only hope that there is something more beautiful than anything we've known on earth.

Again, with all my heart,

Ned

---

*I never found Brian.

Fall, 1976

Letter written by Larry to Lee.

October 26, 1976

Dear Lee:

I believe that Chris had more than ordinary insight into the nature of things and precise and definite (and good) reasons for taking his life (i.e., that he did only what he had to do). And that the exact manner of his death benefitted him in his after-life.

He was the dearest friend I've ever had, and I had hopes of knowing him throughout a long life.

The reason I think these things is a clear and profound way in which he understood Guénon, also his penetrating insights into Flaubert, Hesse, Nietzsche and the so-called traditional school of thought. He seemed always to understand exactly my own thought and was capable of the serenest and loftiest methaphysical conceptions. He fought the living devil and I find myself believing that he (Chris) defeated him at least in a certain respect.

I have communicated with Chris or rather he has communicated with me in dreams, hallucinations, fantasies, etc.

I believe there is a worldwide brotherhood of high-level initiates that control the world (among other things keep spiritual influences flowing into the world). They keep a constant watch over all promising candidates for high things and initiated Chris at a certain point. They have their enemies in the devil and his cohorts who wish ultimately to destroy humankind. Chris and I had certain adventures fighting for Truth against the lie.

My own mistake was to follow the way of drugs (chemical rituals I then called them). I suppose it was my destiny. I don't seem to have the impeccable moral fibre of Chris. Unfortunately I *am* willing to compromise. Well, maybe the next time around. But to cut it all short, if Chris was mad then I am more mad and everyone I know is more mad yet.

I could not have done what he did. I believe that Chris, living and dying the way he did, guaranteed to himself an extra-corporeal prolongation in paradise where he can continue to work for Truth. All is well.

Love,
Larry

Letter from Lee to Larry.

November 8, 1976

Dear Larry:

Thank you so much for your letter of October 26.

I asked Chris toward the end of his life if he thought he had been mentally ill and he answered, "I think I have been what people call mentally ill."

I personally do not feel that people who have the kind of experiences Chris had are suffering from an illness.

In my opinion, Chris was unsettled and unhappy with himself because he had a conflict between his wish for power and prestige, and his wish to love God and to do His will.

Plunging into the depths of oneself is hazardous; it can bring experiences of God, but it can also bring experiences of great evil. Frances Wickes, noted Jungian analyst and writer, says in her book, *The Inner World of Choice*,* that there is no more dangerous journey because of the unknown possibilities that one may encounter.

The end result may be that one becomes a greater person through becoming one's whole self; that one may be lost in the depths; or that one may choose physical death and give oneself back to God.

For Chris, physical death was, in the end, his only option. He did not have the strength to cope with evil in the world and in himself. He never found out that God can absorb evil, and that there are really no opposites. But he did know that he loved God enough to die for Him. He did the highest thing he was capable of doing. He refused to live a life that was full of pretense and joyless, a life not fully in the service of God. So he gave himself back to God; he gave God the best gift of which he was capable, his life.

I believe he reached his highest potential.

Love to you, Larry
Lee

---

*Harper and Rowe, New York

Afterword

I tell you it's better to live joyously for one hour than to live a mechanical lifetime.

Written by Christopher near the end of his life.